Field Visual Merchandising Strategy

Field Visual Merchandising Strategy

Developing a national in-store strategy using a merchandising service organization

Paul J Russell

KoganPage

LONDON PHILADELPHIA NEW DELHI

First published in Great Britain and the United States im 2015 by Kogan Page Limited

2nd Floor, 45 Gee Street	1518 Walnut Street, Suite 1100	4737/23 Ansari Road
London	Philadelphia	Daryaganj
EC1V 3RS	PA 19102	New Delhi 110002
United Kingdom	USA	India

www.koganpage.com

© Paul J Russell, 2015

The right of Paul J Russell to be identified as the author of this work has been asserted by him in accordance with the Copyright, Designs and Patents Act 1988.

ISBN   9780 7494 7 264 1
E-ISBN 9780 7494 7 265 8

British Library Cataloguing-in-Publication Data

A CIP record for this book is available from the British Library.

Library of Congress Cataloging-in-Publication Data

Russell, Paul J.
  Field visual merchandising strategy : developing a national in-store strategy using a merchandising service organization / Paul J. Russell.
    pages cm
    ISBN 978-0-7494-7264-1 (paperback) – ISBN 978-0-7494-7265-8 (ebook)   1. Display of merchandise.
2. Merchandising.   3. Marketing.   4. Stores, Retail–Management.   I. Title.
  HF5845.R87 2015
  659.1'5–dc23
                                                                                                2014041125

Typeset by Graphicraft Limited, Hong Kong
Print production managed by Jellyfish
Printed and bound by CPI Group (UK) Ltd, Croydon, CR0 4YY

CONTENTS

List of figures   viii
List of tables   xi
About the author   xii
How the book is structured   xiii
Preface   xiv

Introduction   1

PART ONE   Fighting the war at retail   5

01   Getting ready for battle   7

Visual merchandisers vs field visual merchandisers   7
The role of merchandising service organizations (MSOs)   8
The leader   8
Defining a field visual merchandising strategy   12
Thinking strategically   14
Strategy vs tactics   24
Chapter 1 checklist   27

02   Skill set of your management team   28

Communicating in the field   28
Project management   29
Visual merchandising directives   32
Planograms   34
Visual retailing software   36
Look books   39
Problem-solving skills   42
Brainstorming and mind-mapping techniques   43
Real-world situation No 1   47
Chapter 2 checklist   50
Tricks of the trade: 'Keeping a bag of tricks'   51

03   Mastering the fundamentals of warfare 55

Merchandise presentations and visual merchandising skills 55
Fixtures and capacity 57
Developing a high taste level 60
Mannequin styling and clothing coordination 61
Mixing patterns in clothing coordination 63
Effects of colour in visual merchandising 68
Design concepts 70
Chapter 3 checklist 72
Tricks of the trade: 'From concept to installation' 73

PART TWO   Planning and initiating your battle strategy 85

04   Components of your strategy 87

Armies for hire 87
The World Alliance for Retail Excellence and Standards 88
Structure of a merchandising service organization 89
Defining objectives and standards 93
Analysing the battlefield 96
Defining store visit requirements 103
Chapter 4 checklist 106
Tricks of the trade: 'How long will it take?' 107

05   Preparing for combat 112

Developing your strategy proposal 112
Selecting the right MSO 118
Request for proposal (RFP) 119
Budgets and contracts 122
Chapter 5 checklist 123
Tricks of the trade: 'You gotta have options' 124

06   Training your troops 130

Setting expectations 130
Training in the field visual merchandising environment 131
Needs assessment 132
Training materials 133
Training documents 135

Product features and benefits   135
Merchandising standards manual   136
Certification test   136
Understanding store visit guidelines   138
Understanding and using the task duration estimate   140
Understanding merchandising directives and planograms   140
Implementing and evaluating the training plan   145
Chapter 6 checklist   156
Tricks of the trade: 'The game of mix and match'   157

07   Planning your combat strategy   162

Defining retailer requirements   162
Developing the strategic plan   169
Real-world situation No 2   191
Chapter 7 checklist   194
Tricks of the trade: 'What's your standard?'   194

PART THREE   Executing the strategy   207

08   Communicating and monitoring the strategic plan   209

Distribution of the strategic plan timeline   210
Monitoring the execution   211
Communicating with sponsors   214
Communicating with your MSO   216
Merchandising service reports   218
Monitoring field visual merchandisers' performance   224
Real-world situation No 3   226
Chapter 8 checklist   229
Tricks of the trade: 'Where's Waldo?'   230

09   Planning and executing tactics and special projects   235

Field visual merchandising tactics   235
In-store tactics   243
Special projects   245
Chapter 9 checklist   250
Tricks of the trade: 'The flawless floor set'   251

References and further reading   262
Index   264

LIST OF FIGURES

FIGURE 1.1   Leader Brand A: Strategic plan   17

FIGURE 1.2   Leader Brand B: Strategic plan   19

FIGURE 1.3.1   Letter from retailer's corporate office to store manager   20

FIGURE 1.3.2   Store visit guidelines   21

FIGURE 1.3.3   Planogram fixture layout   22

FIGURE 1.3.4   Planogram product placement   23

FIGURE 1.4.1   Merchandising standard: Folding   24

FIGURE 1.4.2   Merchandising standard: Sizing   25

FIGURE 1.5   Strategy development process   26

FIGURE 2.1   Project timeline or strategic plan   31

FIGURE 2.2.1   Planogram: Fixture 1 presentation   35

FIGURE 2.2.2   Planogram: Product with style numbers   36

FIGURE 2.3   MockShop rendering: Three views of the proposed fixtures   37

FIGURE 2.4   MockShop software: Screenshot   38

FIGURE 2.5   Example of a look book   40

FIGURE 2.6   MockShop rendering of look book   41

FIGURE 2.7   Brainstorming: List of possible solutions   44

FIGURE 2.8   Mind-mapping: The process   45

FIGURE 2.9   Window display 1: Initial concepts   52

FIGURE 2.10   Completed window display 1   53

FIGURE 2.11   Window display 2: Spin-off concepts   53

FIGURE 2.12   Window display 3   54

FIGURE 3.1   Merchandise presentation   56

FIGURE 3.2   Visual presentation added to merchandising presentation   57

FIGURE 3.3   Wall fixtures with accessories   58

FIGURE 3.4   Wall fixture options with product capacity and number of accessories   59

FIGURE 3.5   Wall presentation   62

FIGURE 3.6   Basic presentation   63

FIGURE 3.7   Layered presentation   64

FIGURE 3.8   Types of patterns   65

FIGURE 3.9   Hooded sweatshirt   66

FIGURE 3.10   Mixing patterns 1   67

FIGURE 3.11   Mixing patterns 2   67

FIGURE 3.12   Mixing patterns: Completed presentation   68

FIGURE 3.13   Concept board: Christmas window   71

FIGURE 3.14   Christmas window display   72

FIGURE 3.15   Initial brainstorming ideas: Menswear with Italian influence   75

FIGURE 3.16   Brainstorming results: Tuscan villa concept   76

FIGURE 3.17   Concept board: Tuscan villa   76

FIGURE 3.18   Complete concept board   77

FIGURE 3.19   Project timeline   78

FIGURE 3.20.1   Visual merchandising directive: Cover   80

FIGURE 3.20.2   Product selection for windows   80

FIGURE 3.20.3   Store visit guidelines   81

FIGURE 3.21.1   Interior presentations   82

FIGURE 3.21.2   Floor layout   82

FIGURE 3.21.3   Planograms   83

FIGURE 3.22   Final window display   84

FIGURE 4.1   Sponsor 1   94

FIGURE 4.2   Sponsor 2   95

FIGURE 4.3   Sponsor 3   95

FIGURE 4.4.1   Merchandising standards manual: Front cover   97

FIGURE 4.4.2   Merchandising standards manual: Sizing instructions   98

FIGURE 4.4.3   Merchandising standards manual: Folding instructions   99

FIGURE 4.5   Merchandising task duration estimate: Chart (Part 2)   106

FIGURE 5.1   Preliminary timeline   116

FIGURE 5.2   MSO score card   121

FIGURE 5.3   Types of fixtures   125

FIGURE 5.4   Types of fixture accessories   126

FIGURE 5.5   Product capacities for fixtures and accessories   126

FIGURE 5.6   Presentation options for 4ft wall   127

FIGURE 5.7   Presentation for 20ft wall   128

FIGURE 5.8   Completed shop presentation   129

FIGURE 6.1   Field merchandising training needs assessment   134

FIGURE 6.2.1   Merchandising standards training: Trainer's instructions   137

FIGURE 6.2.2   Merchandising standards training: Certification   138

FIGURE 6.3.1   Understanding store visit guidelines   139

FIGURE 6.3.2   Store visit guidelines: Example   139

FIGURE 6.4.1   Understanding and using the task duration estimate   140

FIGURE 6.4.2   Merchandiser task list: Example   141

FIGURE 6.4.3   Merchandiser task list: Chart   142

FIGURE 6.5.1 Directive cover page   143

FIGURE 6.5.2 Floor layout   143

FIGURE 6.5.3 Schematic   144

FIGURE 6.5.4 Product listing   144

FIGURE 6.6 Sizing hanging apparel: Side hung   149

FIGURE 6.7 Sizing hanging apparel: Faced out   150

FIGURE 6.8 Merchandiser's training log   155

FIGURE 6.9 Catalogue and store front with two windows   161

FIGURE 7.1 Sample retailer letter of introduction   166

FIGURE 7.2 Strategic plan: Phases, goals and timelines   171

FIGURE 7.3 Developing the launch plan: Initiation phase tasks   174

FIGURE 7.4 Developing the launch plan: Initiation phase timeline   176

FIGURE 7.5 Developing the launch plan: Planning phase timeline   180

FIGURE 7.6 Developing the launch plan: Execution phase timeline   182

FIGURE 7.7 Developing the launch plan: Timeline detail checked   185

FIGURE 7.8 Developing the launch plan: Monitoring phase timeline   189

FIGURE 7.9 The launch plan: Amending the timeline   192

FIGURE 7.10 Revised launch plan   193

FIGURE 7.11 Developing a merchandising standards manual: 3D rendering   196

FIGURE 7.12 Developing a merchandising standards manual: Sizing instructions   197

FIGURE 7.13 The completed merchandising standards manual   198

FIGURE 7.14 Reviewing the manual: 3D rendering vs instructions   204

FIGURE 8.1 In-store service schedule   219

FIGURE 8.2 In-store survey   221

FIGURE 8.3 Weekly store visit summary   222

FIGURE 8.4 Field visual merchandiser's performance evaluation chart   226

FIGURE 8.5 T-shirts planogram   227

FIGURE 8.6 Review process: Materials needed   232

FIGURE 9.1 Strategic plan timeline: Snail tactic   236

FIGURE 9.2 Store measurements and fixture dimensions   255

FIGURE 9.3 Numbering fixtures   256

FIGURE 9.4 Zoning groups   256

FIGURE 9.5 Planograms of fixtures   257

FIGURE 9.6 Merchandising times for one fixture   258

FIGURE 9.7 Time frames for complete floor set   259

FIGURE 9.8 Calculating merchandising time   259

LIST OF TABLES

TABLE 4.1 Merchandiser's task list 101

TABLE 4.2 Merchandiser's task list: Estimated completion times 102

TABLE 4.3 Merchandiser's task list: Amended 103

TABLE 4.4 Task breakdown 104

TABLE 4.5 Merchandiser task duration: Estimate for 1-hour merchandising service (Part 1) 105

TABLE 4.6 Merchandiser task duration: Associated time frame 108

TABLE 4.7 Merchandiser task duration: Estimate for two fixtures in children's department 110

TABLE 6.1 Example: Test passing score 147

TABLE 6.2 Field merchandising training programme requirements 153

TABLE 6.3 The game of 'mix and match' 159

TABLE 8.1 SWOT analysis chart 212

TABLE 8.2 Task duration estimate 228

TABLE 8.3 Store selection 231

TABLE 8.4 Store visit report checklist 233

TABLE 9.1 Calculating merchandising time 260

ABOUT THE AUTHOR

For more than two decades, Paul Russell has been involved in the development and execution of field visual merchandising strategies. Paul grew up in Germany, where at an early age he became captivated with art and fashion. After returning to the United States, he decided to study fashion merchandising in college and started his career in visual merchandising for a national men's clothing retailer.

After being encouraged to provide his expertise to smaller retailers, Paul started a visual merchandising consulting business. He began by visiting retail stores, making visual assessments and presenting retailers with proposals on how to increase their sales through the visual merchandising techniques and unique training he offered.

His success in the consulting realm led to an opportunity to work for a world-renowned athletic brand. He trained, developed and managed a large team of field visual merchandisers while gaining a wealth of knowledge in this field.

Paul immersed himself in all the materials he could find on training, project management, visual merchandising and strategic planning. His efforts paid off and through the years Paul has worked for leading apparel brands and developed field visual merchandising strategies on a national and international level.

Paul currently serves on the Manufacturers Advisory Council for the World Alliance for Retail Excellence and Standards and was also the Chairman of the 2014 Retail Merchandising and Marketing Conference.

HOW THE BOOK IS STRUCTURED

The book is divided into three parts.

Part One: Fighting the war at retail

This book provides insight into the war at retail and the partnership that retailers have developed with brands to enhance their store presentation. It offers a description of a field visual merchandising (FVM) strategy, the skills of the management team and mastering the fundamentals of visual merchandising and clothing coordination. It finishes with a scenario that provides insight on taking a visual merchandising concept from development to implementation using your outsourced FVM team.

Part Two: Planning and initiating your strategy

Here you will be taken through the process of developing and initiating your strategic plan and learning the importance of defining your objectives and analysing the battlefield. It also focuses on the details of sourcing and selecting the right Merchandising Services Organization (MSO), training your field team, defining the requirements and planning strategy.

Part Three: Executing your strategy

The final part will address the execution process, communicating with your MSO and monitoring the execution. We will discuss merchandising service reports and explain the difference between a project and a tactic while defining the steps in the development and execution process.

PREFACE

Over the past 20 years, I have had the opportunity to develop and execute strategies that involved outsourcing to a merchandising services organization (MSO). Throughout the process, I have made a lot of mistakes and have learned invaluable information from each situation. During my career, I have searched for books on developing field visual merchandising (FVM) strategies to help fine-tune the many tasks it takes to execute a strategy of this nature. Although I haven't found any books directly relating to the subject, I have documented and implemented many best practices that have proven to be successful when incorporated into programmes. Two of these practices will be forever stamped in my memory.

I initially began my career in visual merchandising with a menswear retail chain that had stores throughout the United States. To execute the visual merchandising strategies, we would develop window and interior presentations in our flagship store, and then conduct a walk-through with senior management to gain approval before moving forward. After approval was granted, we would bring in a photographer to take pictures of each presentation. Subsequently, directives would be written, attaching the corresponding photos and then packets would be mailed to all stores and the visual merchandising teams. At this point, my responsibility was to travel the country visiting stores to ensure my visual team and the retail stores were following corporate guidelines and directives.

Although I managed a team of district visual merchandising managers based in major markets, there were stores where freelance visual merchandisers were employed to execute our corporate visual strategies. These freelancers had a solid background in visual merchandising, but I quickly learned not to assume that a person knew how to effectively complete a task just because they had experience. They may have had experience working ineffectively or may not have a clear understanding of the company's standards. Through this experience, I have learned that it is too easy to fall into the trap of hiring a national FVM team from an MSO without intent to train them. Outsourced employees rarely produce the required results without training on your standards.

The most valuable best practice I have learned came at a time of defeat by a major rival. I worked for a world-renowned athletic brand and managed a team of field visual merchandisers. As did many brands, this company placed concept shops in many retailers to attract the target consumers. These concept shops were mini boutiques housing the best apparel and footwear the brand offered. It was my responsibility to develop the store layout of each concept shop in the region, order custom fixturing and organize the team to install and merchandise each shop.

My team and I were installing a concept shop for a major retailer's grand opening and four of our competitors were installing shops as well. I felt very good about this shop installation because I believed that every detail was planned and going as scheduled. We were given an ideal spot to install our shop and I had my top FVMs assisting with the installation. The fixturing had arrived the day before and the team had almost completed installing all wall and floor fixtures. All we needed to do at this point was to wait for the merchandise to arrive and gladly, it was on the way. Our shop was positioned directly across from our major competitor and their space was empty. The retailer was getting a little concerned because this was the scheduled day for all brands to install their shops and the brand had no fixturing, no merchandisers and no product. It was a great feeling to finally outsmart our major competitor. As my team and I were discussing the floor layout, the front doors of the store flew open and in came six field visual merchandisers. They were outfitted from head to toe in the competitor's apparel and footwear; additionally, each carried a tool bag branded with the company's logo. They all headed to the store's stockroom and came out with huge boxes which I assumed housed their fixturing.

It was soon brought to my attention that each box contained not only fixturing, but also included product, signage and a detailed planogram exhibiting the locations at which merchandise was to be presented. In no time at all, fixturing was installed, signage was placed and all wall and floor fixtures were impeccably merchandised to include mannequins dressed in well-coordinated outfits. It was obvious that a well-developed strategic plan was created to execute this shop. Since that point, I have strived to develop flawless strategic plans from concept to installation. Now, as a result, I often find myself repeating a very important phrase that I have used throughout my career: 'plan your work and work your plan'. This phrase reminds me that the importance of a well-thought-out strategic plan is undeniable.

This experience has also taught me the value of being a life learner. Therefore, I have sought various ways to learn as much as possible about the industry. Not only has my work experience of over 20 years given me invaluable skills, but attending classes, lectures, discussing ideas with experts, reading various materials, teaching and joining industry organizations all have awarded me a wealth of information.

One day, while searching for books on field visual merchandising to add to my library of information, my wife presented me with a challenge. She asked why I hadn't thought of writing a book on the topic myself as opposed to searching for a book that doesn't exist. The thought of writing a book on this subject seemed to be a monumental task, but I accepted the challenge and embarked on this journey.

The retail environment has become a war zone where brands and retailers fight to maintain a strong product presentation in order to be set apart from their competition. But no war is won without a strategy. This book is a comprehensive guide to developing and executing a field visual merchandising strategy using an outsourced MSO. It covers key topics such as developing the strategy, selecting the correct MSO, team training, field communications, store visit guidelines, merchandising standards, planograms, developing the strategic plan and launching the strategy. The book also introduces a section on planning and executing tactics to maintain an advantage over the competition.

Outsourcing FVM services has become a vital positioning strategy for today's retailers and manufacturers who want to survive in a highly competitive marketplace. Most are reluctant to invest in FVM services or don't know they exist. Exceptional retailers and manufacturers understand that this type of strategy doesn't only draw consumers to their product, but educates the customer, creates an inviting shopping experience and increases sales.

In conclusion, I have enjoyed writing this book and hope the contents will help you improve how you develop and execute strategies. I know rolling out a strategy of this nature when using an outsourced organization is not easy. It will require hard work and dedication to keep everything and everyone moving in the same direction. If you get discouraged and lose direction, repeat the phrase that I have used throughout my career: 'plan your work and work your plan'.

So, if your company's sales lie dormant and your customers are passing you by, grab this book and lift your head up: help has arrived.

Paul J Russell

Introduction

Understanding the war at retail

Globally, today's retailers are at war with each other, and to fight the good fight, they have become master planners. They do everything from buying the right merchandise for their customers, to designing stores, buying fixturing and developing signage. The goal of the retailer is to create a unique shopping experience where customers can find everything they need while enjoying the process.

To be competitive, a great deal of attention is given to the visual presentation of product. This involves the overall store layout, the type of fixturing to be used, and the organization of clothing departments, displays and ongoing maintenance of the presentations. Many retailers have partnered with brands to enhance their merchandise presentation and stimulate sales. These brands have conducted extensive research on consumer buying habits and have embraced this strategy as the most efficient means of contact for reaching those target consumers. Major brands have retail marketing and visual merchandising departments to focus on developing in-store strategies. These strategies can consist of anything from in-store signage and promotions, to window displays, custom fixturing and brand concept shops. To understand the war at retail, you need to visit the battlefield.

The retail battlefield

The retail battlefield is where the big brands fight to attract customers and stimulate multiple sales. It's usually a pleasant environment with stimulating music, well-organized departments offering a selection of merchandise by world-renowned brands, but there is more going on than meets the eye.

Within the war at retail, there is a constant battle of the brands to develop and maintain their product presentation and retail marketing strategies. These brands are positioned on the sales floor in close proximity to each other. Therefore, each brand is fighting for the same customers and wants to ensure their merchandise is on the sales floor, sized, folded, hung and presented properly. For brands, this has become much more than a battle: this is war.

Many retailers don't have the manpower to focus on maintaining the product presentation of each brand. Thus, brands are providing the retailers with trained representatives to help with this operation. A few brands have hired full-time field visual merchandisers to visit stores and maintain their product presentation and to ensure the product is pulled from the stock room and taken to the sales floor. Big brands have hundreds of stores that stock their merchandise and have demanded a cost-effective approach to address this matter. These brands have outsourced their product presentation to organizations that employ field visual merchandisers for hire.

Outsourcing merchandising services

Outsourcing field merchandising services is not new to retail. It is a global enterprise that has evolved into a critical part of the retail industry and has proven to be an asset to manufacturers and retailers alike. Companies that perform in-store merchandising and visual merchandising services are called merchandising services organizations (MSO). In the past, these companies generally focused on manufacturers and provided services to a few distribution channels such as food, convenience and drugstores. Retailers within these distribution channels began to see the benefits of using an MSO to execute their in-store strategies and have jumped on board as well. Manufacturers and retailers in the fashion industry followed the trend and began using MSOs to execute field visual merchandising (FVM) strategies globally.

In 2006 a white paper entitled *Partners for Growth: The new role of merchandising service organizations* was produced by MJH & Associates. This study was created for the retail industry as a service for The World Alliance for Retail Excellence and Standards, formerly called the National Association for Retail Marketing Services (NARMS). This white paper provided a description of the industry and expressed how MSOs are providing better retail execution, more services, coverage and compliances. This paper also discussed how the partnership between the MSOs, manufacturers and retailers has been developing and will continue to expand.

There have been numerous studies conducted over the years, revealing that retailers are doing a poor job of maintaining adequate stock levels to meet the needs of their consumers. This is not due to a lack of product, but a lack of having well-trained sales personnel to ensure the product is pulled from stockrooms and presented in a pleasing manner on the sales floor. In a report by Bloomberg News on 2 April 2013, Wal-Mart, the world's largest retailer, received more than 1,000 e-mails from consumers complaining about bare shelves. This scenario is happening in retailers around the world and many are beginning to embrace the use of MSOs by working closely with brands to fine-tune retail strategies and merchandise presentation. As more apparel brands and retailers begin to use MSOs, they are beginning to realize the competition is fierce and the development and execution of FVM strategies are crucial to their success.

The missing link

Some retailers have expressed their discontent with manufacturers using MSO field visual merchandisers. They are frustrated with these manufacturer representatives coming out to service their stores with little or no knowledge or training on the manufacturers' products, merchandising standards and in-store promotions. Some retailers are reluctant to use MSO services based on the same set of circumstances. Most MSOs do a respectable job of developing their field organization, but a strategic implementation plan needs to be built by manufacturers and retailers to ensure the field visual merchandisers are well educated on their company's in-store programmes and promotions.

Likewise, to fulfil the needs of the manufacturer or brand a comprehensive understanding of the manner in which MSOs operate, and the process of selecting the right MSO, should be explored. In addition, processes must be established along with additional training, directives and project management guidelines.

The World Alliance for Retail Excellence and Standards lists over 150 merchandising service organizations that staff a trained field merchandising force to execute in-store marketing activities such as visual merchandising, fixture resets, new store sets, remodels, and point-of-purchase displays. Although these organizations can provide an army of field merchandisers, it is up to the person in charge of the programme to develop a strategic plan that will accomplish their company's objectives. Field visual merchandising is not a well-defined field; it is a combination of many skills and expertise combined to create tools that solve visual merchandising problems. If you are a student of retail marketing, a visual merchandising professional or a business executive in the retail, merchandising or the manufacturing industry, you will benefit from reading this book.

PART ONE
Fighting the war at retail

A field visual merchandising strategy involves developing a plan of action from concept to implementation to entice the company's target consumers and stimulate sales. This concept is the link between your company's product and the consumers. Because a visual merchandising strategy is usually executed in a large geographical area, creative and analytical skills are needed to ensure success. To prepare for battle your first step should be to gain an understanding of the mission, evaluate the skill set of your management team and master the fundamentals of visual presentation.

Getting ready for battle

Imagine stepping onto the battlefield wearing a blindfold. You aimlessly bounce from place to place, attempting to dodge unforeseen bullets. It is impossible to plan an attack or defence. Before going to war with the enemy, it is imperative that you learn the art of strategy. In the same way, before you start developing your field visual merchandising (FVM) strategy, you must gain an understanding of the skills necessary to win the battle against your adversaries and the pertinent information required for your success.

Visual merchandisers vs field visual merchandisers

Before we move forward, let's gain an understanding of visual merchandising and the difference between 'visual merchandisers' and 'field visual merchandisers'. Visual merchandising is the act of creatively presenting products in a manner that will attract consumers and stimulate sales. When an item is on display in a clothing department, in a window or on a mannequin, the creative process of developing the display and coordinating the clothing falls under the umbrella of visual merchandising. Unsurprisingly, this task is usually performed by visual merchandisers. Steve Kaufman, the Editor at Large for *VMSD* magazine, states that:

> Visual merchandisers create the in-store environment that supports the retailer's marketing and merchandising strategies. They set the mood; highlight the merchandise; and invite, attract, welcome, and inform shoppers. They also, somewhat more subtly, make the store a wonderful, joyous place to be.

Visual merchandisers are salespeople who possess the knowledge and understanding to creatively present a company's merchandise using specific techniques and principles. Their goal is to ensure the product is presented according to standards, placed on the correct fixturing, and displayed with accurate signage. In short, they help to build the brand.

Many visual merchandisers have the responsibility of ensuring a product is creatively presented in one or more retail stores. However, these visual merchandisers may also have the title 'field visual merchandiser' and may work for a specific retail chain or manufacturer. The role of a field visual merchandiser is to travel to a group of stores regularly and balance responsibilities such as implementing directives, maintaining the company's high standards of product presentation, training salespeople and developing strong relations with store managers and personnel.

The role of merchandising service organizations (MSOs)

Each clothing manufacturer has a corporate office and a group of sales executives tasked with selling their products to retailers. When purchased, this merchandise is forwarded to the company's chain of retail stores.

To ensure merchandise is presented and displayed in compliance with the company's merchandising standards, the manufacturer may have a team of visual merchandisers who travel to retail stores to assist with presenting the manufacturer's line of product. Manufacturers often provide these merchandising services to many retailers and may hire an outside agency or organization to employ a field team that can accommodate their vast need for coverage throughout many regions. This is usually a merchandising service organization (MSO) that hires a large team of field visual merchandisers. Although the responsibilities may be the same as those of a field visual merchandiser, these jobs are often placed under slightly different titles, such as a 'merchandising specialist' or 'brand ambassador'.

In addition to manufacturers, many retailers also see the value in hiring an MSO to execute their merchandising or visual merchandising strategies. They may employ an approved MSO to service all their stores on a national level. The MSO team may be hired to maintain the product presentation and complete window and interior displays.

The leader

A manufacturer or retailer will usually hire a designated person with the responsibilities of developing and executing a strategy at retail with a team of field visual merchandisers. In this book, we will refer to this designated person as 'the leader', but there are a variety of titles for such a position: director of field visual merchandising, FVM manager, director of visual merchandising, retail marketing manager or director. The leader is the mastermind behind the operation and is usually responsible for creating and overseeing the development and execution of the strategy.

This leader should have both creative and analytical skills. It takes innovative thinking and an artistic eye to present a product in a manner that attracts consumers. Analytical skills are essential in developing and executing a strategy over a large geographical area. So, as the leader, one must be meticulous with details and systematic in one's approach to solving visual merchandising problems. There is a plethora of additional skills that are generally acquired while in the field of visual merchandising that aid in the development of winning strategies.

Leaders that excel in the apparel FVM industry usually possess very similar proficiencies and experiences. As the leader, one should constantly develop expertise in every area associated with the development and execution of FVM strategies. In addition to managing and being a mentor to the team, it is imperative that one masters the eight specific skills below. Let's discuss these key abilities and experiences:

- understanding the brand's DNA;
- uncovering the visual merchandising culture in the organization;
- staying up-to-date on industry knowledge;
- understanding standard and custom fixturing;
- directives, planograms and look books;
- developing training programmes and curriculums;
- window displays and interior presentations;
- sourcing vendors.

Understanding your brand's DNA

You should have a clear understanding of your brand's DNA, regardless of whether you work for a clothing manufacturer or a retailer. This DNA consists of everything from how your company started the product or service it offers, to knowing all aspects of your company's target consumer. Corporate DNA deals with the personalities of the company: the way a company does business, its motivation, the drive behind the force of behaviour. It is important to understand where your company sees itself within the retail industry. What is your brand's weakness? What methods or concentrations do the senior executives seek to improve? Is your brand seeking to grow or are you content with the current position you hold in the market? Your company may compete in a particular market and may sell product in numerous trade channels or it may be a speciality retailer, department store or a big box retailer. Whatever the case, understanding the DNA of the organization will help you develop strategies that are focused and true to the company's mission statement.

Understanding the visual merchandising culture in the organization

Every company has a corporate culture. Similarly, there is evidence of a visual merchandising culture within several organizations. An article in the *Houston Chronicle* made mention of the fact that this type of culture is a mindset that is established and put into motion by the CEO. This mentality is communicated to the senior management team and meanders throughout the organization. It requires that business functions and strategies be developed and executed with visual merchandising in mind.

Within the retail industry, visual merchandising plays a major role in identifying with a company's target consumers. If functions are executed with a visual merchandising approach, the final presentation will blend together and integrate a well-thought-out process that is appreciated by the target consumer. When a strong visual merchandising culture exists in your organization, the development of a field strategy will be embraced by all levels of management. If there is not much value given to this area in your organization, it will be evident in the structure of the company. When an organizational chart has visual merchandising near the bottom of its hierarchy, it may be difficult to establish this type of culture.

Staying up-to-date on industry knowledge

The world of visual merchandising is forever changing. There are always new trends in merchandise presentation, store design, fixturing, signage and fashion. To stay abreast of current industry knowledge, look at the entire business environment surrounding the fashion and retail industry. Create a library of books on subjects pertaining to visual presentation and pay specific attention to industry developments. A few great books to add to your collection are *Silent Selling* (4th edition) by Judy Bell and Kate Ternus; *Visual Merchandising and Display* by Martin M Pegler; *Dressing the Man* by Alan Flusser; *Deep Dive: The proven method for building strategy, focusing your resources, and taking smart action* by Rich Horwath. In addition, it would be beneficial to subscribe to trade publications such as *VMSD*, *DDI* and *Retail Environments*. I also encourage you to attend conferences and trade shows such as Global Shop and the Retail Merchandising and Marketing Conference. Consider joining an industry organization such as the World Alliance for Retail Excellence and Standards.

Understanding standard and custom fixturing

It is imperative to understand the many types of floor fixturing when developing field visual merchandising strategies. Many retailers use standard fixturing to present their merchandise. Therefore, you must familiarize yourself with various styles or types that are commonly used within the organization and learn which accessories are used with these fixtures. In addition to standard fixturing, many retailers and manufacturers develop a custom fixturing programme that is rolled out to numerous stores. Those individuals involved with the in-house visual merchandising team and the field visual merchandisers should be aware of exactly how to present product on these fixturings.

Directives, planograms and look books

A visual merchandising directive is the communication vehicle that provides direction to the field visual merchandising team. This written document provides essential instructions for accomplishing a given product presentation. Usually, a visual directive includes a planogram, which is a diagram or a 3D image of whatever the visual presentation should resemble when completed. In addition, a directive may include a look book. This book is a visual aid which illustrates the retailer or manufacturer's line of product to be manufactured or distributed within a specific season. Examples and details on developing these documents will be discussed in Chapter 2.

Developing training programmes and curriculums

Training is one of the most important steps in developing an FVM strategy. Developing training programmes will help to ensure everyone involved in the presentation process is adhering to the same procedures and merchandising standards for servicing stores. Having a comprehensive understanding of the necessary training methods and materials will help determine the type of educational resources needed for the team. We will go through an in-depth discussion on training in the field environment in Chapter 6.

Window displays and interior presentations

The knowledge necessary to develop window displays and interior presentations should be mastered by the leader and his or her direct reports who are in the field. This is the vehicle for stimulating multiple sales and attracting the target consumers. One should be able to recognize well-put-together displays and have the knowledge to develop innovative presentations. It may become necessary for one to possess a thorough knowledge of visual presentations and understand effective methods for training the team. Again, with retail always changing, it is essential to stay abreast of new trends and techniques as this is an unyielding truth if one intends to be successful.

Sourcing vendors

To source vendors, one must be efficient in identifying, evaluating and selecting the best merchants to participate in the development and execution of the strategy. The main vendor to be sourced in field visual merchandising is the MSO, whom you will hire to provide merchandising services to the respective retailers. We will discuss more about the MSO in Chapter 4. In addition to an MSO, one may have the responsibility of sourcing companies that provide installation service and produce in-store signage. To locate these organizations, one should be prudent and learn as much as possible about the type of companies needed to accomplish the chosen strategy and be well versed on the services they offer. Also, one should be prepared to articulate the exact requirements needed from vendors and be astute at writing an RFP (request for proposal) to aid in identifying the right partners to join with and help make the strategy a success. We will discuss more particulars of these documents in Chapter 5 as well.

Defining a field visual merchandising strategy

A field visual merchandising strategy should be based on your organization's DNA, consumer insight, market research, vision and mission statement. Many companies gather extensive research to identify their target consumers and to analyse the needs of the customer. This information is used to develop the company's vision and mission statement which will provide direction for your strategy.

Forbes.com is one of the most trusted information resources for business leaders. In an article on 28 May 2013, '5 Lessons for Mastering Your Mission', the author explains that 'a clearly articulated mission statement tells your employees what your company's goal is and how everyone should work to achieve it. It defines why you are in business and what principles guide you'. As the leader, gaining a clear understanding of the company's mission and being able to translate that mission into an FVM strategy is an important task. Let's look at an example.

Nike is a world-renowned athletic brand with a mission statement that defines every aspect of their brand, Nike's mission statement is 'To bring inspiration and innovation to every athlete in the world'. (If you have a body, you are an athlete.) Nike has retail stores globally that reflect every part of their mission statement. If you visit a Nike store anywhere in the world, you will see creative and inspiring presentations with graphics of active athletes: mannequins in action pose, playing basketball or running in Nike footwear and apparel.

The store design is very innovative and reflects the image of the company. In addition to these retail locations, Nike has concept shops placed in retail stores throughout the globe that are serviced by field visual merchandisers. Every Nike retail store and every concept shop echo the words presented in their mission statement. As the leader of your strategy, it would be wise to adopt the same philosophy and strive to bring your company's mission to life by translating it into a field visual merchandising strategy.

A strategy

Before we move forward, it is imperative that you understand what is meant by the word 'strategy'. The online Oxford dictionary defines strategy as 'a plan of action or policy designed to achieve a major or overall aim'. The term is derived from the Greek word for 'generalship' or leading an army. Another definition states that a strategy is 'the art of planning and directing military operations and movements in a war or battle'. In ancient Greece, it was the 'art of the general'.

An FVM strategy is a plan of action designed to achieve an overall aim using visual merchandising principles in the field. It's actually a well-calculated process of visual merchandising that involves the selection of the correct steps to accomplish the goals as listed in your company's mission statement. A strategy is much more in-depth than a plan. A plan is simply a list of steps, but a strategy involves identifying risk, using insight and creative thinking on each detailed step chosen in order to reach the desired destination. Many strategies are unsuccessful due to a lack of understanding of the involved retail environment.

Before beginning the development process, performing a thorough probe of the retail store where your strategy will be executed can provide invaluable knowledge and lay a foundation to establish a strategy that will be focused and well defined. One suggestion is to visit stores in each retail account to get an understanding of the environment and their operations. This will help you evaluate the store layout in each retail account, define objectives and formulate a strategic plan in conjunction with the necessary goals of your organization. In addition, invaluable contacts will be made during these visits. Many can become allies to help in the execution process. These allies will want to see the strategy succeed, so they may offer valuable information that can be applied in the planning process.

Thinking strategically

A strategic plan is a document which the leader develops to define and communicate the strategy. This document lists in detail the goals and the tactics needed to achieve the strategy during the planning process. The strategic plan is usually broken down into phases. Each phase includes a sequential list of goals, but to develop this document, you need to know how to think strategically rather than just chronologically.

Strategic thinking is defined as the ability to produce effective plans in line with an organization's objectives within a particular economic situation. Strategic thinking helps business executives review policy issues, perform long-term planning, set goals, determine priorities, and identify potential risks and opportunities.

Thinking strategically involves determining the best way to move forward in order to reach the objective. In field visual merchandising, the process starts with five essential steps: researching, identifying risk, developing a road map, communicating the strategy and coordinating the execution with your FVM team. Let's look deeper into the process:

1 **Researching**: Researching involves reviewing information such as the store environment, the fixturing, the retailer's processes and the target consumer to determine the type of service to provide to the retailer. Knowing this information will provide direction as to what steps should be taken to accomplish the desired goal.

2 **Identifying risk**: As with researching, one of the most significant components of the process is identifying risk. This aspect is very important and can make or break a strategy. It involves using forethought, visualizing the end result, and working backwards to distinguish the necessary actions and procedures needed to fulfil the overall objective. This includes developing a list of activities to be

executed. By analysing these activities, the leader becomes equipped to identify the risk associated with each task and may formulate procedures to address these concerns prior to the launch of the strategy. There are numerous strategic thinking practices used to execute a strategy once a risk has been identified.

3 **Developing a road map:** For this portion of the process, you must evaluate the details of each activity you identified, determine the best execution steps needed and categorize these steps in sequence to one another, moving in the direction towards the objective. These activities will be converted into goals.

4 **Field communication:** This is where directives are developed and provided to the field team to ensure a consistent message permeates the field and all participants possess a comprehensive understanding of the desired result to be accomplished.

5 **Coordinating the execution:** The final step involves coordinating the deliveries of all items conducive to executing the strategy with the field visual merchandisers and the retail store personnel.

Example of thinking strategically

When taking a road trip one would normally obtain written directions to get from point A to point B and follow the directions to get to the desired location. This is a plan, not a strategy. If this were a strategy, one would have approached the road trip in the following manner:

1 Obtain the written directions to go from point A to point B.

2 Research the route to determine if and when traffic would be too difficult.

3 Identify alternative routes and determine the best time to travel to avoid heavy traffic.

4 Obtain written directions on alternate routes to have on-hand if needed.

5 While driving, look ahead at traffic to ascertain when or if to take the alternative route.

Thinking strategically also involves asking questions and gathering information from numerous resources before making a decision and developing the processes. Additionally, it involves ensuring that clear direction is provided to everyone on the team and mechanisms are in place to continuously update involved parties on changes to the strategy.

Example

If a field visual merchandiser arrives at a retail location and informs the manager on duty that he or she is there to set the merchandising presentation for Brand A, the manager on duty may not be aware that Brand A was sending a merchandiser to the store to perform this task. Therefore, the manager on duty may want to contact their corporate office to seek approval.

Ultimately, this action would cause a time lag in the presentation execution. If the leader had identified this risk prior to the execution, a process could perhaps have been implemented such as drafting a letter to be signed by an officer from the retailer's corporate office prior to the date of the launch. This letter would be forwarded to inform all involved retail stores and field visual merchandisers of the execution. The field visual merchandisers would have this letter on hand to present to each store manager upon arrival. By identifying risk, a major obstacle can be foreseen and eliminated prior to the actual activity taking place.

Although an FVM strategy is much more complex than these models, let's look at two instances and determine which leader used strategic thinking and identified risk when developing their strategy. Remember, a plan provides a list of steps and a strategy presents well-thought-out activities selected to get from a starting point to the destination.

Example of plan vs strategy

Scenario

On July 4 two competing apparel brands, A and B, are launching a new assortment in a department store with 200 locations. The retailer has provided both brands A and B with designated fixturing across the aisle from each other on the sales floor. Each will basically have the same size space to include a presentation of product on a nested table, one two-way fixture and a mannequin. Each brand has a field merchandising director or manager (the leader) responsible for developing execution strategies and providing direction to the field teams.

Objective

Both apparel brands have the objective of ensuring their product is presented correctly with signage on the designated floor fixtures and merchandised properly to attract the company's target consumer while stimulating sales.

Strategy: Brand A

Leader A has developed a strategy to accomplish the objective and has included a timeline. This timeline is also called the 'strategic plan' that reflects each phase of the rollout such as the initiation, planning and execution. Below each phase, goals are listed that should be accomplished to complete each phase.

The complete strategy is documented in the timeline and becomes a road map to have the promotion up and ready by the July 4 launch (Figure 1.1).

To provide direction to the FVM team, this leader has developed a directive to instruct the team as to what should be accomplished. This directive also provides stock numbers for the product and guidelines on the placement of merchandise.

FIGURE 1.1   Leader Brand A: Strategic plan

Strategy for In-Store Promotion			
STRATEGIC PLAN	**DURATION**	**START**	**FINISH**
July 4th Strategy for In-Store Promotion	33 days	Mon 6/1/12	Wed 7/3/12
Initiation	**14 Days**	**Mon 6/1/12**	**Thu 6/14/12**
– Obtain Store List from Account Executive	1 days	Fri 6/1/12	Fri 6/1/12
– Obtain ETA on Product Delivery to All Stores	5 days	Mon 6/4/12	Fri 6/8/12
– Obtain ETA on Signage Delivery to All Stores	4 days	Mon 6/11/12	Thu 6/14/12
Planning	**7 days**	**Tue 6/15/12**	**Thu 6/21/12**
– Develop Visual Merchandising Directives for Field Team	1 day	Tue 6/15/12	Tue 6/15/12
– Develop Store Visit Schedule for Field Team	3 days	Mon 6/18/12	Wed 6/20/12
– Review and Obtain Approval from Account Executive	1 day	Thu 6/21/12	Thu 6/21/12
Execution	**12 days**	**Fri 6/22/12**	**Wed 7/3/12**
– Forward Visual Directives & Schedule to MSO	1 day	Fri 6/22/12	Fri 6/22/12
– Review Documents with MSO Management Team	1 day	Mon 6/25/12	Mon 6/25/12
– MSO to Review Directives & Schedule with Field Team and Confirm Dates	3 days	Tue 6/26/12	Thu 6/28/12
– In-store Execution	2 days	Mon 7/2/12	Wed 7/3/12

Field visual merchandising programme

Store visit guidelines for July 4 promotion:
Moors Department Store

When you arrive at the store:

- Enter through the employee entrance.
- Sign in at the customer service desk.
- Locate the department, review the planogram and identify what is required in order to complete the merchandise presentation.
- Determine where your time needs to be allocated.
- Note what fixtures, signage and product should be located in the back stockroom and brought to the department floor.

Before you start merchandising:

- Locate the store contact and communicate your priority to set the Aerdana product presentation for the July 4 promotion.
- Ask for assistance with locating the stockroom where the product, fixturing and signage is housed.
- Locate the items to complete the presentation.
- Ensure the products below are presented.

Product stock numbers and fixtures needed for presentation:

- Nested table: A jeans, 3 colours Blue, Black and Faded Ash, Aj68259, Aj 50221 and Aj50885;
- 2-way fixture: short-sleeve skate shirt two colours, SSS 572 and SSS579;
- Mannequin: Top SSS572, Bottom Aj50885.

Strategy: Brand B

Leader B has developed a timeline (strategic plan) to accomplish the objective as well, and has included the same type of information as the leader of Brand A. Additionally, this leader has added one additional phase, Compliance, to the timeline. In this process, the MSO will submit a report providing details that took place during the launch, including before and after photos. The phases and goals in this strategic plan are documented and the plan therefore becomes a road map towards completion by the 4 July launch date (Figure 1.2).

FIGURE 1.2 Leader Brand B: Strategic plan

Strategic Plan for In-Store Promotion			
STRATEGIC PLAN	**DURATION**	**START**	**FINISH**
July 4th Strategy for In-Store Promotion	**80 days**	**Mon 4/9/12**	**Mon 7/9/12**
Initiation	**17 days**	**Mon 4/9/12**	**Mon 4/25/12**
– Obtain Store List from Account Executive	2 days	Mon 4/9/12	Wed 4/10/12
– Obtain Contact at Retailer's Corporate Office	1 day	Wed 4/11/12	Wed 4/11/12
– Confirm Dates, Fixturing and Space with Retail Contact	1 day	Thu 4/12/12	Thu 4/12/12
– Obtain Product Delivery Information	5 days	Mon 4/16/12	Fri 4/20/12
– Obtain Ship to Addresses for each Field Visual Merchandiser	3 days	Mon 4/23/12	Mon 4/25/12
Planning	**25 days**	**Tue 5/1/12**	**Fri 5/25/12**
– Develop Visual Merchandising Directives and Planogram for Field Team	8 days	Tue 5/1/12	Tue 5/8/12
– Develop Merchandising standards for Product Presentation	3 days	Wed 5/9/12	Fri 5/11/12
– Draft Introduction Letter to Stores and Forward to Retail Contact and Field Team	2 days	Mon 5/14/12	Wed 5/15/12
– Develop Store Visit Schedule for Field Team	3 days	Wed 5/16/12	Fri 5/18/12
– Review and Obtain Approval from Account Executive	1 day	Fri 5/25/12	Fri 5/25/12
Execution	**37 days**	**Mon 5/28/12**	**Wed 7/3/12**
– Forward Visual Directives, Planogram & Schedule to MSO	1 day	Mon 5/28/12	Mon 5/28/12
– Review Documents with MSO Management Team	2 days	Tue 5/29/12	Wed 5/30/12
– MSO to Review Documents with Field Team and Confirm Dates	6 days	Thu 5/31/12	Tue 6/5/12
– Ship All Signage to Field Team and Obtain Tracking Numbers	5 days	Mon 6/11/12	Fri 6/15/12
– Confirm Receipt of Signage from Each Team Member	4 days	Mon 6/18/12	Thu 6/21/12
– Field Visual Merchandising Team to Conduct Pre-Calls	3 days	Mon 6/25/12	Wed 7/27/12
– Field Team to Complete Execution and take Before and After Photos	2 days	Mon 7/2/12	Wed 7/3/12
Compliance	**1 day**	**Mon 7/9/12**	**Mon 7/9/12**
– MSO to Submit Compliance Report including Before and After Photos	1 day	Mon 7/9/12	Mon 7/9/12

Likewise, leader B developed documents to ensure the success of the execution:

- Letter from the store's corporate office approving the execution that will be forwarded to each store's management team and field merchandiser (Figure 1.3.1).

- Directive and store visit guidelines for field team, which includes written instruction (Figure 1.3.2).

FIGURE 1.3.1   Letter from retailer's corporate office to store manager

Moors Department Stores
2145 W. Morris Street
Denver, CO 80203

To: Store Manager
From: Tom Harden, Menswear Sales Manager
Date: 5/13/2012
Subject: Bossman July 4th Visual Presentation and Floor Set

We are very pleased to announce that Bossman has selected your store to receive merchandising service. An Associate from Bossman's Merchandising Service Organization will be servicing your store during the period of 7/2/2012 to 7/3/2012 to execute our July 4th Visual Presentation and Floor Set.

The Bossman Associates' primary responsibilities will be to ensure the correct signage is up, restock, restore, resize and refold Bossman's merchandise and to take before and after photos of their work. Prior to the store visit, you will receive a call indicating the date of the store visit.

On the day of the store visit the Stock Squad representative will sign in at the Service Desk and ask for a member of Store Management. Please provide your support and access to your inventory so they can maximize sales in your store. Should you have any questions regarding the store visit, please contact me at Headquarters.

Thank you in advance for your support.

Sincerely,

Tom Harden
Menswear Sales Manager
817-256 -8172
Tom.harden@moors.com

- Planogram that provides visual instructions for fixture layout (Figure 1.3.3), product placement and product style numbers (Figure 1.3.4).

Furthermore, leader B provided merchandising standards for the field team (Figures 1.4.1 and 1.4.2). This process ensures that the presentation of the product meets the requirements of Brand B and creates consistency throughout all 200 stores.

When comparing the strategy timelines of both leaders, it is apparent that leader of Brand B utilized a great deal of forethought to identify potential

FIGURE 1.3.2 Store visit guidelines

Field Merchandising Programme
Store Visit Guidelines for Macy's

Scheduling Your Visit with the Store:
  ➢ It is mandatory that you call at least one week in advance of your appointment to schedule your visit with the department manager.
  ➢ Ask the department manager the location of the employee/vendor entrance.
  ➢ Ask the department manager who your contact should be if they will not be available during your visit.

When you Arrive at the Store:
  ➢ Enter through the employee entrance
  ➢ Sign in on the Vendor Log at the security or customer service desk. At this time you will be given a vendor ID badge that must be worn at all times during your visit.
  ➢ Locate the department area and determine where your priority of work should be. This will help determine how to allocate your time correctly based on the department needs. (i.e. restocking, reorganizing, refolding and resizing).

Before You Start Merchandising:
  ➢ Review your task duration estimate to know your objectives.
  ➢ Locate your store contact and check in with them. Let them know that your priority is to help restock and restore the Bossman product presentation to the planogram. Walk them through the changes you plan to make to the Bossman presentation.
  ➢ Ask them to show you the location of the stockroom, where Bossman product is housed, and where damaged product should be placed, if found on the floor.
  ➢ Ask if the store has any special merchandising requests.
  ➢ Ensure you take your before photos before you start restoring the presentation.

FIGURE 1.3.3 Planogram fixture layout

risk when developing the timeline. By visualizing and analysing every goal in the strategic plan, leader B identified six potential risks and developed processes to address each:

1 **Store management uninformed of the execution:** A procedure was developed to identify a contact person at the retailer's corporate office that held authority to offer guidance to the store's management team. This contact drafted a letter from the store's corporate office approving the execution that would be forwarded to each store manager and field merchandiser.

2 **Retailer unclear on the details of the execution:** Confirmed the dates of the set-up, fixturing and space allocated with corporate contact to ensure everyone received a clear understanding of the execution.

3 **Signage lost due to shipping or misplaced in each store:** Obtained ship-to addresses for the field visual merchandisers and shipped signage to each team member's home. With the signage in hand, the field team would not need to locate the signage in each store.

FIGURE 1.3.4 Planogram product placement

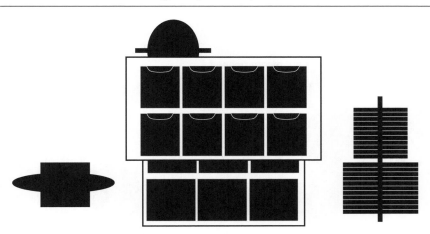

Fixture #	BOSSMAN #	DESCRIPTION
1	BB 459245	Big Boy Pocket T-Shirt 8 colours
2	BB 459245bb	Big Boy Pocket T-Shirt Baby Blue
2	BJ345899blu	Boss Skinny Jeans
3	BJ345899	Boss Skinny Jeans 3 colours
4	BB 459245	Big Boy Pocket T-Shirt Baby Fire Red
4	BJ345899FDG	Boss Skinny Jeans Faded Gold
5		Logo Sign 24"x 48"

4 Field merchandisers unclear on the execution: Developed visual merchandising directives that included the approved letter, detailed planograms and merchandising standards to ensure the field merchandisers had a well-defined understanding of what must be executed.

5 Product and fixturing delayed in shipping: Directed the field merchandisers to conduct a pre-call to each store to confirm product and fixturing was received at each location prior to visiting the store.

6 Confirmation that the execution was successful: A procedure was developed to assure compliance. Upon completion, the MSO will provide a report containing before and after photographs of the performance. This report and photos would be forwarded to the leader for review.

Leader B has a great strategy in place and has addressed the risk associated with the execution of the strategy. The next step in the process is to determine the tactics that will be used to accomplish each goal in the strategy timeline.

FIGURE 1.4.1   Merchandising standard: Folding

FOLDING

To maintain clean and well-presented displays involving folded apparel, the use of folding boards are recommended.

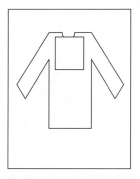

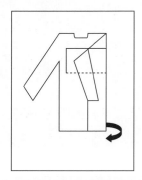

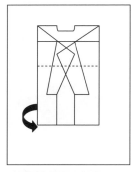

- Centre the folding board vertically on the top of the shirt.

- Fold the right sleeve over the folding board.

- Fold the left side the same way.

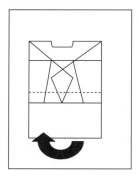

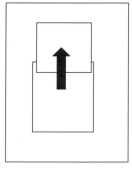

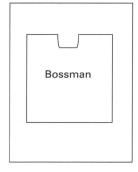

- Fold the bottom of the shirt over the sleeves.

- Remove the folding board.

- Turn the shirt over.

Strategy vs tactics

A tactic is a breakdown of how each goal in the strategy is to be executed. An article on the Management Innovations website outlines several key differences between strategic and tactical planning. Executives are usually responsible for developing strategies, as they have a bird's-eye view or an elevated perspective along with pertinent information that is specific to the

FIGURE 1.4.2 Merchandising standard: Sizing

SIZING

Sizing apparel is an important step in making the shopping experience easy for the customer. When possible, make sure there is a complete size run of every item, as this will promote strong sell-through.

Face outs

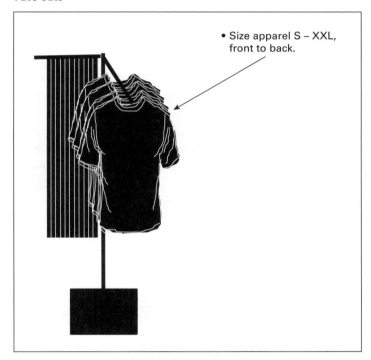

• Size apparel S – XXL, front to back.

mission the company desires to accomplish. Lower-level managers may not be privy to such information, though they may have a better understanding of the day-to-day operations and are usually responsible for carrying out the tactics.

In an FVM environment, the process is essentially the same. Generally the leader develops the strategy while the tactics are executed by managers, MSO management, the FVM team or a vendor. Vendors are usually responsible for executing a portion of the tactics such as developing and shipping signage or installing fixturing, just to name a few. The details of each tactic should be clear and concise.

Example

One goal in the planning phase of leader B's timeline is to develop a visual merchandising directive and planogram for the field team (Figure 1.2). The technique of how these documents are developed and the tools needed make up the tactic. If a goal of the strategy is to provide merchandising services for different retail accounts that each have multiple stores, a different tactic may be used for each account. One account may be serviced once a month and the other twice a month, although the overall goal is to provide merchandising services to both accounts.

Often, tactics may change, but the goal within a strategy will stay the same. In Chapter 9, we will address several types of tactics and explain the means by which these may be used to outsmart the competition.

Let's recap: When developing a strategy, the first step should be to gain an understanding of your organization's mission statement. After the mission statement is clear, develop the strategy and timeline (strategic plan). Then, determine the goals and develop the tactics to complete each goal. The chart in Figure 1.5 depicts the order of the process.

FIGURE 1.5   Strategy development process

Chapter 1 checklist

- Do I have an understanding of my company's DNA? If not, do I know where to obtain the information I need to gain a comprehensive understanding?
- Does my company have a strong visual merchandising culture?
- Have I adequately appraised my skills and identified the additional expertise needed to enhance my abilities for developing FVM strategies?
- Am I up-to-date on current industry knowledge, or are there additional materials I need to obtain to keep me abreast of trends that can enhance the strategies I am developing?
- Am I aware of the type of fixturing my company uses to present our merchandise? Is it standard fixturing or do we have a custom fixturing programme?
- Do I understand the type of training needed for my field visual merchandisers and my internal managers?
- Have I given thought to how I will train my team to develop window and interior presentations?
- Do I understand the importance of visual directives, planograms and look books and the way these documents will aid in providing direction to my field team?
- Do I know where to source materials and vendors to use in executing my strategy?
- Do I know and understand my company's vision and mission statement?
- Have I gained a clear understanding of a strategy and am I prepared to apply those principles to developing an FVM strategy?
- Do I have a solid understanding of my company's mission statement to translate it into an FVM strategy?
- Do I understand the processes of strategic thinking and am I equipped to apply these practices when developing the strategic plan?
- Do I understand the phases, goals and tactics within a strategy and how they are incorporated?

Skill set of your management team

Depending on the structure of your organization, you may be responsible for the complete development of a field visual merchandising strategy and utilize an outsourced FVM team for execution. Many manufacturers and retailers have an in-house FVM team reporting to the leader, and an outsourced FVM team executing their initiatives. If you have an in-house management team, it would be wise to evaluate your management team's skill set to identify strengths and weaknesses pertaining to the execution of your strategy.

One crucial skill required, especially when hiring an outsourced MSO, is communication. The first step is to identify the most effective means to communicate the initiatives to the field visual merchandisers in a manner that can be understood by everyone involved in the strategy. The initiatives will not be accomplished if effective communication is not provided to those involved who are required to complete the execution. Therefore, the management team must have adequate skills and tools to communicate in an FVM environment.

Communicating in the field

It may become necessary for the management team to communicate with individuals on many levels and with various types of people outside your organization. The methods and appropriate times of communication are very important. Before selecting your approach, it is wise to find out the objective and weigh the data required to attain the desired result.

Once the objectives are understood, consider the audience, the information they would need to know and decide the most effective manner to communicate those objectives so that everyone interprets the information in the manner in which the message was intended. If communicating to a group that is not acquainted with visual merchandising, refrain from using terms or acronyms that may not be familiar to your audience. Sit back sometimes and imagine being on the receiving end of the communication, determine if the information is clear and represents the message to be relayed. When preparing an FVM strategy, you and the management team may employ numerous methods for field communications in conjunction with the normal e-mails, conference calls and face-to-face encounters.

Alternative methods of communicating will keep the FVM team clear on objectives and deadlines and maintain a strong, consistent brand message in the retail locations. On that point, we will discuss five methods of communication:

- project management;
- visual merchandising directives;
- planograms;
- visual retailing software;
- look books.

Project management

If I had to list the most important skill used in executing field merchandising strategies, project management would be number one. It's the glue that keeps the strategy together. I encourage you to take advantage of project management courses if possible. The skills developed in project management help to establish clear, achievable targets and provide a road map to the desired destination. Many of the processes developed will keep the management team, field visual merchandisers and vendors on time, on budget and aid in identifying obstacles and potential mistakes.

Project management plan

In general, a project is a plan that has a start and a finish date. It starts at a particular time and has a distinct completion date. The goal of project management is to organize, coordinate and manage the many details required to ensure a project is on time, on budget and achieves the desired goal. Often, the process involves coordinating the execution with external partners who may not be aware of the complete rollout and may not have worked with every stakeholder involved in the execution. Thus, the leader who is assigned the project is responsible for making sure all participating parties are aware of the role they play in the execution process. For this reason, the leader will need to contact each participating party to determine the time frame required to execute their respective part of the project.

With this information, the leader can begin analysing each organization's time frame and start placing each task in the proper sequence or schedule. This also includes ensuring each time frame does not conflict with another or with the expected completion date.

To simplify the process of organizing FVM activities and scheduling, it is recommended that project management software be utilized. There are many types of computer-based project management software packages on the market such as MS Project and Turbo Project. MS Excel could also be utilized. Project management software not only assists with the organization process, but it also furnishes a means of communicating the complete execution from start to finish so that everyone possesses a well-defined understanding of their role in the implementation process.

Project management schedules

A project management timeline or schedule is a document that provides everyone involved with a quick visual on what task should be taking place at a particular time and who should be executing those tasks. Everyone involved will be able to identify where their task is located in the execution process and the time allotted for execution of their task. We will refer to this document as the strategic *plan*. Also, once this document has been completed, it can be used to identify risk associated with the execution. It is possible to glean insight for developing procedures to address those risks that may have surfaced. Overall, this document becomes a road map to stay on time and on schedule. Let's look at an example of project management software being utilized to plan the set-up and execution of a concept shop in a major retailer.

Example

Your team is setting up a concept shop in a major sporting goods retail store that involves the delivery and installation of fixturing, graphics and product. The installation for the shop is to be completed by 28 April 2014. To ensure everything is executed systematically, the leader or a designee must coordinate the delivery and installation of fixturing, product, signage and FVM services with the retailer. Everyone involved should be presented with the details of the execution. Therefore, the leader or someone assigned by the leader, develops a project timeline to communicate the activities that are expected to take place (Figure 2.1). This timeline communicates the start and finish date of the project and each activity involved in the implementation. Additionally, it notes the responsible party for each activity.

FIGURE 2.1 Project timeline or strategic plan

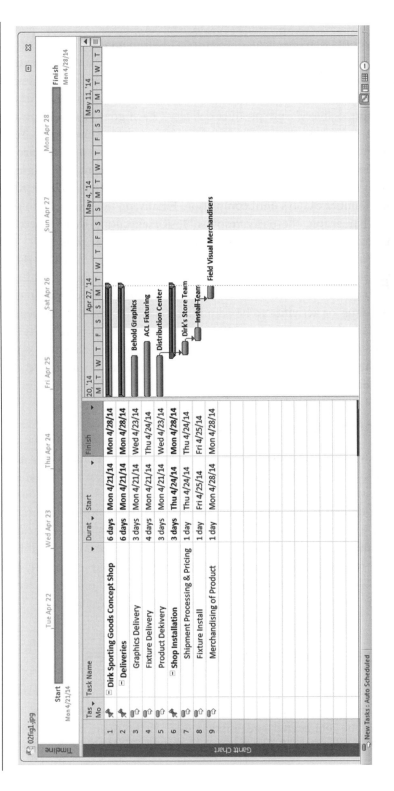

As per the timeline created, the project will require six full days to complete starting on April 21 2014 and ending on April 28 2014. This execution has two phases. Phase 1 involves the deliveries and Phase 2 comprises the shop's installation. Goals are listed under each phase such as 'graphics delivery', 'fixture delivery' and 'product delivery'. Each goal has duration to the side of it indicating the number of days expected for completion. To the right of the duration you will find the start and finish dates for the project.

To the right of the finish date, the timeline presents the commencement and ending date for the entire strategy and a bar graph that stretches across the number of days until completion. Finally, on this example, to the right of the bar graph, the party responsible for executing that respective goal is listed. This process is replicated throughout the next phase.

The timeline becomes a working document and is used by the leader to keep abreast of present and future tasks. This document should be shared with all involved parties within this execution. If it becomes necessary for the dates or activities to be adjusted to meet the deadline, the leader should update this document and forward it to the team. The skills learned in project management will be a tremendous aid in executing any strategy if the team has the discipline to put a timeline in place and monitor it regularly.

Project Management Institute

If one becomes serious about career development, consider joining the Project Management Institute (PMI). PMI is the world's leading organization for project management professionals and has over 2 million members worldwide. By joining, one can obtain a wealth of information on developing and executing projects like an FVM strategy and beyond. The rules learned are the same principles used in many organizations around the globe to create and roll out projects using strategies. By becoming a member, one would receive access to publications to stay well informed of new project management information, tools, research and career development.

Visual merchandising directives

Field visual merchandisers travel from store to store to complete visual assignments and it is imperative to give clear, precise directions that can easily be interpreted and implemented. If the team is executing a project in 200 stores, the field visual merchandiser should be able to quickly view a directive and understand the instructions. If the directive is unclear to one or two people, the presentation in those stores will most likely be presented incorrectly. Therefore, simplicity is very important.

The directive below is incorrect; it communicates through two large paragraphs and would require the reader to review the document several times to grasp the directions to be accomplished. The goal is to ensure everyone on the team has a clear understanding of the objectives in order to complete the strategic plan.

Bossman Clothing Company

Directives for new signage

Start date:	August 15 2012
End date:	August 15 2012

Ensure that signage is current for the new floor set and that the fixtures are signed appropriately as outlined on the planogram. We have new shelf talkers in place to help the customer identify the available styles of product and where they are located on a shelving fixture or folded back-wall presentation. Every category of product must have signage identifying the product. Ensure that all sale signs are placed on the fixtures at all times.

Complete the store visit as required, review the planogram with the store contact to ensure the product is set in the correct area of the store. Ensure all styles, colours and sizes are represented and all possible stock is on the floor during your visit. Ensure that the overall presentation is restored to attract the target consumer. Ensure that all product is sized from smallest to largest, front to back, left to right, and top to bottom. Ensure that all product stacks are arranged consistently by size so that items can easily be found. Ensure that all hanging product is sized and presented on the correct hangers.

The following directive is clear and the headings make it known that there are two major objectives to be achieved. The bullet points provide details on achieving each objective. This document is much cleaner to read and makes it possible to carry out the directive correctly.

Bossman Clothing Company

Directives for new signage

Start date: August 15 2012
End date: August 15 2012

1 Ensure that signage is current for the new floor set and that the fixtures are signed appropriately as outlined on the planogram:

   – Bossman shelf talkers (12ft x 3ft): we have new shelf talkers in place to help the customer identify the available styles of product and where they are located on a shelving fixture or folded back-wall presentation.

   – Headers (24ft x 5.5ft): every category of product must have signage identifying the product.

   – Price point signage: ensure that all sale signs are placed on the fixtures at all times.

2 Complete the store visit as required:

   – Review: discuss the planogram with the store contact to ensure the product is set in the correct area of the store.

   – Restock: ensure all styles, colours and sizes are represented and all possible stock is on the floor during your visit.

   – Remerchandise: ensure that the overall presentation is restored to attract the target consumer.

   – Resize: ensure that all product is sized from smallest to largest, front to back, left to right, and top to bottom.

   – Refold: ensure that all product stacks are arranged consistently by size so that items can easily be found.

   – Hanging: ensure that all hanging product is sized and on the correct hangers.

Planograms

A directive usually includes a planogram, which is a visual reference of the instructions given in the directive. Much has been written about planograms. In the book *Visual Merchandising for Fashion* by Bailey and Baker, the authors point out that planograms are particularly useful to visual merchandisers within larger, multiple-brand retailers because they illustrate the type of fixture required and how the product should be laid out to maintain brand equity across a variety of stores.

Planograms provide clear direction, showing the fixture, the product with style numbers and how the product is to be merchandised (Figures 2.2.1 and 2.2.2).

FIGURE 2.2.1   Planogram: Fixture 1 presentation

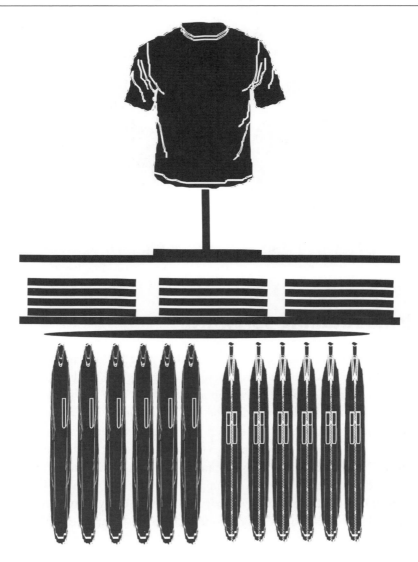

FIGURE 2.2.2   Planogram: Product with style numbers

Ss8976

Ls8977   Lk8723

Visual retailing software

Planograms are essential tools to ensure that your FVM team has a clear understanding of the objectives. Therefore, the method used to communicate planograms is particularly important. MockShop is visual retailing software, specifically designed for the fashion industry. It is a state-of-the-art technology that gives complete creative freedom by letting the user build 3D stores and planograms of any size (Figure 2.3).

In the MockShop software, you can drag and drop virtual fixtures, garments and graphics to provide a complete visual guide to every fixture in the virtual store. The software clearly shows how every fixture should be merchandised and provides foolproof instructions that even the newest member of your FVM team will be able to follow (Figure 2.4).

FIGURE 2.3 MockShop rendering:
Three views of the proposed fixtures

FIGURE 2.3   *continued*

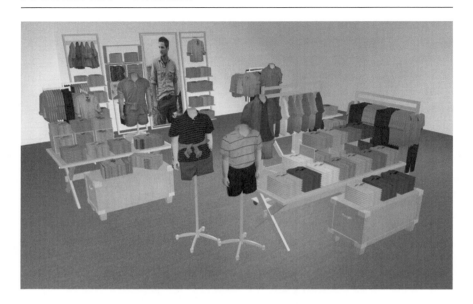

FIGURE 2.4   MockShop software: Screenshot

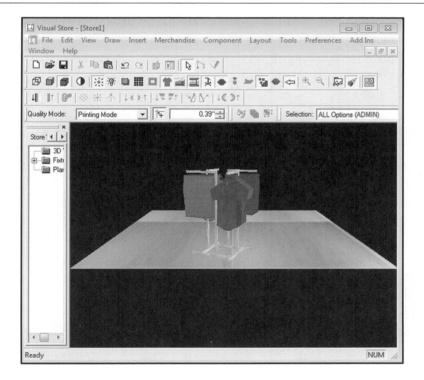

The benefits of using MockShop for field visual merchandising communication

- Improved communication: MockShop uses pictures instead of words. Pictures eliminate language barriers and ensure ideas and instructions are received clearly by your field merchandising team.

- Consistent brand identity: You can create as many planograms as you want, for stores of any size and in any location. This gives you complete control over your brand identity, worldwide.

- One size fits all: MockShop can model any store, of any size, allowing you to visualize your entire store portfolio. It's quick and simple.

- Efficient store layouts: Layouts for store openings and planogram updates can be created quickly and more efficiently.

- Solve visual merchandising issues in the field: Issues in the field can be alleviated by producing as many fixture variations as required to determine the best course of action.

- Standard and custom fixturing uploaded to the software: Custom and standard fixturing can be uploaded to the software to project your brand image in every store layout developed.

- Image processing: Imaging and importing tools automatically convert photos and computer aided design (CAD) sketches into correctly scaled garment silhouettes.

Look books

The online Oxford dictionary defines a look book as a set of photographs displaying a fashion designer's new collection, assembled for marketing purposes. Look books are used by both apparel manufacturers and retailers to communicate not only the line of product they offer, but to present a feeling or a story to show just how a new product assortment is coordinated together. They're usually developed seasonally to showcase a new product line and can be included in a visual directive to provide the FVM team with new product information in a visual format (Figure 2.5).

When including a look book with a visual directive, it is always beneficial to include a MockShop rendering to show in what manner the product can be merchandised (Figure 2.6).

FIGURE 2.5 Example of a look book

MEN'S CLASSIC LOOK BOOK FALL 2012

FIGURE 2.6   MockShop rendering of look book

2013 LOOK BOOK SPRING SUMMER

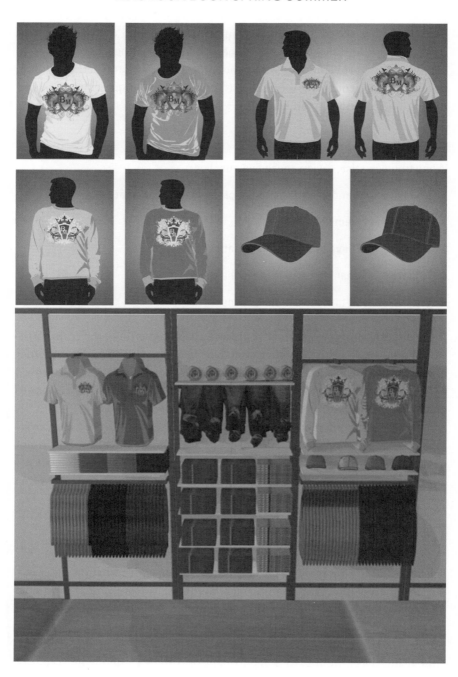

Problem-solving skills

When developing and executing an FVM strategy, the team will encounter problems and issues on a regular basis. It will be an asset to the organization if the team has the ability to make smart decisions and analyse problems quickly. These troubles may arrive one at a time or altogether. The key to resolving these problems is to direct the team to concentrate on the solution, not on the problem. It is a sound idea to prepare a list of questions to review that will help them stay on track.

Example

When troubles arise, review these five questions:

1   Do I have a clear discernment of the problem or situation at hand?

2   What is the objective?

3   How long do I have to rectify this situation?

4   Is there more than one way to solve the issue?

5   Who will I need to involve in the process?

If the situation involves several problems at the same time, the team's process should be to prioritize these problems, placing them on a list by order of importance or in succession. Many times one problem needs to be solved before moving to the next issue. So, if this is the case, it will be crucial to place these in succession to one another.

For example, a merchandiser is required to travel to a store on an overnight trip to accomplish a major execution at short notice. If you do not have authority to approve travel, you may want to get these arrangements approved by your superior before contacting your MSO about identifying an available team member for the trip.

Merchandising problems

It is essential for the team to develop skills in solving merchandising issues. For instance, if the field team is merchandising a store and the product quantity is more or less than what is required in the planogram, this would be the time to make a wise merchandising decision quickly to solve the problem. For a training session, visit a store in your local shopping mall with your team, select an area of a department or a fixture and create scenarios and have the team determine the best way to remerchandise the product. This exercise will keep your team prepared for the inevitable.

It is always beneficial to have a plan of attack when problems arise. Having problem-solving techniques in place helps the team to be prepared for the unexpected that may arise at any time. It is impossible to discuss every problem that may be encountered while merchandising; however, I have found a couple of techniques that work hand-in-hand: brainstorming and mind-mapping.

Brainstorming and mind-mapping techniques

One of the most widely utilized tools for creative problem-solving is brainstorming. There have been numerous studies conducted regarding the effectiveness of this technique and its approach to generating ideas. Brainstorming was invented in 1939 by Alex Osborn, who was an executive vice-president of advertising. He crafted the technique as an alternative to business meetings that did not embrace new ideas and imagination.

Brainstorming

The brainstorming technique can be conducted in a group setting or individually. It involves quickly generating ideas and getting the information out of your mind and putting it onto paper. Upon writing down an idea, another one may come to mind; write that one down and the process continues. When you visually see the ideas you have produced, it is fitting to do a process of elimination and only maintain the solutions you believe will solve the problems.

Example

The FVM team is setting new signage in 200 stores in time for a special in-store promotion that takes place in 5 days. You were just notified that the signage for 10 stores came in damaged. It is very important that signage is set 100 per cent in all 200 stores. The signage company has extra signage that is available to be shipped. Thus, you will need to find the best way for getting the signage to your merchandising team in order to complete the project in time for the promotion.

1　To brainstorm, quickly list all possible solutions on a piece of paper (Figure 2.7).

FIGURE 2.7   Brainstorming: List of possible solutions

2   Go through a process of elimination and only keep the solution that best solves the problems:

   a   Ship overnight to stores – although this option may work, there is a possibility the signage could be misplaced by the store personnel once received.

   b   Ship to MSO then to merchandisers – this is a good option because it will ultimately get the signage in the hands of the merchandisers, but to ship the signage to the MSO and then to the merchandisers may require more time and might surpass the deadline.

   c   Ship direct to merchandisers – this is the best solution because it will get the signage to the merchandisers quickly and in time to meet the deadline.

3   After you have made a selection, move to mind-mapping.

Mind-mapping

A report developed by the Study & Learning Centre at RMIT University in 2007 revealed that mind-mapping utilizes both sides of the brain and stimulates richer concepts. Mind-mapping and brainstorming work together in the planning process. Mind-mapping consists of quickly organizing the important details of your solution and linking these details together in sequence. Once you have the details in sequence, you can see every step in the process of solving your problem (Figure 2.8).

Example

1   Place your solution in the centre of a piece of paper and circle.

2   Write each important detail moving around the circle and underline each one.

FIGURE 2.8   Mind-mapping: The process

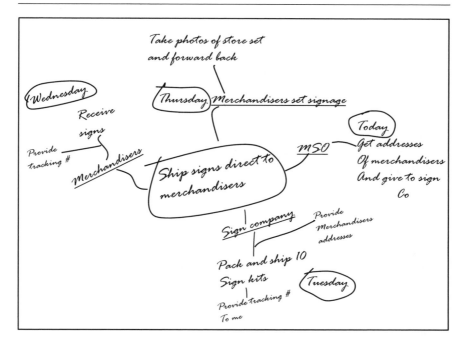

3 Draw a line from your solution to each of the important details.

4 Visualize the steps to complete each important detail.

5 Draw a line connecting each detail to each step in that process.

6 Draw smaller lines to link smaller details.

7 List the sequence or order of execution for each important detail and circle with the execution date.

This process will provide a quick view of your solution and the steps necessary for execution. When completed, your solution can be produced in a formal format that can provide direction to those involved in the execution.

Formal format of the solution

Ship signs directly to the field merchandisers' homes for the store-set on Thursday.

1 Today: Contact MSO to obtain home shipping addresses for merchandisers who service the 10 stores.

2 Tuesday: Contact the signage company to overnight 10 sign kits, one to each merchandiser and then to provide the leader with tracking numbers.

3 Wednesday: Provide tracking information to field merchandisers to identify arrival times of signage.

4 Thursday: Field merchandisers to visit stores to set signage and take pictures.

Once a solution has been determined, provide direction to all parties involved and follow up on the outcome to ensure the project was executed properly. Once results have been obtained, provide feedback to the account executive or sales personnel responsible for that retailer.

E-mail communication to all parties involves:

From:	Taylor Bell
Sent:	Monday, January 16 2012 12:35 pm
To:	Jack Johnson, Tammy Green
Subject:	Friday's in-store promotional signage

Tammy and Jack,

I believe the solution below will get us back on track to get the signage up by Friday's in-store promotion. We need to overnight the signs directly to the field merchandisers' homes to set the store by Thursday. They will carry the signs into the store for installation. See details below:

1 Today – Tammy to provide shipping addresses of the merchandisers who service the 10 stores.

2 Tuesday – Jack to pack and overnight 10 sign kits, one to each merchandiser, and then provide me with tracking numbers.

3 Wednesday – Field merchandisers to track the shipment for arrival times and receive signage.

4 Thursday – Field merchandisers to visit stores to set signage and take pictures for compliance.

Thanks for your help in executing this project.
Let me know if you have any questions.
Thanks,
Taylor

Real-world situation No 1

To develop winning FVM strategies, a leader must be well trained. In Parts 1, 2 and 3 of this book you will be presented with real-world situations that will require strategic thinking in order to analyse and solve the proposed problems or to provide answers to the questions. These are conceptual, but reflect situations that take place on a daily basis in the industry. Each will incorporate information presented in previous chapters.

The challenges

The challenges you face will be to analyse each situation and develop the best answers to the questions. When reviewing and analysing these situations, utilizing the following procedures will aid in developing a habit that will be beneficial in making the process uncomplicated.

1 Read through the entire case study several times to gain a comprehensive understanding.
2 Identify the objective.
3 Identify the problems and document each one.
4 Brainstorm solutions to the problems (use brainstorming techniques if needed).
5 List your solutions and the steps needed to complete each one (use mind-mapping to organize your steps and place them in sequence).

To validate your selected solution and confirm that you are moving in the right direction, use the five essential steps of strategic thinking that are explained in this chapter:

1 Researching.
2 Identifying risk.
3 Developing a road map (use the mind map to help develop your road map).
4 Field communication.
5 Coordinating the execution.

If after going through the five essential steps of strategic thinking you have concerns about your solution, repeat the process until you have a solution that you believe will work.

Remember, thinking strategically involves determining the best way to move forward towards the vision in order to reach the objective. Using this process over and over again will prepare you for the real world of developing and executing FVM strategies. These situations will not include the solutions to the problem.

The solution to the problem will be based on your expertise and applying the information provided in this book. Give it your all to solve the problem. Keep in mind, these are real-world situations that may appear to have a simple solution, but going through the process will help you identify unforeseen problems that should be addressed.

Situation one

Merchandising service requested for re-opening of a retail store

Background Information

You manage a large FVM programme for your company and one of the retail accounts of your FVM team service is a sporting goods retail chain named Millers. The account executive for this retailer would like your assistance with providing merchandising services for the re-opening of this store after a remodelling.

Millers has 120 stores located in shopping centres throughout the south-east. Your field merchandising team services 100 of these stores and your company's product is selling very well in the locations you service. There are 20 stores that your team does not currently service. The account executive originally obtained approval to add this account to your merchandising service store list due to the account's lack of maintaining a strong product presentation of your company's apparel.

You received the following e-mail today:

From:	Mickey Goodman
Sent:	Wednesday, February 15 2012, 9:37 am
To:	Taylor Bell
Subject:	Millers store grand re-opening

Taylor,

My buyer has approached me about merchandising assistance for the Millers store in Savannah, GA. I know we do not currently service this location, but could you possibly help? This store has been recently remodelled and Millers has requested we send in a few merchandisers on 5 March to remerchandise our concept shop prior to the grand re-opening on 7 March. Our shop has two 4-way fixtures, a nesting table and a 4ft wall section. This store visit would be to guarantee we look our best for this grand re-opening event. I will be at the re-opening along with our new VP of Sales.

Later today, I will e-mail you the current product and photos of our concept shop when it was originally set up and provide any additional information you may need.

Let me know if you have any questions.

Millers Store Address: 4722 W Broad St, Savannah, GA 61102

Thanks,

Mickey

Situation:

After reading through the e-mail and analysing the background information, you have identified the following:

1 Your team does not currently service this Millers store location.

2 You are aware the account does not do a good job of merchandising.

3 The objective is to remerchandise the concept shop prior to the grand re-opening.

4 You have 13 days until execution.

5 The team will be remerchandising two 4-way fixtures, a nesting table and a 4ft wall.

6 Today you will receive a list of product and photos of how the shop originally looked.

7 The Account Executive and the new VP of Sales will be at the grand re-opening on March 7.

The challenge

Your team should have a comprehensive understanding of all the details associated with this execution. They need to know where to go, what time to be there, the objective, how the product needs to be presented and how long they have to complete the execution.

Your challenge is to develop a strategic plan that will incorporate the information required by your FVM team and other parties involved in this execution along with how much time it should take to develop and execute your strategic plan.

Assumptions

The problem that frequently occurs in this type of situation is that the leader assumes that, to solve the problem, all that is required is to call the account manager at the MSO and request two merchandisers be sent to the store on 5 March to remerchandise the concept shop. It is very important that, as the leader, you provide clear direction with details of what should be accomplished and the objectives.

Chapter 2 checklist

- Have I evaluated the skills of my management team?
- Does my management team have the communication skills necessary to assist in the development and execution of this strategy? If not, what training do I need to provide?
- Does my management team have solid project management skills? Is anyone on the team a certified project manager? Would it be beneficial to send individuals to project management training?
- Does my management team have the expertise in developing visual merchandising directives? Should I provide additional training in this area?
- Is everyone on the team familiar with using and developing planograms?
- How does my company communicate planograms? Do they use software?
- Does my company use MockShop visual retailing software? If not, should I obtain this software and get everyone trained or just a few key managers?
- Does my company use or produce seasonal look books? If so, where can I obtain copies for my team?
- What type of problem-solving skills does my team utilize?
- Is my team familiar with mind-mapping and brainstorming techniques? If not, should I provide training?

Tricks of the trade: 'Keeping a bag of tricks'

There have been numerous occasions in my career when I was pressed for time and coming up with creative ideas for window displays were just not working. There have been other occasions when my creative juices flowed like a tap and I came up with more ideas than the project actually demanded. This operation became a roller-coaster and I soon saw that many of the big ideas I came up with were lost in my memory, forgotten or I could not remember the details. I became frustrated with my inability to recall these great ideas when I needed them and so I began writing them down. I soon found out that reading my notes did not stimulate my creativity in the manner I anticipated. Therefore, I was back where I started.

Everything changed one day when I saw a picture in a magazine. I said to myself, wow, this would make a great window display. I quickly ripped the picture from the magazine and created a file folder labelled 'window display ideas'. This process became a ritual of mine and as I travelled through airports and malls, I would purchase fashion and art magazines in search of stimulating ideas. I also subscribed to visual merchandising periodicals, took pictures of interesting objects and cut out illustrations. Anything and everything that stimulated ideas went into my folder of window display ideas. I began taking it with me when I travelled and whenever I needed to come up with creative ideas, I went to my folder. I soon found out how valuable this folder had become.

The situation

My company was opening a new flagship store and the window displays had been planned for months. My team and I were flying in for the store set-up and were at the airport when I received the call. The props for the window displays would not arrive in time for the grand opening. My heart dropped because the president of the company and an entourage of senior executives were coming to the grand opening. As I informed my team of the situation, one of my team members said something that put a smile on my face. She said, 'Well Mr Russell, what do you have in your bag of tricks now?' With that statement, I realized that a new concept needed to be developed quickly and I knew where to go find it – my 'window display ideas' folder. The grand opening was a success and my folder became known as my 'bag of tricks'. Keeping a bag of tricks means developing and maintaining a file of ideas that you can pull from at any given time should the need arise. I have found that my best window display concepts are taken from one idea then applied to another. Let's look at three examples.

Window display: Idea 1

The first idea derived from five images pulled from my bag of tricks. In my view at the time, these images all related to each other because they gave me the impression of being caught in a storm (Figure 2.9).

FIGURE 2.9 Window display 1: Initial concepts

Now that we had the concept, the question was: could this be applied and duplicated in 300 stores by field visual merchandisers on a low budget? Using the brainstorming technique that we discussed earlier in this chapter coupled with experimentation, the concept worked (Figure 2.10).

Window display: Idea 2

This next concept was a spin-off from the first idea (Figure 2.11). Although it was only executed in a few stores, with clear instructions, training and having all props packed in kits and shipped to each store, an FVM team could set up this display in 30 minutes.

FIGURE 2.10 Completed window display 1

FIGURE 2.11 Window display 2: Spin-off concepts

Window display: Idea 3

The more images you place in your bag of tricks, the more you have to choose from (Figure 2.12).

FIGURE 2.12   Window display 3

There are those who feel setting up window displays like the ones discussed should not be executed by an outsourced FVM team because one cannot be certain about the calibre and experience level of each person in the field. However, the key to success in any execution is training and providing clear instructions. If you purchase new software or toys for kids, they all come with instructions. If the instructions are clear and cover all the details needed to complete the task, this should minimize your problems. The problems are usually due to ill-defined instructions rather than to the person's failure to follow them correctly.

Mastering the fundamentals of warfare

Everyone in the fashion industry will state that they are aware of the fundamentals of visual merchandising, but many times, this is not the case. While creative talent is prevalent, developing a visual presentation that truly identifies with your company's target consumer takes practice and a concentrated effort. You and your management team will have the responsibility of providing direction to a team of field visual merchandisers. While many on your team may have strong visual merchandising skills, there may be some beginners who need additional training. Therefore, you and your management team should have a comprehensive understanding of these fundamentals in order to provide direction.

Merchandise presentations and visual merchandising skills

The purpose of developing and executing a field merchandising strategy is to ensure that merchandise is presented in a manner to attract the target consumer in numerous retail stores. This can be achieved by combining two crucial aspects: merchandise presentation and visual merchandising. To master these skills, you must commit yourself to constant research and application. Leaders and their teams should never assume they know all there is to know about these subjects. New techniques in merchandise presentation and visual merchandising are ongoing and improved ideas are constantly being developed.

In his book *Visual Merchandising and Store Design Workbook*, Greg Gorman presented the difference between a 'merchandise presentation' and 'visual merchandising'. The two terms are occasionally confused. Let's discuss the differences and look at a few examples.

Merchandise presentation skills

A merchandise presentation focuses on presenting merchandise in a uniformed, balanced manner that is pleasing to the eye. Merchandise may be folded and stacked neatly or hung in a colour sequence from left to right, flowing from light colours to dark. There are countless ways to create merchandise presentations (Figure 3.1).

The product in this merchandise presentation consists of T-shirts, long-sleeve T-shirts, hooded sweatshirts and a table presentation of jeans. Although not visible, the side-hanging product is sized from small to large, going from left to right. The product facing the customer is visible from the front and is sized from small to large, from front to back. The folded T-shirts and the jeans are sized from small to large, from top to bottom. This merchandise presentation gives the customer easy access to the product and the size they need or desire.

FIGURE 3.1   Merchandise presentation

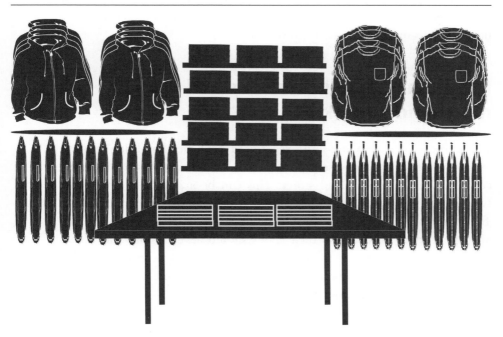

FIGURE 3.2   Visual presentation added to merchandise presentation

Visual merchandising skills

Visual merchandising focuses on the creative process of drawing the consumer to the merchandise in a display or on a mannequin. When a visual presentation is added to the table (Figure 3.2), both techniques work together to create a great shopping experience for the customers. Both techniques require mastering in order to provide direction to FVM teams.

Fixtures and capacity

Visual merchandising involves presenting product on fixtures in a pleasing manner to attract your target consumers. The product of a particular brand is often presented on standard fixturing, but many brands and retailers develop their own custom fixturing in order to set themselves apart from the competition. There are several types of standard fixturing used to present merchandise; therefore, it is very important to gain an understanding of what type will be used and their capacity.

One key to developing good merchandising skills is to understand how to utilize each type of fixturing to present merchandise in a creative manner. This involves knowing how the fixturing is designed and how to use all the accessories such as hang bars, straight arms, cross bars and shelving (Figure 3.3).

Occasionally, field merchandisers will need direction on how to merchandise product on specific fixturing in different situations. Therefore, it is a good idea to develop a book of options showing techniques for presenting product on fixtures and always include the accessories which would maximize the fixture capacity. When giving direction, these techniques can be utilized to provide a clear understanding in a short span of time. When options are pre-planned, more thought can be applied to the creative process involved (Figure 3.4).

The fundamentals of merchandise presentation and visual merchandising include many unique methods of presenting apparel on fixtures, on

FIGURE 3.3   Wall fixtures with accessories

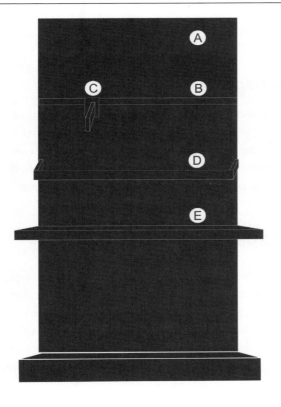

A. Wall Fixture
B. Straight Arm
C. Face Out Bar
D. Hang Bar
E. Shelf

FIGURE 3.4   Wall fixture options with product capacity and number of accessories

Option 1

QTY	PART	PART CAPACITY	TOTAL UNITS
1	Hang Bar	60 Hanging	60 units
2	Shelf	40 units, 4 stacks of 10	80 units
1	Shelf	40 Hats, 4 rows of 10	40 units

Option 2

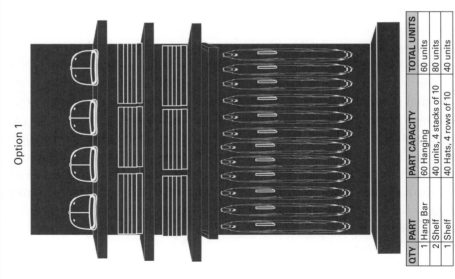

QTY	PART	PART CAPACITY	TOTAL UNITS
1	Hang Bar	60 Hanging	60 units
	1 Cross Bar,		
3	2 Straight Arms	44 Hanging, 2 rows of 22	44 units
1	Shelf	40 Hats, 4 rows of 10	40 units
1	Shelf	Use as Cap shelf	

mannequins and in windows. One of the best ways to learn these techniques is to walk round the shopping mall or along the high street. Here, you can observe the ways in which multitudes of product are presented. Take notes and develop files for yourself. Observe different ways of folding, layering and hanging and unique ways of presenting apparel. Experiment and add your own twist and flair, but keep in mind that whatever technique you utilize must be easily duplicated by field merchandisers.

To stay abreast of industry trends, it would be a good idea to develop a library of books on subjects pertaining to visual presentation, subscribe to publications and attend appropriate trade shows and conferences (see page 11 for detailed suggestions).

Developing a high taste level

If you and your team will be developing apparel presentations and providing direction to field visual merchandisers, having a keen eye for co-ordinating clothing is paramount. When we say that a person has a high taste level or good taste in clothing, we mean that the person has very good judgement in selecting clothing and is sensitive to what colours and patterns coordinate together. In the fashion industry, there are many people who are truly gifted with this ability; but if not, with hard work and a strong sense of style, clothing coordination can be developed.

When selecting products for a visual presentation, you will normally make your selection from a large assortment of merchandise. Since the assortment is usually very large, it is important to have a keen eye for pulling the right combinations together in order to identify with your company's target consumers. We all have walked into a store and seen a display on a mannequin that was exciting and unique, with the apparel coordinated using stylish combinations of colours and patterns that we ourselves would not have put together. Just imagine the impact a display can have when the presentation is duplicated in 300 stores, stimulating sales across the country.

One of the best ways to develop a high taste level is to look constantly through fashion magazines. The goal should not simply be to identify the latest styles, but to evaluate how colours, patterns and textures are mixed and matched. The more you expose yourself to ideas, the better you will become at identifying the right and wrong of clothing coordination.

There are many good books on the market that provide a good understanding of these subjects such as *Interiors: An introduction* (2nd edition) by Karla Nielson and David Taylor. This is an interior design book that provides insight on developing good taste and style. Also, *Dressing the Man: Mastering the art of permanent fashion* by Alan Flusser. Although these books have been on the market for quite some time, they will provide a wealth of information for developing a high taste level.

Mannequin styling and clothing coordination

Mannequin styling and clothing coordination involves selecting the right merchandise for a display. Display forms or mannequins are often used to provide the consumer with a view of what the clothing looks like when it is worn and to present coordinated outfits that stimulate sales. Pulling together clothing for a display appears to be easy, but there is a thought process that goes into the execution. If the goal is to select merchandise for two separate displays, most retail assistants will select an outfit for one display before moving to the next. This process creates two unique outfits in the presentation, but the bigger question to ask is, do the two outfits complement each other? It is important, however, to make sure the wardrobes are complementary. When both outfits complement each other and the items in the presentation can be mixed and matched between the two outfits, the customer is more likely to purchase more items than those presented in one display. One of the best ways to stimulate multiple sales is to layer the merchandise to present multiple items that coordinate with each other.

Example

If the goal is to pull merchandise from the following wall presentation (Figure 3.5) for two display forms, what would the presentation look like?

A basic presentation could be created in the following manner (Figure 3.6), but such an example falls short when it comes to stimulating multiple sales. Although the merchandise can be mixed and matched, not much was done to entice the customer.

There are only four items selected for this presentation with many more that could have been used to stimulate sales and make the presentation exciting.

One of the best ways to proceed is to select one item from the wall presentation and build an outfit for one of the display forms. Once an outfit

FIGURE 3.5   Wall presentation

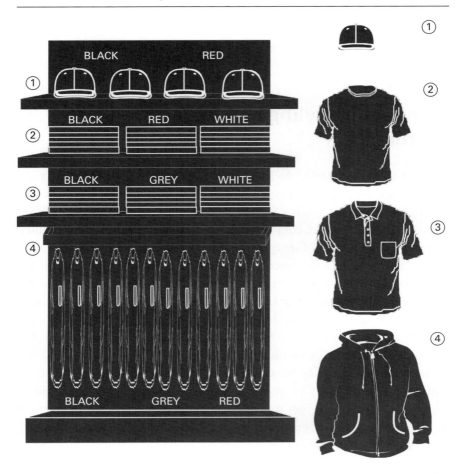

is created, items must be added to build a wardrobe. This process must be repeated until you have many of the items on the wall worked into the presentation.

The next step is to lay out all the items and determine what merchandise can be layered to create a well-coordinated presentation. In the process, try not to use the same item twice, but keep the colour scheme the same in both outfits.

By layering the merchandise and adding more items for the customer to select, the presentation becomes more appealing and presents more possibilities for stimulating multiple sales. We now see nine items in the

FIGURE 3.6   Basic presentation

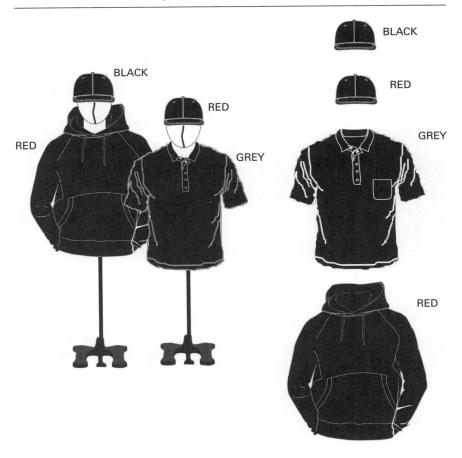

presentation and a more appealing display that provides numerous options for the customer (Figure 3.7). This is distinctly more effective than the four items in the previous presentation.

Mixing patterns in clothing coordination

One of the most exciting ways to create eye-catching displays is to incorporate all patterns in visual presentations. In the book *Dressing the Man*, Alan Flusser explains that if one wants to develop a unique and enduring dressing style, familiarity with the prerogatives of patterns is a must. The goal is to

FIGURE 3.7 Layered presentation

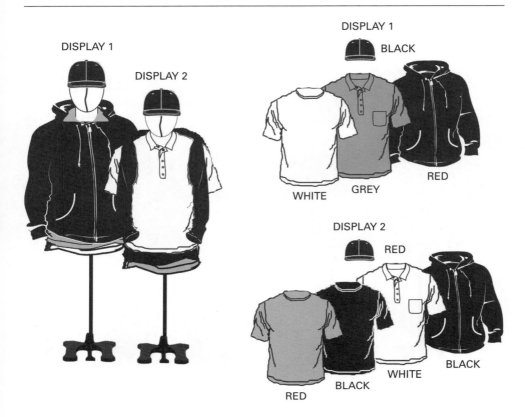

DISPLAY 1

DISPLAY 2

DISPLAY 1

BLACK

WHITE GREY RED

DISPLAY 2

RED

RED BLACK WHITE BLACK

pull together colour-coordinated outfits using multiple patterns. This can work very well when the patterns are in different scales. It would be very beneficial to learn the names of many types of patterns and be able to identify these patterns when they are seen. A few of the most common patterns are presented here (Figure 3.8).

It is fairly easy to put an outfit together using solid colours, but taking the jump to coordinate visual presentations using all patterns within the same colour scheme takes more practice and expertise. Although this seems scary, it can be very successful in stimulating sales if executed properly.

The first rule of thumb to remember is not to select patterns that are of the same size. This will destroy the concept and look too busy to the customer. The key is to skilfully select patterns in different scales.

FIGURE 3.8 Types of patterns

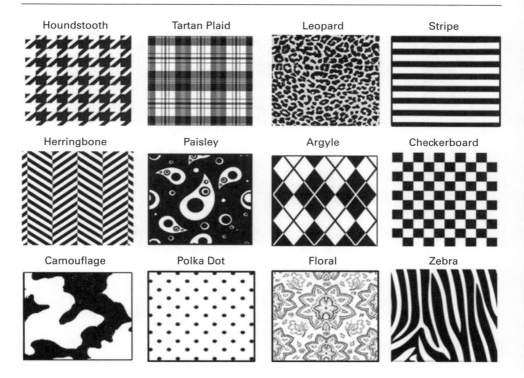

Houndstooth	Tartan Plaid	Leopard	Stripe
Herringbone	Paisley	Argyle	Checkerboard
Camouflage	Polka Dot	Floral	Zebra

Example

Let's go through the same process previously discussed, but use all patterns as opposed to solid colours.

Let's say the first selected item in your presentation is this black and white houndstooth patterned sweatshirt with a black and red printed logo on the front (Figure 3.9). Knowing that your colour scheme is black, white and red, you start selecting items within the same colour scheme that contain patterns. In the process, each item you select is placed next to the other items you have selected to ensure the patterns are larger or smaller than the previously selected items. In this presentation, the plaid cap is a larger pattern than the houndstooth pattern in the sweatshirt and is within the same colour scheme.

FIGURE 3.9   Hooded sweatshirt

As you move through the process of selecting items with patterns of different sizes, staying within the same colour scheme, you began to lay out all the items and determine which merchandise can be layered to create a well-coordinated presentation. When completed, you have developed an outfit for the first display form (Figure 3.10).

For the second display form, you would continue the process by selecting more items that can coordinate with the previous items, ultimately creating a wardrobe that works together (Figure 3.11).

The completed display forms presented together show a unique, well-coordinated display that is designed to stimulate multiple sales. This process takes practice, but can be mastered by reviewing well-coordinated outfits in magazines and developing files on how unique patterns are mixed together to create well-coordinated outfits (Figure 3.12).

FIGURE 3.10   Mixing patterns 1

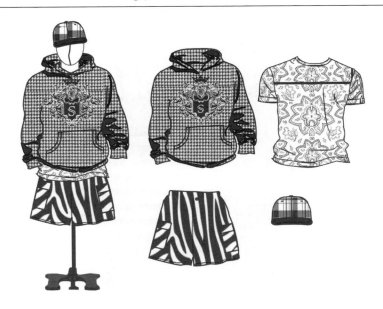

FIGURE 3.11   Mixing patterns 2

FIGURE 3.12 Mixing patterns: Completed presentation

Effects of colour in visual merchandising

A good understanding of colour is very valuable when developing visual presentations. You may want to start by learning basic colour theory, such as:

- primary and secondary colours;
- colour tones, tints and shades;
- colour harmony;
- bright, cool, pastels and neutral colours;
- basic colour schemes.

Purchase a colour wheel to use as a tool when developing your displays; it will help in stimulating ideas for presentation. Colour can create a mood;

therefore, knowing how to create a desired mood in a presentation can stimulate sales.

Let's look at the common moods that can be created through colour:

RED

Intense red:	Danger, passion, love, excitement, conspicuousness.
Dark red:	Wealth, power, sometimes evil.
Pink:	Cheerfulness, youth, festivity.
Light or pastel pink:	Femininity, innocence, relaxation, delicacy.

ORANGE

Orange:	Friendliness, warmth, celebration, clarity.
Dark orange:	Wealth, success, fame, rich depth.
Light or pastel orange:	Stimulation (to the appetites), security, relaxed euphoria (sense of well-being)

YELLOW

Yellow:	cheerful optimism, sunshine, springtime, renewal, intense, demanding, revealing, warmth, intellect, stimulation.
Golden yellow:	Wealth, affluence, status, distinction, high esteem.
Middle to light yellow:	Intelligence, wisdom, compassion, freshness, cheerfulness, optimism, goodness, clarity, cleanliness.

GREEN

Green:	Nature, calmness, friendliness, integrity, practicality, frankness.
Dark green:	Solidity, anchored, tenacity, security.
Blue–green:	Sea and sky, cleanliness, nostalgia, calmness.
Yellow–green:	Youthfulness, freshness, happiness.

BLUE

Blue:	Loyalty, honesty, integrity, royalty, stimulation, restlessness.
Deep blue:	Sincerity, conservatism, safety, peacefulness, kindness, compassion.
Light or pastel blue:	Tentativeness, cleanliness, calm, expanded time and space, lack of security.

PURPLE OR VIOLET

Purple or violet:	Optimism, imagination, royalty, dignity, poise, renewal, commitment.
Dark purple or violet:	Depth, richness, security, sternness, soberness, sobriety, dullness.
Light or pastel purple:	Freshness, springtime, flowers, imaginativeness, femininity, kindness, sensitivity.

Design concepts

If your company has numerous retail stores or if you work for a brand that sells product to retail chains, you may be tasked with developing and implementing window displays. When developing a window presentation, the first step is to determine the direction for the project, otherwise known as the concept. Concept development usually starts with understanding the space where the presentation will be installed by conducting a site survey. This would require you to take measurements and pictures of the window in order to determine how much space is available for the display. After the measurements and the site survey have been performed, you should have a clear understanding of the size of the space. Start by brainstorming and researching to generate ideas. Your ideas can be quickly sketched out or written on paper, as there is no need to stop to fine-tune your thoughts. The primary purpose of this process is to consider and organize the many approaches available because one idea could stimulate another and lead to a successful final product.

Once you have identified the best idea, fine-tune the sketch and guesstimate if the concept can be implemented in all of your chain store windows. This process will help you visualize the concept and stimulate ideas on how it can be executed. If your sketch does not work, start the process over. You may need to repeat it multiple times in order to develop the best conceptual

FIGURE 3.13   Concept board: Christmas window

Concept Board: Christmas Window

drawing. With the conceptual drawing in hand, start sourcing props to bring your design to life while gaining an idea of the price involved with executing the window display in your stores. Depending upon varying window sizes, you may need to develop numerous options. If you are presenting your concept to your management team or a group of sponsors, you may want to develop a concept board (Figure 3.13). This would give everyone on the team insight on the concept, the direction, and the next steps.

When the window is complete, it should resemble the concept you created (Figure 3.14). This Christmas window display was developed for an airport gift shop. The concept was to present a winter wonderland in a small window that would highlight some last-minute gifts for the shopping season.

If your concept is being installed in one store window, you could develop or purchase very elaborate props for your presentation, but if you are rolling out the concept to 50 stores, your props would need to be shipped and easily installed. Therefore, you should source props that your FVM team can set up easily within a given time frame.

FIGURE 3.14   Christmas window display

Chapter 3 checklist

- Do all my managers have strong fundamentals in visual merchandising?

- Does my company have custom fixturing? If so, does my team understand how to put the fixturing together and know the capacity of each fixture?

- Is a high taste level essential to success in my department?

- Can I identify anyone on my team who has a high taste level for coordinating clothing?

- How important is clothing coordination in the type of visual presentations that we develop?

- Would additional training in clothing coordination be beneficial to my team?

- Does my team have an understanding of the fundamentals of mixing patterns in clothing coordination?

- Is mixing patterns an area that I should review or provide additional training for?

- Is my management team well versed in mannequin styling? Is additional training needed?

- Currently, is colour being used effectively by my team when developing visual presentations?

- Does my team have a comprehensive understanding of how to use colour when developing visual presentations?

- Is 'developing a concept' understood among my team?

- What techniques are we currently using to develop concepts?

- Does my team have a solid understanding how to apply brainstorming and mind-mapping when developing a concept?

- Has my management team developed and executed a project from concept to installation?

- Can my team walk me through the process of developing and executing a project?

- How many projects have my team executed in the past year?

- How many of those executions were successful?

- Should I provide more training on rolling out a national programme?

Tricks of the trade: 'From concept to installation'

I have always loved developing concepts, but when one is given the task of developing a concept and taking it from the initial stage to rolling it out in 100 stores in a short period of time, it can be challenging. It would be fairly easy if the windows and shops in each store were all the same size, but usually this is not the case.

In the Preface of this book, I stated that I have documented and implemented many best practices that have proven to be successful whenever incorporated into programmes. Let's walk through a scenario to give you a look at how to apply many of these practices.

The scenario

Your company is launching a new line of men's suits and sports coats with an Italian influence. This is a major advertised launch that will draw customers and celebrities from around the country. To support this launch, the account executive for a major retail account has secured display windows and space for concept shops in 100 stores. You have been asked by senior management to develop a window concept and shop layout along with a timeline of how this can be executed, using the outsourced FVM team you have in place. You will be presenting your concept to senior management in two weeks and they are excited to see how you plan to make this happen by the launch date of July 13.

Step 1

The first step is to acquire an understanding of the size of each window and the amount of floor space that the account executive has gained. Therefore, you obtain a store list that includes the address and phone number of each store location. In addition, you ask the account executive to provide a letter from the stores' corporate office, giving permission for field visual merchandisers to visit stores to take site surveys. This information is forwarded to your MSO account manager with details of the project. Your goal is to have field visual merchandisers visit each store on the list to conduct the site survey. At the site survey, each field visual merchandiser will take measurements of the window where the presentation will be installed and take four pictures: one front view, one view of each side, and one view of the ceiling inside the window. In addition, they will ask the manager to identify the floor space where the concept shop will be placed and take measurements and photos as well. While your MSO is obtaining this information, you begin Step 2.

Step 2

If you have a management team, your next step is to set up a meeting with your team to develop conceptual ideas. Before the meeting, send an e-mail to your management team explaining the situation. Attach a look book to exhibit the new product line and ask each team member to brainstorm and bring to the meeting one or two ideas that would present an Italian influence in a window presentation. At the meeting, when the brainstorming session starts, ask each team member for their ideas. As you list each idea, ask everyone to keep in mind that whatever props are included in the selected concept will need to be shipped to the stores and easily installed by the FVM team. Therefore, all items should be lightweight, cost-effective and packed in kits to eliminate numerous boxes shipping from several locations.

You and the team began to review and discuss each idea, determining which best reflects the Italian influence, complements the product presented in the look book and can easily be shipped and installed (Figure 3.15).

The team decides that the 'Tuscan Villa' concept would work the best and has several options for props that can be sourced and developed in a short time frame.

FIGURE 3.15   Initial brainstorming ideas: Menswear with Italian influence

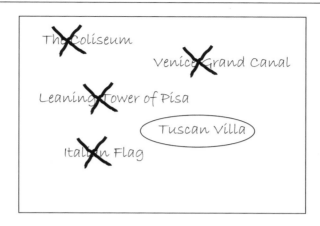

Step 3

The next step is to use mind-mapping to identify several options for props and materials that can be packed in kits and shipped together (Figure 3.16).

With the mind map in hand, you and your team can begin researching to develop a concept board. The concept board is a grouping of pictures and quick sketches that provide a mood or direction for the concept. This will be used along with the mind map when sourcing props and materials for the window displays (Figure 3.17)

Step 4

By this time you should follow up with your MSO to obtain the site survey information. Once you receive site surveys containing the measurements and photos of each store window and floor space, you can determine the sizes for the window displays. The layout for the concept shop can easily be adjusted if the same size space has not been allotted in all 100 stores.

When the sizes have been determined, proceed with sourcing props and fine-tuning the concept using MockShop visual retailing software. Your goal is to present a complete concept board that includes visuals of the window concept, interior presentation and the window presentation kit (Figure 3.18).

Step 5

With the concept board developed, props and materials selected and everyone aware of the execution, the project timeline can be prepared to meet the launch date of July 13 (Figure 3.19).

FIGURE 3.16   Brainstorming results: Tuscan villa concept

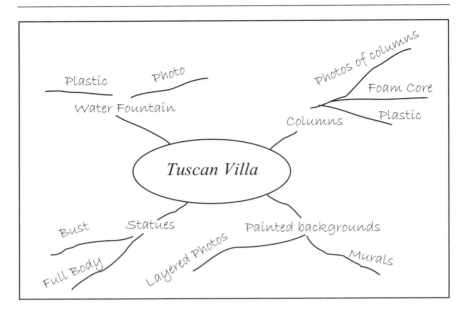

FIGURE 3.17   Concept board: Tuscan villa

FIGURE 3.18 Complete concept board

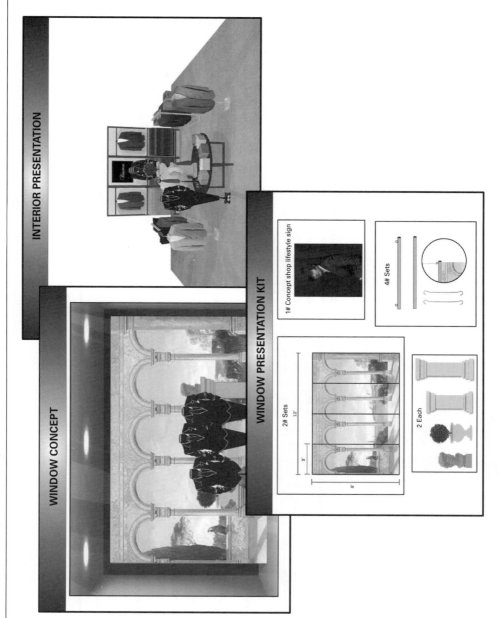

FIGURE 3.19 Project timeline

ID	❶	Task Name	Duration	Start
1		WINDOWS & CONCEPT SHOPS FOR 100 STORES	86 days	Mon 3/12/12
2		PRODUCTION & SHIPPING PROPS FOR KITS	20 days	Mon 3/12/12
3		PRODUCTION OF COLUMNS & GRAPHICS	20 days	Mon 3/12/12
4		SHIPPING OF PLASTIC PLANTERS	14 days	Mon 3/12/12
5		SHIPPING OF MURALS	14 days	Mon 3/12/12
6		SHIPPING OF SCULPTURE	10 days	Mon 3/12/12
7		SHIPPING OF HARDWERE KITS	12 days	Mon 3/12/12
8		PACKAGING KITS & SHIPPING TO STORES	45 days	Mon 4/9/12
9		PACKAGING 100 KITS	7 days	Mon 4/9/12
10		SHIPPING 100 KITS TO STORES	20 days	Wed 4/18/12
11		PROVIDE SHIPMENTRACKING INFORMATION	1 day	Wed 5/16/12
12		PRE-CALL TO STORES TO CONFIRM DELIVERY	7 days	Thu 5/17/12
13		PRE-CALL REPORT DUE	1 day	Mon 5/28/12
14		SCHEDULE WINDOW INSTALLATION FOR TEST STC	1 day	Tue 5/29/12
15		SCHEDULE INSTALLATION DATES FOR 99 STORES	7 days	Wed 5/30/12
16		INSTALLATION SCHEDULE DUE	1 day	Fri 6/8/12
17		WINDOW AND CONCEPT SHOP INSTALLATIONS	29 days	Wed 5/30/12
18		TEST STORE WINDOW INSTALLATION	3 days	Wed 5/30/12
19		PHOTOS OF TEST STORE WINDOWS DUE	2 days	Mon 6/4/12
20		WINDOW & SHOP INSTALLATIONS FOR 99 STORES	7 days	Mon 6/18/12
21		FINAL PHOTOS AND REPORT DUE	9 days	Wed 6/27/12

This timeline provides everyone involved with a quick visual of which task should be taking place at a particular time and who should be executing the task. Everyone involved will be able to identify where their task is located in the execution process and the time allotted for execution.

The timeline will be executed in three phases that will take 86 days to execute.

Phase 1: Production and shipping props for kits

In this phase all props and signage will be produced and shipped to the signage company.

Phase 2: Packaging kits and shipping to stores

The signage company will pack all items into individual kits and ship to each store location. In addition, your MSO will:

- conduct a pre-call to each store and confirm delivery of each kit;

- schedule installation dates for one test store and the additional 99 stores;

- provide the leader with a schedule of when each installation will be executed.

Phase 3: Window and concept shop installations

In the last stage, your MSO and FVM team will complete the installations for the one test store and forward photos. The additional 99 stores will then be executed and your MSO account manager will forward a complete report to include photos of the additional stores.

Step 6

Your last step is to develop a visual merchandising directive that provides your FVM team with complete instructions on the set-up and installation of the window presentations and the concept shop. This is a major launch and you want to ensure that everyone on your field team has a clear understanding of the objectives and visual instructions.

Your instructions for the window presentations consist of four documents:

1 Store visit guidelines (Figure 3.20.3).

2 A rendering of the windows that need to be executed.

3 A list of all items included in the window presentation kit (Figure 3.20.2).

4 Product selection for each window.

FIGURE 3.20.1 Visual merchandising directive: Cover

FIGURE 3.20.2 Product selection for windows

FIGURE 3.20.3 Store visit guidelines

STORE VISIT GUIDELINES

These guidelines have been developed to provide instructions on servicing this retailer. In addition to the information below, please review the attached 'sales floor rules' and govern yourself accordingly. Prior to visiting the store, pack your task duration estimate, planograms, signage or any point of purchase materials needed.

Scheduling Your Visit with the Store Management:
- It is mandatory that you call at least one week in advance of your appointment to schedule your visit with the store or department manager.
- Ask the manager the location of the employee/vendor entrance.
- Ask the manager who your contact should be if they will not be available during your visit.

When you Arrive at the Store:
- Enter through the employee entrance.
- Sign in on the Vendor Log at the security or customer service desk. At this time you will be given a vendor ID badge that must be worn at all times during your visit.
- Locate the department area and determine where your priority of work should be. This will help determine how to allocate your time correctly based on the department needs. (i.e. restocking, reorganizing, refolding and resizing).

Before You Start Merchandising:
- Review your task duration estimate to know your objectives.
- Locate your store contact and check in with them. Let them know that your priority is to help restock and restore the Bossman product presentation to the planogram. Walk them through the changes you plan to make to the Bossman presentation.
- Ask them to show you the location of the stockroom, where Bossman product is housed, and where damaged product should be placed, if found on the floor.
- Ask if the store has any special merchandising requests.
- Ensure you take your before photos before you start restoring the presentation.

You should also offer instructions for the concept shop installation. This would consist of several documents such as:

1 Interior presentation rendering (Figure 3.21.1).

2 Floor layout (Figure 3.21.2).

3 Planograms of each fixture that includes the product and style numbers (Figure 3.21.3).

FIGURE 3.21.1   Interior presentations

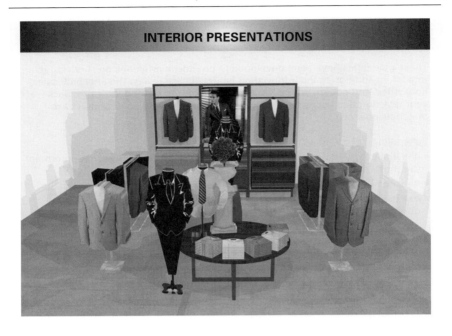

FIGURE 3.21.2   Floor layout

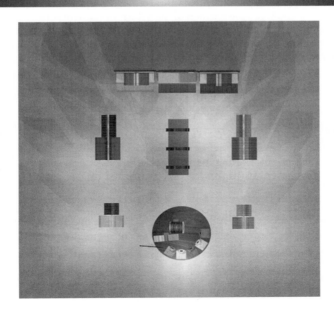

FIGURE 3.21.3 Planograms

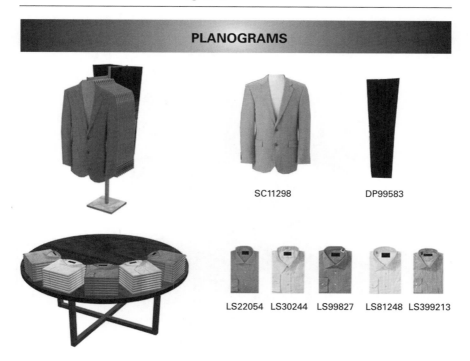

When complete visual direction is offered along with a detailed project time-line, your FVM team becomes an extension of your brand, ready to carry out turnkey projects on a steady base. What makes it all worthwhile is to see the visual directives come to life in the photos you will receive later (Figure 3.22).

If you survey all of Part 1 of this book along with this scenario, you will acquire an understanding of how to utilize these practices and an idea of how valuable they are to the success of your FVM strategy. In this 'tricks of the trade' section, we applied the following skill sets and fundamentals:

1 Communication in the field.

2 Mind-mapping and brainstorming.

3 Visual merchandising directives.

4 Planograms.

5 MockShop visual retailing software.

6 Project management.

7 Merchandise presentation and visual merchandising skills.

FIGURE 3.22   Final window display

It would be beneficial for you, as the leader, and for your team to gain a broad understanding of how to apply these practices as you continue to develop and execute strategies using the field visual merchandising team.

PART TWO
Planning and initiating your battle strategy

It's important to recognize that before you can plan an FVM strategy you should acquire an understanding of the components needed to plan the details. No battle is won without an army and no war is won without a strategy. In field visual merchandising, the same logic applies. Therefore, to plan the strategy, one should know how to select an MSO and gain knowledge of their capabilities if one intends to utilize their services to execute the strategy. The FVM team must be well prepared and outfitted for the battle and it is essential for the leader to be focused on the goals and tactics to fulfil the objectives of the strategy.

Components of your strategy

To produce a strategy, one must have a clear understanding of the components necessary to develop the strategy. First of all, it is paramount to recognize the structure and capabilities of the chosen army. Next, one will need to set clear objectives, stress what is to be carried out and emphasize the standards. Last but not least, one should know the battlefield where combat will take place and define the requirements to participate in the fight while remembering that the battle isn't won without an army.

Armies for hire

The clothing industry is extremely competitive and apparel manufacturers are unyielding when it comes to satisfying the demands of their target consumers. These executives seek out the best talent from universities all over the world and hire the greatest designers, marketers and salespeople with hopes of producing the right product for their target consumers. Manufacturers develop in-store marketing campaigns and spend billions of dollars, pounds or euros to ensure their product has a winning presence in stores. To do this, contributions are made from many other industries such as transport companies to take the product from the manufacturer to the retailer. Outside workers are involved in manufacturing the product, shipping merchandise all over the world, pricing, packaging the product and participating in a host of other activities that go into bringing a garment to life and presenting it in a retail store.

Millions of garments are produced on a daily basis and the success of a garment lies in the hands of sales assistants who are responsible for getting this product from the stockroom to the sales floor. One could only imagine the frustration of clothing manufacturers if they discover their product did not sell because it did not make it from the back stockroom to the sales floor in time to coordinate with marketing campaigns.

This scenario happens more frequently than we would like to believe. Outsourcing involves hiring an outside agency to perform work that is usually completed by a company's in-house employees. Many companies outsource services to take advantage of the features and benefits of using an outside organization. Outsourcing has become a cost-effective way for companies to take their vision to the next level. Many organizations have been developed to offer outsourcing services to a host of industries.

Field visual merchandisers are the road warriors and silent soldiers not seen by most customers. Most are well trained and are the face of the brands they represent. They are the eyes and ears of the brand who gather invaluable market intelligence on a regular basis. In many instances, retail sales personnel do not see executives from the manufacturer or brand, but instead they will meet and communicate with an field visual merchandiser who represents the brand. These road warriors build strong relationships with store management and sales assistants turning them into brand advocates. Due to local residency of field visual merchandisers, brands and retailers are seeing a decrease in travel time and related expenses when outsourcing to a merchandising service organization (MSO).

MSOs play an important role in the retail industry and are being hired by manufacturers and retailers. They hire, train and manage a large team of field merchandisers who provide merchandising services to retailers on behalf of many of the top brands. Retailers are using MSOs to execute their in-store strategies. An important part of developing an FVM strategy is having an understanding of the MSO's capabilities. The World Alliance for Retail Excellence and Standards is one organization that provides a list of outstanding MSOs to help with those services.

The World Alliance for Retail Excellence and Standards (www.worldalliance-retail.org)

This is a global organization that brings together retail service providers, manufacturers and retailers. They have a comprehensive website that supplies a list of retail services providers that perform many types of services up to and including field merchandising. Their website also provides industry research, educational information and a wealth of knowledge on industry operations. They also have an annual conference to provide insight, contacts and valuable information on developing and executing strategies.

There are many benefits to joining an organization of this type. A retailer, manufacturer or MSO would have the opportunity to network with industry professionals and discover valuable information that will prove to be beneficial when developing and executing strategies. One significant benefit is its ability to provide key information needed to identify an MSO to meet your demands.

Merchandising service organizations are not all alike and in the past decade, identifying the right MSO partner was a guessing game. No one would provide recommendations and everyone wanted the business. It was difficult to obtain information on which MSOs were in good standing with retailers, and which organization could or could not manage your expectations. To address this issue, the World Alliance for Retail Excellence and Standards developed the World Alliance Gold Certification programme.

World Alliance Gold Certification

The Gold Certification programme is a retail service management standard which identifies retail member companies that have completed the documentation process to become a certified retail service provider with World Alliance. The certification addresses the company's operational functions, delivery of services, policies, internal controls, training, and many other functions associated with being an exceptional retail service provider. The gold certification criteria were created by a national organization that specializes in developing certification programmes.

As you develop your strategy, it is necessary to know the capabilities of MSOs and their function. A certification programme is a means to help one identify the right MSO, but a basic understanding of how these organizations are structured is needed to make a wise and informed decision. Keep in mind the organization you select will represent your brand in all retail locations, and with this partnership they must have a clear understanding of your company's objectives.

Structure of a merchandising service organization

The goal of every MSO is to provide superb service and ensure every retailer and brand's product is presented in the best manner possible. Many MSOs have a large FVM team located throughout the country, servicing many types of retailers, representing many brands. Although merchandising is a major portion of the service provided, MSOs may also hold expertise in other areas such as fixturing installation and event marketing, to name just two. MSOs are not all structured similarly. Although they all have account managers, field managers, trainers and field merchandisers, it's important for a leader to understand the structure of a basic MSO organization.

Levels of management

Many MSOs have between 500 and 1,000 merchandisers in the field. Each MSO has multiple layers of management with different types of responsibilities. Although titles and responsibilities may vary, the basic field structure looks similar to the following:

Account/programme managers

Account or programme managers will be the point of contact for everything within the MSO organization. He or she will usually work out of the MSO's corporate office and will communicate the needs of the leader to the field organization. This person will forward any information from the field back to the leader or to a designated person. Account managers are very detail oriented and many have years of industry experience. The account manager should be well versed on the hiring company's standards and possess details of the strategy and its execution process. This individual will also provide store visit reports, alerts or red flag issues and any feedback information a leader needs from the field merchandisers.

Directors, regional managers/field service managers

Directors, regional managers or field service managers hire and train the field management teams. These individuals may also assist in the recruiting process for field visual merchandisers and are responsible for ensuring all stores in the programme are serviced with qualified field team members.

District managers, field training managers and team leaders

Depending on the size of the MSO, they may employ several levels of field managers such as district managers, field trainers and team leaders. This team is responsible for training and reviewing reports to ensure the leader has pertinent data on each store visit. They guarantee before and after photos of their work and ensure that all facets of the strategic plan are in compliance with the leader's directions. Many perform store visits to certify the merchandising standards are upheld and the leader receives the quality services that are expected from an MSO.

Types of field visual merchandisers

An FVM team should be an extension of the brand; therefore, it's vital for the leader to visit stores that are being serviced on a regular basis to confirm the product is being presented as directed. It is wise to have knowledge regarding the different types of merchandisers, so as to select what's best for your strategy.

Apparel field visual merchandisers

The overall goal of an apparel field visual merchandiser is to ensure the product is pulled from the stockroom, creatively merchandised in a manner that attracts the company's target consumers, while placing signage correctly in its proper place and taking before and after photos. They also develop a solid relationship with the retail store sales assistants while communicating new initiatives forwarded by the brand. After the store visit, the merchandiser will complete a store visit report to provide information such as low stock levels on product, signage needed, the quantity of product pulled from the stockroom and much more.

Apparel field visual merchandisers usually visit stores on a bi-weekly rotation and service multiple brands. Depending upon the request, stores may be serviced once a week, twice a month, quarterly or seasonally. The time frame for each store visit is determined by the specifics negotiated between the hiring company and the MSO. Each merchandiser is focused on a geographical area and usually services stores within a 30-mile radius from their home. Most are employed part-time, Monday to Friday, and provide an array of services for different retailers from merchandising for one brand to product training for another.

Apparel brand ambassadors/merchandising coordinators/merchandising specialists

Apparel brand ambassadors may be called merchandising coordinators or merchandising specialists. They are similar to apparel field visual merchandisers, but are only focused on providing merchandising services for one specific brand. Some brands have numerous stores in a major market; consequently, a brand ambassador is the next best thing to a full-time employee. In addition to merchandising product, they serve as brand advocates to provide support for all retail marketing and branding initiatives at the retail level. While a brand ambassador services stores for one particular brand, many times they may be outfitted from head to toe, dressed in that manufacturer's product as a walking billboard for the brand.

Additional tasks of field visual merchandisers and brand ambassadors

In addition to regular services provided by the field merchandisers and brand ambassadors, they are often used for product training and merchandising for brand shop installations, store openings and resets:

- Product training: When a brand introduces a new product, they usually use merchandisers or brand ambassadors to provide product knowledge training to store personnel.

- Merchandising services for brand shop installations: Brand shops are designated areas within a department, highlighting one particular brand. When a brand plans to install custom fixturing or a new brand shop in a retail store, a group of merchandisers may be requested to merchandise the new product.

- Store openings and resets: Groups of merchandisers are also used for new store openings and are utilized to reset merchandise for an entire department.

- Point-of-purchase displays and signage: POP displays and signage are used to attract consumers and provide information on the features and benefits of a product and price. Field merchandisers are also used to set POP and signage in numerous stores prior to an in-store promotion.

Store visits

The number of store visits and the time frame of each visit are determined by what is negotiated between the retailer/manufacturer and the MSO. The size of the area and the number of fixtures is also considered. A manufacturer may have two fixtures in an account that has 300 stores and a brand shop with floor fixtures and a wall presentation in another account that has 500 stores. Store visits may also take place once a week, twice a month, monthly or once a quarter. It all depends on the strategy, the cost and what activities are needed in each account.

Example

A brand shop consisting of five floor fixtures may take 1 hour 30 minutes to service. The time includes pulling product from the stockrooms, and merchandising the product on the five fixtures. If sales are very good, the retailer/manufacturer may need field merchandisers to provide services once a week.

Defining objectives and standards

It's time to get down to business to define the objectives and obtain clear-cut information to prepare for the battle. First, a leader should gather an understanding of which accounts the field merchandising team will need to service, how many stores each account has and a list of store addresses. This information is collected from the sponsors.

Sponsors

Sponsors will generally be executives who are responsible for funding the strategy. Normally, these are senior executives in the organization that have the authority to decide fiscal and budgetary allocations. A leader should meet with each sponsor to gain an understanding of their expectations. Every sponsor should be open to provide any information required and willing to become involved in the development and implementation process. Keep in mind that sponsors may have different expectations for each account. Thus, you must document this information to ensure all parties are on the same page. A leader should have an understanding of the structure of a retail merchandising strategy and be aware of what can and cannot be accomplished. Always be prepared to offer guidance to sponsors if their expectations and targets are unrealistic.

A leader should establish a trusting relationship with sponsors. Usually they want to know who is responsible for the outcome of the strategy and to be certain they can trust the leader to make sure their expectations will be met. Some sponsors prefer to be kept informed on details and should be provided with regular updates on the milestones as they are accomplished. In order to succeed as the leader of your strategy, you should focus on building a solid relationship and becoming an advocate for the sponsors.

Sponsor expectations

Sponsors have their own expectations and the leader's goal is to define these expectations and document this information.

For example: there are three sponsors and each one has an account in a different trade channel. Develop an account profile and document key information around what type of visual merchandising service each demands. The account profile should include the following information (Figure 4.1).

FIGURE 4.1   Sponsor 1

Sponsor 1	Account Profile

Account Type	Department Store
Total Number of Stores	400
Total Stores Needing Service	200
Total Urban Stores	10
Total Suburban Stores	175
Number of Key Cities	5

Sponsor 1 is an account executive responsible for a department store chain that has 400 stores The company's product is carried in 200 stores. This sponsor would like the FVM team to service these 200 stores twice a month to ensure that the product is pulled from the back room and merchandised on the sales floor with the correct signage in place.

The product should be merchandised on four floor fixtures that will be dedicated to the brand. Request a store address list for the 200 stores to be serviced. When asking for a store list, be sure to request that the information be furnished in a spreadsheet format, such as MS Excel. This cuts down on typing errors when transposing information and can easily be developed into a master store list.

The sponsor will probably contact the account to obtain an accurate store address listing. Ask the sponsor to provide you with the name and contact information of a go-to person at the account's corporate office in case approvals are required. Additionally, as plans are developed, this go-to person can assist with passing down information needing to be transferred to the retail store. When providing information to accounts, always copy in sponsors to keep all responsible parties in the loop on information or data obtained and forwarded.

The second sponsor is an account executive for a specialty store chain that has 500 stores (Figure 4.2). The company's product is carried in 200 stores. This sponsor would like the FVM team to service these 200 stores once a month to ensure the product is pulled from the back room and merchandised on the sales floor with the correct signage in place. The brand has a 300sq ft concept shop in each of the 200 stores with two mannequins. Also request a store address list of the 200 stores that will be serviced.

FIGURE 4.2 Sponsor 2

Sponsor 2	Account Profile
	Account Type	Specialty Store
	Total Number of Stores	500
	Total Stores Needing Service	200
	Total Urban Stores	50
	Total Suburban Stores	150
	Number of Key Cities	8

The last account executive is responsible for a superstore chain that has 475 stores (Figure 4.3). The company's product is carried in 200 stores. This sponsor would like the FVM team to service these 200 stores twice a month to ensure the product is pulled from the back room and merchandised on the sales floor with the correct signage in place. The brand has a 225sq ft concept shop in each of the 200 stores. It would be beneficial to request a store address list of all 200 stores needing to be serviced.

FIGURE 4.3 Sponsor 3

Sponsor 3	Account Profile
	Account Type	Big Box
	Total Number of Stores	475
	Total Stores Needing Service	200
	Total Urban Stores	0
	Total Suburban Stores	200
	Number of Key Cities	5

Evaluating sponsor expectations

The leader should have a clear understanding of the sponsor's expectations and maintain open communication with them on a regular basis.

After evaluating the overall expectations and objectives, the strategy will start to take shape. For now, the leader has the following information:

- The FVM strategy will be focused on servicing 600 stores in three trade channels: department store, specialty store and superstore.

- There are 200 stores in each account with locations throughout the country that include suburban, urban areas and major cities.

- Two of the accounts have brand concept shops in 200 stores each and the department store account has four fixtures in a designated area.

All three sponsors have the same expectations: each wants to ensure the company's product is pulled from the back room of each store and merchandised properly on the sales floor in the designated area. As the leader, your goal should be to create a consistent product presentation in all 600 of these retail locations.

If the target consumer visits a store in New York and travels to a store in Georgia, they should see very similar product presentations in both stores. This is why the FVM team should be presented with the company's merchandising standards.

Merchandising standards

These standards are very important and helpful in communicating the methods in which the merchandise should be presented in all stores. Many retailers have their own merchandising standards for their stores, but often these principles may not reflect the manner in which your company's product should be presented. To communicate your standards, it is wise to develop a merchandising standards manual (Figures 4.4.1, 4.4.2 and 4.4.3). This manual can be used to train the field merchandising team and offer guidance for retailers on the way the product presentation should be maintained.

Analysing the battlefield

Once merchandising standards have been developed, visit stores within the retail accounts that will be serviced by your FVM team to gain an understanding of how the product is currently being presented. To do this, a master store list should be developed utilizing the list obtained from each of your sponsors.

FIGURE 4.4.1   Merchandising standards manual: Front cover

Master store list

A master store list should give the name of the store, the address, the phone number and if possible, the name of the store manager at each location.

Once this list is in hand, select two or three stores from each account and make travel arrangements. Visit each store to analyse the presentation of the product and develop an estimate as to the length of time each store visit should take.

FIGURE 4.4.2   Merchandising standards manual: Sizing instructions

SIZING APPAREL

When apparel is sized and a full size run is offered, the customer has a great shopping experience. The customer can easily locate their size and move to the payment point or fitting room. The following sizing instructions will help you create and maintain this atmosphere for your customers.

Apparel should be sized left to right, small to large or front to back, small to large.

SIDE HUNG

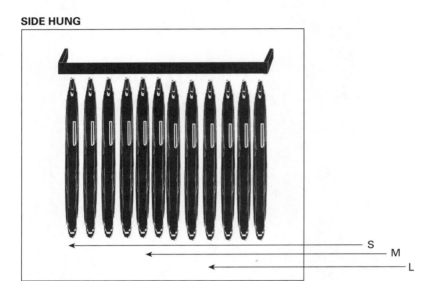

FACED OUT

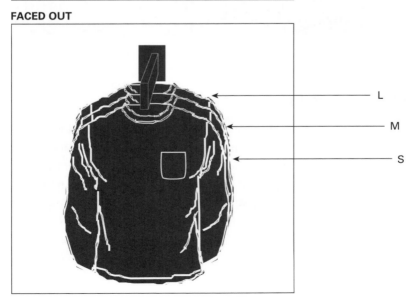

FIGURE 4.4.3 Merchandising standards manual: Folding instructions

SHIRTS
To maintain clean and well-presented displays involving folded tops, the use of folding boards are recommended.

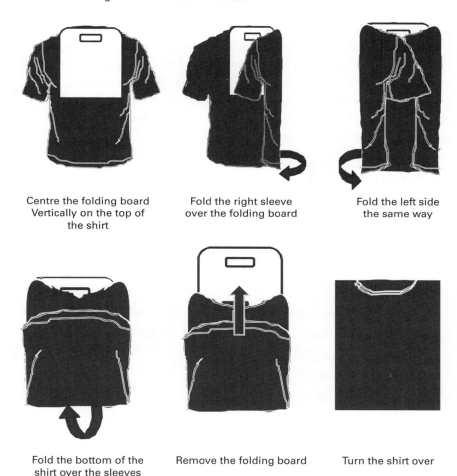

Centre the folding board Vertically on the top of the shirt

Fold the right sleeve over the folding board

Fold the left side the same way

Fold the bottom of the shirt over the sleeves

Remove the folding board

Turn the shirt over

Bring the following items to help develop an estimate:

- camera: to take pictures of the area where the product is presented;
- stop watch: to estimate the time it will require to finish each task;
- measuring tape: to measure the area where the product is presented;
- pen and pad: to document findings and to draw the floor layout;
- merchandising standards manual.

Keep in mind the goal is to obtain an approximation of the time the store visit should take. Remember, the allotted area in each account will probably not be the same size in all stores. Therefore, visit a few stores in each account to develop a good estimate.

Prior to going to each store, it is advisable to contact the manager on duty to confirm the purpose of the visit. Retail management teams are very protective of their stores and do not welcome just anyone in their stockrooms or allow visitors to take pictures without permission. The goal is to build a relationship with the store personnel and obtain approval to perform the tasks necessary to estimate the time of a store visit. When visiting a store, ask for the store manager and confirm that permission has been given to enter the store's stockroom and take pictures of the area where the product is presented.

Visual assessment

Locate where the brand's product is merchandised on the sales floor and complete a visual assessment. Walk through the area and make a note of the layout of the department and where the product is merchandised. Afterwards, complete the following tasks:

- Get a photo of the area where the product is presented.
- Measure the length and width of the area and draw out the floor plan.
- List how many fixtures of product are on the sales floor.
- Take a picture of each fixture to have a record of the way the product is merchandised.
- Observe the type of signage being utilized.
- Observe the location of the competitors' products.
- Document the time to walk from the department to the stockroom using the stopwatch.
- View the stockroom and estimate how long it would take to locate the product, hangers and a cart for transporting these items to the sales floor.
- Document the time it takes to get back to the department.

Next, estimate the time it would take to place signage or any graphics needing to be changed. Determine and document the number of pictures and shot angles the merchandisers should take. Estimate the time it would require to complete the pictures. These pictures will be included with each store visit report.

When walking through the area at which competitors' products are located, observe the way their products are presented and where their area is located in relation to your brand. Document any information about competitors that field visual merchandisers would need to provide after each store visit.

Relevant questions can be added to the field visual merchandiser store visit report: Eg what competitors are nearby or how big is their area? You should inquire about any other information that might be helpful to increase sales. Likewise, be sure to document any questions around the brand, such as the amount of product taken out from the stockroom to the sales floor and whether the correct signage is posted.

Merchandiser's task list

As observations are made, list the tasks the field merchandiser would need to complete to ensure product is presented in compliance with the merchandising standards. Keep in mind the objectives of each sponsor associated with the account. Be sure to include these objectives when putting together your task list to ensure completion of all expectations at each store visit.

The task list should resemble the list in Table 4.1.

TABLE 4.1 Merchandiser's task list

Task
Visual assessment
Take before photos
Work product and signage from the stockroom to the sales floor
Merchandising of the area
Take after photos
Total

Time study

Conducting a time study will reveal how long a store visit should take, based on the tasks to be completed. Again, keep in mind this is an estimate because each store in an account will not be the same size. Do not overlook this step because the cost of a store visit is associated with the total time it takes to complete the task. In addition, this time study does not include provision for reporting. Gathering market intelligence will add time to the study; therefore, once you have selected an MSO, don't forget to discuss time needed for this task.

Using your best judgement, estimate how long it should take a merchandiser to complete each assignment and list that time on the task list. Once all tasks and estimated completion times have been documented, total the times and re-evaluate. The estimates can be fine-tuned later, but this should provide an idea of how long it should take to complete a store visit in this account.

The task list with estimated completion times should resemble the list in Table 4.2.

TABLE 4.2   Merchandiser's task list: Estimated completion times

Task	Estimated completion time
Visual assessment	5 minutes
Take before photos	5 minutes
Work product and signage from the stockroom to the sales floor	20 minutes
Merchandising of the area	25 minutes
Take after photos	5 minutes
Total time for store visit	*60 minutes*

Defining store visit requirements

Once a time study for each account is completed, the next step is to define the store visit requirements by analysing each time study and placing all tasks in the proper sequence. For example, if the time study revealed that a store visit is estimated to take one hour, provide step-by-step instructions on the most efficient way to complete each store visit within an hour.

Defining merchandiser task list and priority

When analysing a time study, determine which task might take longer than others and make adjustments to provide additional time for that task. In addition, think about the communication the field merchandisers should have with the store manager. An example would be having merchandisers conduct a walk-through of the area with the store manager after all has been completed. Be sure to include time for this task as well. Also, once completed, place each task in sequence based on the order in which they should be executed.

Review each task to determine if additional time needs to be allocated. Place all tasks in sequence and don't forget any of them (Table 4.3).

TABLE 4.3   Merchandiser's task list: Amended

Task	Estimated completion time
Visual assessment	5 minutes
Take before photos	5 minutes
Work product and signage from the stockroom to the sales floor	28 minutes
Merchandising of the area	25 minutes
Walk-through with department manager or manager on duty	5 minutes
Take after photos	5 minutes
Total for this store visit	*73 minutes*

If the overall completion time increases after making changes, it is wise to increase the store visit to an hour and a half or re-evaluate each task and make adjustments. Keep in mind that time is money.

Task breakdown evaluation

To provide detailed instructions to the field merchandising team, break down each task and explain exactly what needs to be accomplished. In addition, list smaller tasks under others that can be associated together. For example, 'taking before photos' can be associated with 'visual assessment' because they both take place at the start of the store visit. In this case, 'visual assessment' could be the task and 'taking before photos' could be a breakdown of that task. Let's look at an example in Table 4.4:

TABLE 4.4   Task breakdown

Main task	Detailed tasks	Time estimate
Visual assessment of area		**6 minutes**
	1. Walk through the area and make a list of activities to be accomplished (eg re-fold T-shirts on gondola etc)	3 minutes
	2. Take before photos	3 minutes

Once a breakdown evaluation for each task has been completed and the estimated time each task will take has been determined, it is time to develop the 'task duration estimate'.

The task duration estimate is the document that field merchandisers will use at the store visit to provide step-by-step directions on what activities should be completed. It is the formalized version of what was created previously.

This document will also be used when developing the overall cost of merchandising services for the strategy. In addition, it will be presented to your sponsors to confirm what will be accomplished on each visit and all cost associated.

Developing merchandiser task duration estimates

The merchandiser's task duration estimate is presented in two parts. The first part (Table 4.5) is a breakdown of each task in sequence with an explanation of what needs to be accomplished, and the estimated time associated with completing each task during the overall store visit.

TABLE 4.5 Merchandiser task duration: Estimate for 1-hour merchandising service (Part 1)

Main task	Detailed tasks	Time estimate
Visual assessment of area		**6 minutes**
	1. Walk through the area and make a list of activities to be accomplished (eg re-fold T-shirts on gondola etc)	3 minutes
	2. Take before photos	3 minutes
Merchandising area		**20 minutes**
	1. Folding: re-fold and size product according to merchandising standards	10 minutes
	2. Hanging: re-fold and size product according to merchandising standards	10 minutes
Work product from back room to sales floor		**28 minutes**
	1. Locate and pull product, hangers and POS from back room	10 minutes
	2. Transport all pulled items to sales floor	8 minutes
	3. Work pulled product and POS into merchandise presentation	10 minutes
Final walk-through		**6 minutes**
	1. Walk through and explain the task you have completed to store manager	3 minutes
	2. Take after photos	3 minutes

The second part of the task duration estimate is an organization chart that presents all tasks broken down in a manner that can quickly be viewed and understood (Figure 4.5). You should develop a merchandiser's task duration estimate for each account.

FIGURE 4.5   Merchandisers task duration estimate: Chart (Part 2)

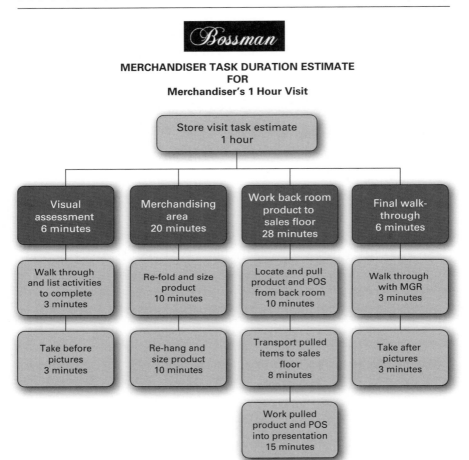

Chapter 4 checklist

- Have I identified the components to prepare my combat strategy?
- Do I have a clear understanding of the structure of a merchandising service organization?
- Have I gained an understanding of the role of the account manager in an MSO?

- Do I understand the role of the MSO's management team and their responsibilities?

- Based on my understanding, do I know the type of field visual merchandisers I need to execute my strategy?

- Would outsourcing to an MSO be beneficial to my company?

- Am I aware of the role of the World Alliance for Retail Excellence and Standards?

- Have I visited their website to explore the features and benefits offered?

- Would my company benefit by joining this organization?

- Do I understand the role of my sponsors?

- Do I have a comprehensive understanding of my sponsor's objectives?

- Have I evaluated my sponsor's expectations?

- Do I have a clear understanding of what retail stores my field visual merchandisers will service?

- Do I understand the importance of obtaining a store list from each of my sponsors?

- Am I clear on using the store list I have obtained to develop a master store list?

- Do I comprehend the importance of developing a task duration estimate to determine the length of time for each store visit in the various retail accounts my team will service?

Tricks of the trade: 'How long will it take?'

The task duration estimate is a valuable tool in determining how long a store visit should take in order to meet the objective. This tool is also used to determine the overall cost of the programme. For example:

In one retail account with 300 stores, your task duration estimate calls for a one-hour store visit in each store twice a month. This equals 600 one hour store visits each month in this account. If you are paying £20 for a one-hour store visit in this account, it will cost you £12,000 a month for services in this retail account.

Once your strategy is up and running, your FVM team cannot take on added responsibilities and meet the objectives of your sponsors without you obtaining additional funding. As the leader, you will need to address these issues when they occur and take the appropriate action to eliminate confusion. Let's look at a scenario that you may need to address.

The scenario

Your field team provides visual merchandising services to one of your sponsor's retail accounts that have 300 stores. The team visits these stores twice a month for one hour to merchandise the company's product in the men's clothing department. This retailer just purchased your company's new line of children's product that will be placed in the children's department in the same 300 stores your FVM team services.

You received a call from your sponsor asking if your field team could stop by the children's department on each visit to merchandise the two fixtures of hanging product the retailer just purchased. Rather than saying yes immediately, it is wise to evaluate the situation and tell the sponsor that you will follow up with an answer.

Step 1

As the leader, if you have not done your homework, you would not see the complication with saying yes to this question. If you review the task duration estimate, you will see that there is a time frame associated with each task on the list (Table 4.6):

TABLE 4.6   Merchandiser task duration: Associated time frame

Main task	Detailed tasks	Time estimate
Visual assessment of area		**6 minutes**
	1. Walk through the area and make a list of activities to be accomplished (eg re-fold T-shirts on gondola etc)	3 minutes
	2. Take before photos	3 minutes
Merchandising area		**20 minutes**
	1. Folding: re-fold and size product according to merchandising standards	10 minutes
	2. Hanging: re-fold and size product according to merchandising standards	10 minutes

TABLE 4.6 *continued*

Main task	Detailed tasks	Time estimate
Work product from back room to sales floor		**(28 minutes)**
	1. Locate and pull product, hangers and POS from back room	10 minutes
	2. Transport all pulled items to sales floor	8 minutes
	3. Work pulled product and POS into merchandise presentation	10 minutes
Final walk-through		**(6 minutes)**
	1. Walk through and explain the task you have completed to store manager	3 minutes
	2. Take after photos	3 minutes

The total time to complete all tasks at each store visit will take the full one hour. Therefore, if the sponsor wants the FVM team to service the two fixtures in the children's department, there are two options:

1 The first option would be to provide additional funding to service the two fixtures.

2 The second option would be to cut back on the time needed to service the men's department. This option is not recommended.

Before you call the sponsor back with an answer, best practice would be to contact the MSO and have the field team conduct a task duration estimate for the service of the two fixtures. Once you receive the estimate from your MSO, review it for accuracy and approach the next step with caution.

Step 2

After review, you estimate it will take an additional 35 minutes to service the children's department (Table 4.7). Normally, an MSO will not provide service to a store for 35 minutes because it is not cost effective to have a team member drive to a location for such a short period of time. As your field team already services this account, the additional 35 minutes should not be a problem if funding is provided.

TABLE 4.7   Merchandiser task duration: Estimate for two fixtures in children's department

Main task Subsidiary task	Time estimate
Visual assessment of area	**2 minutes**
1. Walk through the area and make a list of activities to be accomplished (eg re-fold T-shirts on gondola etc)	1 minute
2. Take before photos	1 minute
Merchandising area	**10 minutes**
1. Folding: re-fold and size product according to merchandising standards	5 minutes
2. Hanging: re-fold and size product according to merchandising standards	5 minutes
Work product from back room to sales floor	**20 minutes**
1. Locate and pull product, hangers and POS from back room	6 minutes
2. Transport all pulled items to sales floor	8 minutes
3. Work pulled product and POS into merchandise presentation	6 minutes
Final walk-through	**3 minutes**
1. Walk through and explain the task you have completed to store manager	2 minutes
2. Take after photos	1 minute
Total store visit task estimate	**35 minutes**

As you review the task duration estimate for the two fixtures in the children's department, try to anticipate questions the sponsor may have and prepare your answers:

1 Sponsor: Why is there additional cost to service only two fixtures? Your answer: In order to meet the objectives for servicing the men's department, it takes the full one-hour service. (Provide the original task duration estimate to confirm).

2 Sponsor: Why are you saying it will take 35 minutes to service two fixtures of children's product when the product is hanging? Your answer: To merchandise the product it will only take 10 minutes, but the visual assessment, working the product from the back room to sales floor and the final walk-through added an additional 25 minutes to the service. This is needed to meet your objectives. (Provide the task duration estimate for servicing the two fixtures).

Once you have anticipated all the questions and prepared your answers, you are ready to contact the sponsor and provide a well-thought-out reply to the question. Imagine answering this question if the task duration estimates did not exist.

Preparing for combat

Once you gain an understanding of the components related to your strategy, it is essential to look back, assess and document the information that has been gathered, and then obtain support from your sponsors before preparing for combat. At this point, the leader is aware of the following information:

1 The field merchandising team will service 600 stores in three trade channels (the department store, specialty store and superstore).

2 There are 200 stores in each account; these stores are located throughout the country in demographics such as suburban areas, major cities, and urban areas.

3 Two of the accounts have brand concept shops in 200 stores and the department store account has four fixtures in a designated area.

4 A master store list has been developed that provides addresses for each store location.

5 The sponsors' expectations for each account have been obtained and documented.

6 The task duration estimate for each account has been developed. Remember this is the information outlining the tasks that need to be completed and the length of time each store visit should require.

7 A merchandising standards manual has been developed to provide direction and guidelines for the product presentation at retail.

Developing your strategy proposal

After collecting, reviewing and assessing the information you acquired, it is important to obtain backing from your sponsors by developing a strategy proposal. This proposal will serve as the foundation for the strategy and provide direction to everyone involved. The purpose of this proposal is to persuade your sponsors to embrace your direction and ideas for moving forward. In other words, you are selling your ideas at this point. Your objective is to ensure the sponsors have a clear understanding of the direction you are taking, that they agree with and support the process. A strategy proposal should present a complete overview of the leader's direction thus far and provide the following information:

- strategy overview;
- objective;
- scope;
- merchandiser task duration estimates;
- competitive advantage;
- stakeholders;
- budget development;
- strategic direction;
- MSO information;
- contract review and approval.

1 **Strategy overview**: An overview should be a brief summary stating the importance of the FVM services and the specifics of the strategy.

2 **Objective**: State the overall goals of the strategy. Some details of this information can be obtained from information provided by your sponsors. It should also state that to achieve this objective, a field merchandising team would be established to service the 600 stores on the list. In addition, provide a preliminary launch date for the strategy.

3 **Scope**: The scope should provide the details of the type of services your field visual merchandisers will provide to retailers – from merchandising to pulling product and completing reports.

4 **Merchandiser task duration estimates**: State the purpose of the task duration estimates and include copies of each.

5 **Competitive advantage**: State the competitive advantage of offering an FVM service to retail accounts that would ensure the product is presented and maintained in a manner to attract the company's target consumers.

6   **Stakeholders:** List the stakeholders that will be involved in the strategy. In addition to the MSO you select, stakeholders are the organizations that will play a role in the execution of the strategy such as graphics companies and fixturing installation companies. Stakeholders have a vested interest in the success of the strategy.

7   **Budget development:** Make certain that budget development will take place once an MSO has been selected with details providing the cost of each store visit, training and the number of stores to be serviced.

8   **Strategic direction:** The direction at this point should be to identify an MSO to provide merchandising services, select that MSO, and develop a budget for the strategy and a launch timeline.

9   **Selecting an MSO:** Provide information on the type of services an MSO will provide and explain the benefits of providing visual merchandising services to the company's retail accounts. Also state the number of MSOs to be included in the selection process. In addition, state that you will choose a committee to aid in identifying the right MSO for the strategy.

10   **Contract review approval:** State the approval process, the estimated time it will take for the approval process, contract review and signing.

Proposal outline

Once you have an understanding of the information your proposal should include, it is a good idea to develop an outline. An outline will help you organize your material and establish the flow of information from beginning to end. As stated, your proposal should be persuasive; therefore, you want to remove doubts that may be in the minds of your sponsors.

One way to remove doubts is to play the role of the sponsor and try to think from that point of view. Now think what questions would you want answered? If you make a list of questions and answer these doubts in your proposal, you will possess a solid probability of acquiring the support of your sponsors. Once you have your list of questions, use these as headings in your proposal outline and answer the questions by adding the material previously developed under the appropriate heading. Let's take a look at the following outline:

A proposal to develop an FVM strategy to service retail accounts

What is the purpose of the field visual merchandising strategy?

- strategy overview;
- objective.

What are the major features of the strategy?

- scope;
- merchandiser task duration estimates.

Why is this proposal needed?

- competitive advantage.

Who will be involved in the strategy?

- stakeholders.

What will the strategy cost?

- budget development.

Where do we go from here?

- strategic direction;
- proposal sign-off;
- MSO selection committee;
- selecting an MSO;
- contract review and sign-off.

Preliminary timeline

With your proposal, always include a timeline. A preliminary timeline should be a detailed document that displays the time it should take to identify and select an MSO, develop the budget and get contracts signed. This document will serve as the road map to the approval of the strategy proposal (Figure 5.1). Based on this timeline, it will take 74 days.

FIGURE 5.1   Preliminary timeline

ID	Task Mode	Task Name	Duration	Start	Finish
1		**MSO Selection Process**	**74 days**	Mon 4/30/12	Thu 8/9/12
2		**RFP Process**	**43 days**	Mon 4/30/12	Wed 6/27/12
3		Develop RFP	5 days	Mon 4/30/12	Fri 5/4/12
4		Obtain RFP Approval	2 days	Mon 5/7/12	Tue 5/8/12
5		Select Five MSOs	7 days	Wed 5/9/12	Thu 5/17/12
6		Forward RFP to MSOs	2 days	Fri 5/18/12	Mon 5/21/12
7		Submit Proposals by End of Day	3 days	Tue 5/22/12	Thu 5/24/12
8		Proposal Review	5 days	Fri 5/25/12	Thu 5/31/12
9		Select Three MSOs to Present	7 days	Fri 6/1/12	Mon 6/11/12
10		Presentations from MSOs	5 days	Tue 6/12/12	Mon 6/18/12
11		MSO Selection Process	7 days	Tue 6/19/12	Wed 6/27/12
12		**Budget Development**	**13 days**	Thu 6/28/12	Mon 7/16/12
13		Review Breakdown of Cost	5 days	Thu 6/28/12	Wed 7/4/12
14		Confirm Store Coverage with Selected MSO	3 days	Thu 7/5/12	Mon 7/9/12
15		Budget Approval	5 days	Tue 7/10/12	Mon 7/16/12
16		**Contract Review & Signing**	**18 days**	Tue 7/17/12	Thu 8/9/12
17		Obtain Contract from MSO	3 days	Tue 7/17/12	Thu 7/19/12
18		Review Contract with Legal	5 days	Fri 7/20/12	Thu 7/26/12
19		Finalized Contract	5 days	Fri 7/27/12	Thu 8/2/12
20		Obtain Contract Sign Off	5 days	Fri 8/3/12	Thu 8/9/12

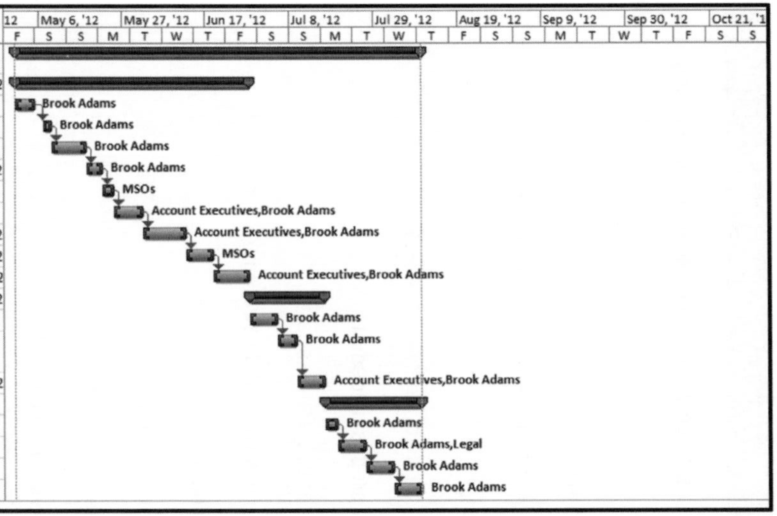

Other doubts to consider

Before you start writing, there may be a few other doubts that you may want to address in your proposal. Often, sponsors are unsure of moving in a new direction because it requires changing from the way they have operated in the past. Therefore, be sure to anticipate other questions that may cause doubt in the minds of your sponsors. Let's look at a few additional questions that you may want to address in your proposal.

1. Is this strategy realistic?

If your company has never used an outsourced company for visual merchandising services, some of your sponsors may have doubts. As visual merchandising is of a creative nature, a sponsor may have fears about trusting the merchandise presentation of the company's product to people that do not have a comprehensive understanding of the brand. Therefore, you may want to include a section on training your FVM team.

2. Is this the right time to allocate funds to this type of strategy?

If there have been concerns about allocating a budget for this type of strategy, it would be wise to incorporate a section titled 'Why the time is right'. In this section you should discuss how visual merchandising stimulates multiple sales and explain what the consequences will be if the strategy is not launched now.

3. Does this strategy line up with the company's goal?

In Chapter 1, we explained the importance of gaining a clear understanding of the company's mission and of being able to translate that mission into an FVM strategy. If you have embraced this philosophy, include a section that discusses how the strategy is in line with your organization's mission statement.

4. Will there be an increase in sales if this strategy is successful?

To provide an answer to this question, you will need to conduct research. It would be a good idea to investigate how visual merchandising has increased sales in other companies or possibly in your own organization. If you have access to a sales analyst, state that you would use this individual to gather sell-through information on retail accounts. Include this in a section titled 'Benefits of the proposed strategy'.

5. How will the success of this strategy be evaluated?

To be persuasive, it may be beneficial to include a section on what methods you plan to utilize to evaluate the strategy. You might also want to provide details on how often the evaluation will take place: once a month, every quarter or every six months. Explain the type of evaluation you plan to conduct and the manner in which the results will be communicated to the sponsors.

Strategy sign-off

In the last section of your proposal titled 'Where do we go from here?' it would be wise to provide a sign-off deadline date. One can sign in order to specify the proposal has been read and the reader agrees with the content and signs off on moving forward. The sign-off deadline date informs the sponsors that they will need to articulate their approval to move forward by a specific date indicated in the proposal.

MSO selection committee

If your proposal is accepted and your sponsors have signed off on moving forward, your next step is to start the process of selecting your MSO. It is recommended that you create an MSO selection committee that would be involved in the selection process of determining the best MSO for your strategy. The committee should be made up of your sponsors and anyone in your organization that you and your sponsors feel would add value in the selection process.

Selecting the right MSO

To identify the right MSO one can research the internet, contact other manufacturers or retailers or heed recommendations from peers in the industry. In Chapter 4, we discussed an organization called the World Alliance for Retail Excellence and Standards. By joining such an organization, you will have access to a large directory of MSOs listed on their website. On this site you can identify and select MSOs that offer FVM services. I encourage you to select a few companies and start researching. Start the process by contacting each MSO to obtain information about their company. After receiving information from selected MSOs, start the evaluation process by comparing each company to narrow down the selection to the top three.

Depending on how much information each MSO provides, you should compare information such as:

- How long has the MSO been in business?
- How many merchandisers do they have in the field?
- Do they have adequate merchandiser coverage to render services for the geographical area needed?
- Do they have apparel merchandising experience?
- Do they currently provide services to apparel manufacturers?
- Do they perform shop installations?
- How many managers and trainers do they have in the field?

If needed, do additional research to help narrow down the MSOs to three. Once the finalist has been selected, the next step would be to draft a request for proposal.

Request for proposal (RFP)

The RFP is a procurement document developed by a brand or retailer and forwarded to a number of MSOs requesting each to provide a proposal and a bid for merchandising services. The RFP should include detailed specifications on the type of services requested in order for the MSO to develop a proposal that will meet the needs of the brand/retailer. The RFP should include the following information:

1 Company overview and history of the brand: This overview gives the MSO insight into the company and provides a foundation for their proposal.

2 Why merchandising services are being requested: Provide information as to why the company has decided to move in this direction.

3 Statement of work (SOW): A statement of work provides a list of details about the types of services needed and a list of stores to be serviced, such as the information gathered from the sponsors. It also includes the estimated time frame of each store visit, the number of visits per month and the primary responsibilities of each merchandiser. This should include the task duration estimates for stores in each account (see Chapter 4).

4 Store list: Include the store list with addresses of each location. This information will help the MSO to determine if they have adequate field merchandisers to provide coverage and will aid them in preparing a bid.

5 Next steps: Provide a deadline date for all proposals and bids to be submitted and discuss the pertinent elements that should be included in their proposal such as references and a list of stores they are currently servicing.

After forwarding the RFP to the selected MSOs, it is a good practice to follow up in a week by phone or e-mail to confirm their interest in submitting a proposal by the deadline date.

Evaluating the MSOs' proposals

Once all proposals have been received, the first step should be to evaluate each proposal to ensure the requirements requested in the RFP have been met. It is a good idea to develop a scorecard to be used when evaluating each MSO. Additionally, submit this scorecard and a copy of the proposal to your MSO selection committee members who will be involved in the selection process (Figure 5.2).

Confirm that each member of the MSO selection committee will be available to evaluate all proposals and attend a face-to-face meeting with the chosen finalist. If MSOs have provided references, contact these individuals to gain additional information or recommendations. Learn as much as you can about the selected MSOs before having a face-to-face meeting and be sure to share this information with the sponsors.

Face time

Meeting with each MSO is an important step in the selection process. Face time gives the MSO an opportunity to present their ideas and answer any questions from the sponsors. This is also a great opportunity for the sponsors to develop a good rapport and determine which MSO is sincere about becoming an extension of the brand. Be sure to confirm with the MSO the time each will have to present.

As each MSO presents their proposal, make note of the names and responsibilities of their management team. Discuss each person's background in the industry or obtain more information on their expertise. If the MSO's management team has a solid background in the industry, it will be an asset because they will have an understanding of how the industry operates.

FIGURE 5.2   MSO score card

MERCHANDISING SERVISE ORGANIZATION SCORE CARD/EVALUATION

MSO NAME_____   EVALUATION DATE_____

EVALUATOR'S NAME_____

Questions	Yes	No	Comments
Did the MSO seem to understand our brand?	☐	☐	
Did you feel the MSO performed adequate research to obtain an understanding of our needs?	☐	☐	
Did the MSO understand our consumer?	☐	☐	
Did the MSO understand our objective?	☐	☐	
Do you feel the MSO has adequate experience in apparel?	☐	☐	
Did the MSO have adequate field support structure?	☐	☐	
Do your feel the MSO has adequate experience to handle this execution?	☐	☐	
Does the MSO have adequate field merchandising coverage to service our accounts?	☐	☐	
Does the MSO understand the specific needs of our retail accounts?	☐	☐	
Did the MSO understand our frequency of visits, visit length and visit requirements?	☐	☐	
Did the MSO provide adequate infomation on their online report system?	☐	☐	
Did the MSO provide a comprehensive overview of how they are structured?	☐	☐	

SUGGESTED GRAD SCALE: 5 = EXCELLENT   3 = AVERAGE   1 = POOR

EVALUATION SCORE_____

GENERAL COMMENTS

Final selection

After the selection committee has met with the MSO finalist, schedule a meeting to discuss everyone's score card. Review and discuss the team's concerns and add these to the decision process. Also, cost is a major part of the process; obtain an understanding of where every dollar is going in order to compare apples with apples. Once all concerns and expenses have been addressed, select the MSO.

Budgets and contracts

Once the MSO has been selected, start the budget development process by reviewing the MSO's proposal to obtain the cost of field merchandising services. Next, develop a list of additional needs for executing the strategy such as additional training, uniforms and giveaways or promotional products to be given by the field merchandisers to the retail sales assistants when visiting stores. Research the cost associated with each line item on the list and document these costs. Be as accurate as possible and try not to over- or underestimate. MSOs will usually include the cost of training in their proposal. If you think additional training is required be sure to discuss this with the MSO. The MSO will need to provide an additional quote to include the necessary training. This training may involve labour hours, location of venue, possible travel and meals. If online training will be provided consider computer or kiosk capabilities and the cost of producing web-based training. Remember: time is money and there is a cost associated with time spent for additional training of field merchandisers.

The budget may include the following:

- cost of merchandising services provided by the MSO;
- cost for additional training on merchandising standards and product knowledge;
- cost for uniforms or shirts (if applicable);
- cost for developing and producing training materials;
- merchandising kits if applicable, such as folding boards and promotional items.

Once a complete list has been developed, including all new line item totals, review the proposal again for accuracy before moving forward to the MSO contract.

Contract review, negotiations and signing

Once the proposal meets your expectations, the next step will be to obtain a contract from the selected MSO. After receiving the contract, the objective at this point will be to review it with your legal department and evaluate the following details:

1 The terms and conditions of the contract.

2 The cost of every detail in the contract that was agreed upon by both parties.

3 Details of the services to be provided with an explanation of each.

4 Definition of responsibilities of both parties.

5 Launch dates to include timelines.

If there is a need to negotiate cost that seems to be more than you are willing to pay, keep in mind that the goal is to develop a win/win situation for both parties. The process of reviewing and signing the contract may be time-consuming. Therefore, keep an eye on the timeline and keep all parties involved on schedule.

The MSO rejection letter

Do not forget the other MSOs that participated in the RFP process. Send each unsuccessful MSO a 'thank you' letter. In this letter be sure to state that they were not selected to move forward in the final selection process, but thank them for taking the time to submit their proposal.

This is a very important process, not only because it is the right thing to do, but because if for any reason the selected MSO does not work out, the rejected proposal can be reviewed at a later date, at which point the MSO would be invited to present their information again. In addition, it is a good idea to hold on to each MSO's proposal just in case they offer additional services that might be helpful in the future. For example, if the current MSO does not provide fixture installations and the company is in need of that particular service, a contact will have already been established for requesting these services.

Chapter 5 checklist

- Do I understand the purpose of developing a strategy proposal?
- Do I comprehend the 10 parts that should be included in a strategy proposal?

- Does it make sense to create a proposal outline before writing a strategy proposal?
- Do I believe it is significant to include a preliminary timeline with my proposal?
- What should I do to remove uncertainty in the minds of my sponsors who are unsure of this strategy?
- Do I consider it to be important to anticipate questions that may cause doubt in the minds of my sponsors and address those reluctances in my strategy proposals?
- Should I contemplate having an MSO selection committee in the MSO selection process?
- Do I understand how to develop an RFP?
- Have I adequately gained enough information to evaluate an MSO proposal?
- Am I aware of the particular information to seek when reviewing and evaluating an MSO contract?

Tricks of the trade: 'You gotta have options'

As you may have gathered thus far, developing and executing FVM strategies requires preplanning and meeting deadlines. Also, creativity is not a light switch that you can turn off and on at will. So the question is: how do you get these two opposites to work together? In most cases you can't always change the deadline numerous times until you and your team come up with the perfect creative concept. Therefore, 'you gotta have options'. Options are the things that can be preplanned and used over and over again that help you and your team save time in the execution process. Each time you plan an execution, it's not necessary to start from scratch because you have many of the processes in place already.

Planning a store layout or providing your FVM team with merchandising options in a pinch can take less time when you have preplanned presentation alternatives in place. Let's walk through the process of developing options for product presentation.

The scenario

You run a national FVM programme and have six direct reports that assist in the development and execution process. In addition, you have an outsourced MSO that executes your FVM strategies in 1,500 stores. As the leader, you have learned that your team will be rolling out a total of 150 brand shops in the next six months in a major department store. These shops will be a mixture of small, medium and large shops. You and your team have the responsibility for developing store layouts to include product capacity and providing ongoing services provided by your MSO field visual merchandising team. To be proactive, your plan is to develop numerous product presentation options that would aid in developing quick, accurate shop layouts that include the product capacity for each presentation.

Step 1

You began the process by gaining an understanding of the different types of fixtures that will be used in your shop layouts (Figure 5.3).

FIGURE 5.3   Types of fixtures

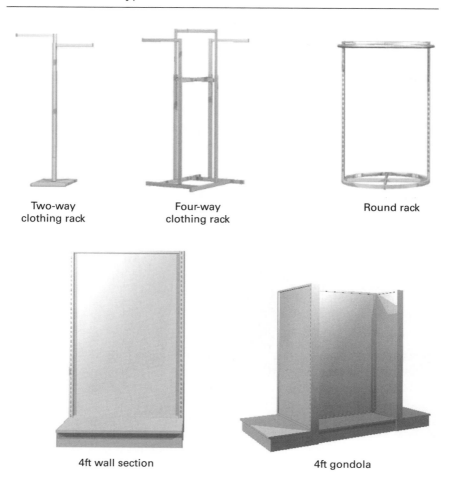

Two-way
clothing rack

Four-way
clothing rack

Round rack

4ft wall section

4ft gondola

FIGURE 5.4 Types of fixture accessories

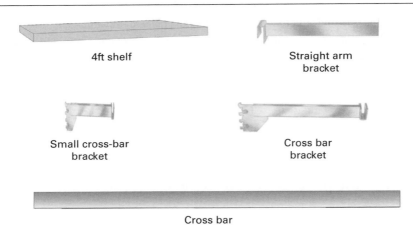

4ft shelf

Straight arm
bracket

Small cross-bar
bracket

Cross bar
bracket

Cross bar

In addition, learn the accessories that can be used on the 4ft wall section and the 4ft gondola (Figure 5.4).

Step 2

Once you have reviewed the types of fixtures and accessories, determine the product capacity for each accessory and fixture (Figure 5.5). These quantities should be documented for future use.

FIGURE 5.5 Product capacities for fixtures and accessories

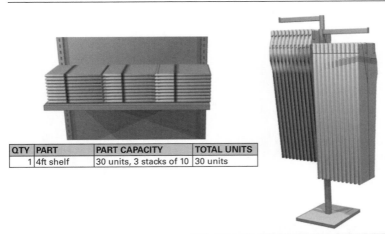

QTY	PART	PART CAPACITY	TOTAL UNITS
1	4ft shelf	30 units, 3 stacks of 10	30 units

QTY	PART	PART CAPACITY	TOTAL UNITS
1	2-way rack	60 units, 30 per arm	60 units

Step 3

Your next step should be to use the information you gathered to develop numerous options for each fixture. If you are developing options for the 4ft wall section, determine the different ways the wall can be merchandised and create several options to include the product capacity and the accessories needed to complete the wall presentation. This information will be useful when determine the overall shop capacity and the number of accessories and fixtures needed when it is time to order fixturing for the shop (Figure 5.6).

FIGURE 5.6   Presentation options for 4ft wall

OPTION 1 – 180

OPTION 2 – 120

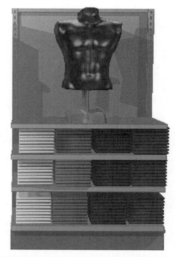

QTY	PART	PART CAPACITY	TOTAL UNITS
6	4ft shelf	30 units, 3 stacks of 10	180 units

QTY	PART	PART CAPACITY	TOTAL UNITS
3	4ft shelf	40 shirts, 4 stacks of 10	120 units
1	Display form	N/A	N/A
1	4ft shelf	Use for display	N/A

Step 4

Now in Step 4, let's walk through how these options can save time when creating a store layout. By using the two options that were previously developed, a back wall of a shop can be planned out and the product capacity can easily be calculated in Figure 5.7, option 1 has 180 units and is used

FIGURE 5.7 Presentation for 20ft wall

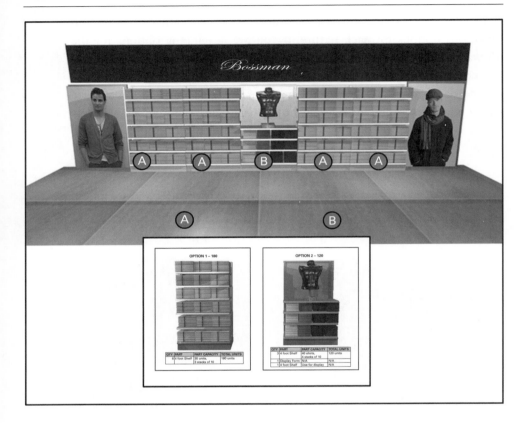

four times in the wall presentation; while option 2 is used once and has 120 units. Each wall section is 4ft long; therefore, the back wall has 20ft of product with 840 units.

Step 5

In this last step, a complete shop can be created including shop capacity using fixture options as guides (Figure 5.8). Let's look at the benefits of creating shop layout such as this one:

1 The account executive has a clear idea of how much product the shop will hold and can calculate the cost of the shop.

2 This layout can be used to determine task duration estimates on how long it would take to install the shop and how many field visual merchandisers will be needed at the installation.

FIGURE 5.8   Completed shop presentation

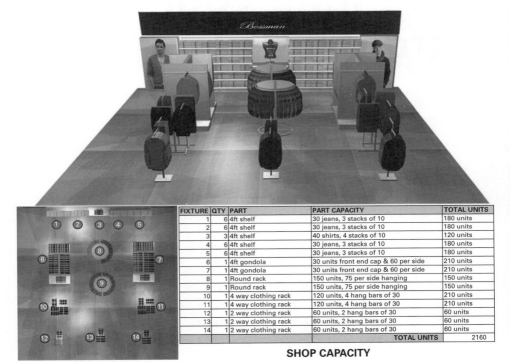

FIXTURE	QTY	PART	PART CAPACITY	TOTAL UNITS
1	6	4ft shelf	30 jeans, 3 stacks of 10	180 units
2	6	4ft shelf	30 jeans, 3 stacks of 10	180 units
3	3	4ft shelf	40 shirts, 4 stacks of 10	120 units
4	6	4ft shelf	30 jeans, 3 stacks of 10	180 units
5	6	4ft shelf	30 jeans, 3 stacks of 10	180 units
6	1	4ft gondola	30 units front end cap & 60 per side	210 units
7	1	4ft gondola	30 units front end cap & 60 per side	210 units
8	1	Round rack	150 units, 75 per side hanging	150 units
9	1	Round rack	150 units, 75 per side hanging	150 units
10	1	4 way clothing rack	120 units, 4 hang bars of 30	210 units
11	1	4 way clothing rack	120 units, 4 hang bars of 30	210 units
12	1	2 way clothing rack	60 units, 2 hang bars of 30	60 units
13	1	2 way clothing rack	60 units, 2 hang bars of 30	60 units
14	1	2 way clothing rack	60 units, 2 hang bars of 30	60 units
			TOTAL UNITS	2160

SHOP CAPACITY

SHOP LAYOUT

3 The layout and the fixture options created can be used as planograms to provide the field team with clear direction on what should be executed.

4 With 150 shops rolling out in six months and ongoing service being provided by the FVM team, having a detailed layout of every shop is invaluable to the account executive, the retailer, the field team and your internal management team.

Creating numerous options for each fixture may be time-consuming now, but the time you and your team will save in the long run will be well worth the effort. These options will not only be used for determining fixture capacity, and the overall capacity for a shop, but will be instrumental if you are conducting a floor reset. In Chapter 9's 'tricks of the trade' section, we will discuss 'The Flawless Floor Set'.

Training your troops

Although MSOs provide basic training to field merchandisers, it's up to the leader to determine expectations and criteria. Ultimately, the leader is responsible for ensuring the team possesses the necessary skills to succeed before they are deployed to execute the strategy. Retailers are disturbed when a field visual merchandiser shows up to their store representing a brand and has no clue about what should be done. Each person on your field team should be well trained and present themselves as an extension of your brand. When these merchandisers are servicing stores, they become the face of the brand. Everyone desires to succeed and field merchandisers should feel confident knowing they are making a difference in each store they visit. Therefore, provide comprehensive training and set clear expectations. These individuals have the capabilities to make a huge impact on a manufacturer's/brand's bottom line. Most possess an engaging personality and will seek out additional ways to increase the brand's presence. They will not hesitate to go the extra mile to ensure the brand is available and positioned in a manner to increase sales. The field merchandisers have to learn to balance the relationships between the manufacturer, the retail store and the MSO. All of these relationships are vital to the success of the strategy.

Setting expectations

Field visual merchandisers should know the objective, how it should be completed, when it should be finished and the time allocated to accomplish the task. To guarantee the team has a well-defined understanding of the responsibilities to be accomplished, a leader should provide detailed training and communicate explicit standards coupled with precise expectations. Every facet of the field visual merchandiser's responsibilities should be addressed and simplified in the training process to ensure brand success and continuity. If field visual merchandisers are to receive planograms (a visual representation of the directive to be executed in stores), develop a training document to convey how to interpret a planogram. For the leader, training is a necessary function in facilitating a flawless execution of the strategy and should not be overlooked.

Training in the field merchandising environment

When an individual decides to take a course in a classroom environment, the goal is for everyone to attend the class, participate, listen to the instructor, take notes, study the material and be prepared to pass a written or oral exam. In the field merchandising environment, merchandisers are usually located throughout the country. Therefore, training cannot be conducted in a classroom setting unless a very large budget is available. This is a time for creativity, so if they can't come to training, then do the next best thing and take the training to them.

When preparing a training programme for the field environment, make sure each team member will be given a clear understanding of the project and be able to physically complete each task to meet the standard that is set forth in the objective.

Extensive training should be conducted and reinforced using the three principles of repetition:

1 **Hearing:** When an individual listens to something over and over again, it becomes part of that person's memory. Example: we have all listened to catchy music on the radio; the more a song is heard, the easier it becomes to remember the words and sing along.

2 **Seeing:** A picture is worth a thousand words. Planograms are visual representations of written instructions to help reinforce the objectives. They are valuable because of their ability to aid individuals who are visual learners by providing a quick glimpse of the information in a pictorial format. It also provides a visual of the presentation after the execution is completed.

3 **Doing:** When a person has been given instructions, shown how to complete a task, and given the opportunity to complete that same task repetitively, the assignment eventually becomes much easier to replicate. Example: we all learned to walk through repetition; the more we walked, the more comfortable we became with the process.

To reinforce each task, use all three principles together when training. Each principle will complement the others and make the information simple to understand. Therefore, the best training programme would involve providing the type of training your field team can see, hear and physically perform while working on the job. To create a programme of this nature, carry out a training needs assessment to identify the specific information to be relayed and ascertain your audience's level of relevant knowledge.

Needs assessment

When developing a training needs assessment, start by analysing every task associated with the field merchandiser's responsibilities to determine the following:

- What type of preparation is required to execute the strategy?
- What set-up or organization should be used to conduct the training?
- What necessary training materials should be acquired or created in order to convey the information?

Chapter 1 lists five steps in the process of thinking strategically. One important step is identifying risk. This requires you to see the end result and to work backwards in order to identify the necessary activities and processes required to meet the overall aim. To start, you must first prepare a list of actions to be performed. Then, you should analyse these activities to find potential issues associated with each task and formulate processes to address these concerns prior to the launch. This process works very well when developing a training needs assessment. By visualizing the task to be completed, a leader can identify and analyse the type of preparation required.

Training needs analysis

Field merchandisers should be trained in the following areas:

1 **Understanding store visit guidelines:** Field visual merchandisers must visit each store and establish strong relationships with the store management and salespeople. This has proven to be a great success. They should gain a clear understanding of the store's protocol and merchandising guidelines, along with their role as representatives of the brand.

2 **Understanding and using the task duration estimate:** Merchandisers must understand the task duration estimate and the ways in which they can use it to accomplish their goals.

3 **Product features and benefits:** They must be acquainted with the merchandise and the product features and benefits because they will be required to communicate this information to sales assistants.

4 **Understanding and meeting merchandising standards:** In order to meet standards, merchandisers need to know how to successfully present the product in a manner that accentuates the brand.

5 **Understanding merchandising directives and planograms:** Directions on the task to be accomplished and guidelines showing how to interpret directives and planograms should be made clear to the group.

6 **Training evaluation:** Merchandisers should be given a test or quiz to confirm their understanding of the information taught and their readiness to be deployed.

With this information, the assessment should be developed to state what instructions are needed, how this coaching will be conducted and a list of the materials needed to facilitate this type of training (Figure 6.1). Keep in mind, the MSO field management team will be conducting this training.

Training materials

Standards and processes should be relayed in a consistent manner while keeping brand initiatives in mind. Likewise, these documents can serve as a reference for field visual merchandisers after training has finished. Having this information on hand as they visit stores could be very helpful and may provide answers to questions which were once reviewed but have been forgotten. The goal is to produce a quality FVM service that is efficient and consistent with brand initiatives to drive sales while providing consumers with a great shopping experience. Therefore, training materials should be clear, concise and easy to understand. Based on the training needs assessment, the following materials should be developed or provided:

- product features and benefits manual (catalogues);
- merchandising standards manual;
- merchandising standards certification;
- store visit guidelines;
- directions for utilization of the task duration estimates;
- merchandising directives and planograms;
- training evaluation test.

FIGURE 6.1 Field merchandising training needs assessment

FIELD MERCHANDISING TRAINING NEEDS ASSESSMENT			
Training Type	What Training Is Needed	How Training Will Be Conducted	What Training Materials Are Needed
Understanding Store Visit Guidelines	Field visual merchandisers must visit each store and establish strong relationships with the store management and sales associates, gain a clear understanding of the stores protocol and merchandising guidelines and understand their role as a representative of the brand.	Field merchandisers will review training document on understanding store visit guidelines.	Training document on understanding store visit guidelines.
Understanding and using the Task Duration Estimate	Field merchandiser must understand the task duration estimate and how to use it to accomplish their goals.	Field merchandisers will review training document on understanding and using task duration estimate.	Training document on understanding and using task duration estimate.
Product Features and Benefits	Field merchandisers need to know the product and the product features and benefits to provide this information to sales associates.	Field merchandisers will review company catalogues to gain an understanding of the brand's product features and benefits.	Company product catalogues.
Understanding and Meeting Merchandising Standards	Field merchandisers need to know how to present product in a manner that meets the merchandising standards.	MSO field management team will conduct one-on-one training in the field with each field merchandiser until standards are met.	Merchandisers standards manual and certification test for evaluation.
Understanding Merchandising Directives & Planograms	Field merchandisers need clear directions on what needs to be accomplished and how to read the directives and planograms.	Field merchandisers will review training document on understanding merchandising directives & planograms.	Training document on understanding merchandising directives & planograms.
Training Evaluation	Field merchandisers should be tested to ensure they are well trained before being deployed.	Field merchandisers will complete and pass written test prior to being deployed.	Written test to evaluate each field merchandiser after training.

Training documents

It is best to provide training manuals the field team can take with them on store visits. Other informative documents can be uploaded to the MSO's website. Online training has become a very worthwhile tool in several industries. Like most businesses, MSOs train many of their employees using an online site that provides easy access from any computer to the necessary training materials. Therefore, creating training documents that can be uploaded to an MSO's website would be most beneficial.

When deciding which material to have electronically and which to have in hard copies, it is always wise to consider printing the manual so that the merchandisers always have one on hand if the need arises. Remember: in the age of digital media, moments can often occur when electrical devices are rendered useless by insufficient battery life or unavailable Wi-Fi. Some documents are well served if obtained electronically. In reviewing the seven previously listed materials, the following documents could be conducted online seamlessly:

- understanding store visit guidelines;
- understanding and using the task duration estimate;
- understanding merchandising directives and planograms;
- training evaluation test.

Product features and benefits

First and foremost, the job of a field visual merchandiser is to present the product in a pleasing manner to stimulate sales and help the brand gain loyalty from their customers. Therefore, product knowledge is a key facet of the preparation process. When a field visual merchandiser visits a retail store representing a brand, they are often met by sales assistants asking questions about the product.

They may get bombarded with inquiries such as, 'are we going to receive the new product and, if so, when?' or 'we are selling out of XYZ, so how might we get more of ABC?' The merchandisers should always strive to be on the cutting edge with information. Staying abreast of the brand's product could prove to be most helpful and could impact the bottom line. It is bad business to have a merchandiser visit a store if that individual is unfamiliar with the brand.

Consider providing each merchandiser with a copy of the company's product catalogues. This is by far the best way to enhance the team's familiarity with the merchandise. If the company has technical product, equip the team with specific training to ensure they possess the knowledge on how the technologies operate. When the company launches a new product, be sure to prepare your team with the latest update. Keep them abreast of any new merchandise and keep in mind that they are your brand advocates and are the eyes and ears in the field. Their communication to sales assistants will become invaluable to the brand.

Merchandising standards manual

The leader should develop a merchandising standards manual for the team. As briefly discussed in Chapter 4, this is done to communicate your brand's initiative and the manner in which your merchandise should be presented. The MSO should use this manual as a training tool and the team will have it on hand while visiting the stores to use as a guide. The ultimate goal of a merchandising standards manual is to create consistency in the way the product is presented in each store across various trade channels. Every product the team touches should have a presentation standard.

The manual should consist of a contents page to provide quick access to each standard. If a field visual merchandiser wishes to quickly identify how shirts are folded, the content page becomes quite useful and saves time.

Certification test

To accomplish this task, each team member should be trained in a consistent manner and possess the skills necessary to complete each merchandising standard as instructed. Therefore, one-on-one exercises are recommended in the field. This training should be conducted on the job by the MSO's field management team.

To ensure compliance, work with the MSO to create a document that provides guidance to the field management team on the best training practices (Figure 6.2.1). This document should include a list of required materials to accomplish the training.

The training manager and the field visual merchandiser being trained should both sign the document to confirm that standards were met. This document certifies the training and the evaluation were both completed (Figure 6.2.2).

FIGURE 6.2.1 Merchandising standards training:
Trainer's instructions

Bossman

MERCHANDISING STANDARDS TRAINING AND CERTIFICATION

Date of Training:_____

Trainer: _____

Field Merchandiser:_____

Training is to be completed by Field Management and repeated until the merchandiser performs each task according to the merchandising standards presented in the Merchandising Standards Manual. Upon completion, the merchandiser should be able to present product on a consistent basis in accordance to the standards learned.

TRAINER'S INSTRUCTIONS

Training should be conducted and reinforced using the following three principles of repetition. To reinforce each task, use all three principles together when training. The principles will complement each other and make the information easier to understand.

- **Hearing** – When a person hears something over and over again it becomes a part of the person's memory. Example: We all have heard songs on the radio and the more the song is heard the easier it becomes to remember the words and sing along.

- **Seeing** – A picture is worth a thousand words. Planograms are visual representatives of written instructions. They are developed because people are visual learners and can quickly grasp information when it is presented visually.

- **Doing** – When a person physically completes a task a few times, they can duplicate the task. Example: We all learned to walk through repetition, the more we walked the easier it became.

To conduct training:
1. Review the subject in the Merchandising Standards Manual with the merchandiser and explain the procedure to be executed.
2. Demonstrater how the task should be completed while explaining.
3. Instruct the merchandiser to complete the task while explaining each step.
4. Review this procedure until the merchandiser has a clear understanding of how to complete the task.
5. Once the merchandiser has reached the standard on how the task should be completed, move to the next task.
6. Sign this document when the merchandiser has completed all task in a manner that meets the merchandising standards as instructed.

FIGURE 6.2.2   Merchandising standards training: Certification

TRAINING GUIDELINES

Materials needed to Conduct Training
- Merchandising Standards Manual
- Folding Board

Training to Be Conducted:

Folding Apparel	**Hanging Apparel**	**Merchandising Fixtures**
❑ Shirts	❑ Shirts	❑ Floor Fixtures
❑ Trousers	❑ Trousers	❑ Walls

Sign to certify that that the merchandiser is certified to perform all tasks presented.

Merchandiser_____

Trainer_____

Understanding store visit guidelines

Each field visual merchandiser should be given instructions so they can comprehend store visit guidelines. These guidelines are provided by retail accounts and list procedures and protocols the field team must follow when visiting stores. Each account will have a different set of guidelines. Therefore, the leader should obtain these procedures from retailers and develop store visit guidelines for each account. These documents will help eliminate confusion and provide direction to your field team on appropriate communication methods for each retailer, and will also stipulate guidelines for entering the store.

Providing instructions on the store visit guidelines and emphasizing their importance will save time and aid in keeping the field team on the same page with you and the retailer (Figures 6.3.1 and 6.3.2). As stated beforehand, the importance of simplicity when communicating to field merchandisers is paramount. All documents should be easy to interpret and provide well-defined instructions. The goal is to have the field team well trained and confident about representing the brand.

FIGURE 6.3.1 Understanding store visit guidelines

UNDERSTANDING STORE VISIT GUIDELINES

Prior to visiting your stores you will receive Store Visit Guidelines. These guidelines are provided by retail accounts and list procedures that each merchandiser should follow when scheduling and visiting a store. Each retailer will have a different set of guidelines.

Therefore, it is important to read and obtain a clear understanding of each retailer's guidelines. These documents will help to eliminate any confusion you may have pertaining to what entrance to use or who to contact once you have entered the store. Below is a sample of how the store visit guidelines documents will look once they have been distributed.

FIGURE 6.3.2 Store visit guidelines: Example

Field Merchandising Programme
Store Visit Guidelines for Macy's

Scheduling Your Visit with the Store:
> ➤ It is mandatory that you call at least one week in advance of your appointment to schedule your visit with the department manager.
> ➤ Ask the department manager the location of the employee/vendor entrance.
> ➤ Ask the department manager who your contact should be if they will not be available during your visit.

When you Arrive at the Store:
> ➤ Enter through the employee entrance.
> ➤ Sign in on the Vendor Log at the security or customer service desk. At this time you will be given a vendor ID badge that must be worn at all times during your visit.
> ➤ Locate the department area and determine where your priority of work should be. This will help determine how to allocate your time correctly based on the department needs. (i.e. restocking, reorganizing, refolding and resizing).

Before You Start Merchandising:
> ➤ Review your task duration estimate to know your objectives.
> ➤ Locate your store contact and check in with them. Let them know that your priority is to help restock and restore the Bossman product presentation to the planogram. Walk them through the changes you plan to make to the Bossman presentation.
> ➤ Ask them to show you the location of the stockroom, where Bossman product is housed, and where damaged product should be placed, if found on the floor.
> ➤ Ask if the store has any special merchandising requests.
> ➤ Ensure you take your before photos before you start restoring the presentation.

Understanding and using the task duration estimate

In addition to understanding store visit guidelines, your FVM team should have clear knowledge of the goal and purpose of the task duration estimate. Although the document may be somewhat self-explanatory, it is a good idea to provide training instructions on usage of this document (Figures 6.4.1, 6.4.2 and 6.4.3).

FIGURE 6.4.1 Understanding and using the task duration estimate

UNDERSTANDING AND USING THE TASK DURATION ESTIMATE

The Merchandisers Task Duration Estimate is broken down into two parts. The first part is the breakdown of each task in sequence and provides an explanation of what needs to be accomplished and the estimated time associated with completing each task and the overall store visit.

The second part is an organization chart that presents everything in part one but broken down in a manner that can be quickly viewed and understood. There is a Task Duration Estimate for each account.

Understanding merchandising directives and planograms

The field team should be informed that merchandising directives and planograms work hand in hand to provide direction for flawless completion of the execution.

Directives provide instructional guidance on specific assignments to be accomplished and the planogram is a visual element that is easily interpreted through a pictorial viewpoint. If a planogram involves a visual for setting up signage, the directives would provide important written information pertaining to the installation of the signage. In other words, these are 'show and tell' documents working together. The directive substantiates that signage should be installed and provides written instructions to carry out the installation. The planogram provides visual guidance for the signage

FIGURE 6.4.2   Merchandiser task list: Example

MERCHANDISER TASK LIST FOR ONE HOUR MERCHANDISING SERVICE

Store Visit Task Estimate: 1 Hour

Visual Assessment of Area : 6 Minutes
1. Walk through the area and make a list of activities that need to be accomplished (*refold trousers on gondola etc*): 3 Minutes
2. Take before pictures: 3 Minutes

Merchandising Area: 20 Minutes
1. Folding: Re-fold and size product according to merchandising Standards: 10 Minutes
2. Hanging: Re-hang and size product according to merchandising Standards: 10 Minutes

Work Product from Backroom to Sales Floor: 28 Minutes
1. Locate and pull product, hangers and POS from back room: 10 Minutes
2. Transport all pulled items to sales floor: 8 Minutes
3. Work pulled product and POS into merchandise presentation: 10 Minutes

Final walk through: 6 Minutes
1. Walk through and explain the task you completed to store manager: 3 Minutes
3. Take after pictures: 3 Minutes

and shows the final arrangement of the fixturing. The field team should be aware that the overall goal of a planogram or directive is to provide guidance on how to present the product in a pleasing manner that makes it easily accessible to consumers and stimulates sales.

Merchandising directives and planograms work hand in hand to provide direction to your team. Directives provide direction on what needs to be accomplished and the planogram is a visual representation that is easily interpreted. If a planogram involves setting up signage, the directives would provide important information pertaining to the installation of the signage.

The overall goal of the planogram is to provide direction on how to present product in a pleasing manner that makes it easily accessible to consumers and to stimulate sales. A planogram has four main components:

1 The cover page: The cover page usually identifies the account name and information pertaining to where the planogram will be used.

FIGURE 6.4.3   Merchandiser task list: Chart

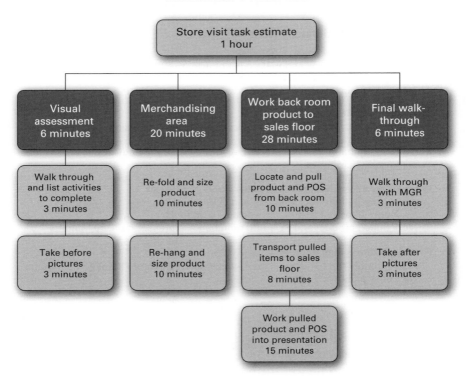

MERCHANDISER TASK DURATION ESTIMATE
FOR
Merchandiser's 1 Hour Visit

2 **The floor layout:** The floor layout shows how each fixture is placed on the sales floor.

3 **Schematic:** The schematic shows how the product is presented on fixtures.

4 **The product listing:** The product listing shows what product is presented and the style number of each.

Figures 6.5.1 to 6.5.4 provide examples of the elements of the directives and planograms.

FIGURE 6.5.1   Directive cover page

Merchandising directives and planograms work hand in hand to provide direction to your team. Directives provide direction on what needs to be accomplished and the planogram is a visual representation that is easily interpreted. If a planogram involves setting up signage, the directives would provide important information pertaining to the installation of the signage.

The overall goal of the planogram is to provide direction on how to present product in a pleasing manner that makes it easily accessible to consumers and to stimulate sales. A planogram has four main components:

1. **The Cover page:** The cover page usually identifies the account name and information pertaining to where the planogram will be used.

2. **The Floor Layout:** The floor layout shows how each fixture is placed on the sales floor.

3. **Schematic:** The schematic shows how the product is presented on fixtures.

4. **The Product Listing:** The product listing shows what product is presented and the style number of each.

Example:

FIGURE 6.5.2   Floor layout

FIGURE 6.5.3   Schematic

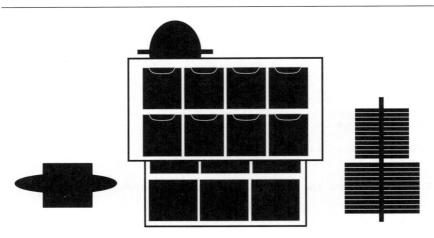

Fixture #	BOSSMAN #	DESCRIPTION
1	BB 459245	Big Boy Pocket T-Shirt 8 colours
2	BB 459245bb	Big Boy Pocket T-Shirt Baby Blue
2	BJ345899blu	Boss Skinny Jeans
3	BJ345899	Boss Skinny Jeans 3 colours
4	BB 459245	Big Boy Pocket T-Shirt Baby Fire Red
4	BJ345899FDG	Boss Skinny Jeans Faded Gold
5		Logo Sign 24"x 48"

FIGURE 6.5.4   Product listing

Implementing and evaluating the training plan

When a training programme has been created, an evaluation test should be produced to guarantee each field visual merchandiser understands the objective of the strategy and has the skills to perform the required task before being deployed.

Before preparing the test, give thought to the duties the field visual merchandisers are to perform at each store visit and the information they are required to know about your organization. Review the training needs assessment and all training materials developed at this point and reference these documents when developing the test. Also give thought to the following:

- How many questions will be on the test?
- What type of questions will be asked? (True or false, multiple choice?)
- How much time will be provided to complete the test?
- Who will administer the testing?
- Where and when will the test be administered?
- Who will grade it and how will the results be provided?
- What score is needed to pass the exam?
- How will scores be calculated?
- Will points be associated with each answer?
- If so, how many points per question?
- If the field visual merchandiser fails the test, can it be retaken and how soon?

Process for developing the test

Why is it necessary to create a process for developing the training evaluation test? The goal of creating a test development process is to ensure that each level of competence is addressed and field visual merchandisers have the knowledge and skills to perform each task at an acceptable level. There are three steps in the development process:

1 Creating the evaluation test directive.
2 Designing the evaluation test.
3 Test administration.

Evaluation test directive

In order to prepare, each field merchandiser should be given adequate information regarding the test and how it will be administered. To confirm your team understands the importance of the evaluation test and what it will entail, develop an outline to distribute to the team prior to administering the test.

The blueprint for this outline can be a one-page document that provides information on the following:

- purpose of the evaluation test;
- test format;
- how to prepare;
- test passing score;
- frequently asked questions.

Purpose of the evaluation test

Providing information on the purpose of the evaluation test helps the team understand the importance of learning the information. Knowing they must pass the test prior to being deployed instils a sense of pride and confidence in the minds of your team once they have completed the test.

Test format

The test format should describe the number and type of questions on the test, such as '50 true or false' or '50 multiple choice'. If there is a time limit, state the amount of time that will be given to complete the test.

How to prepare

To help the team prepare for the test, it is a good idea to provide a short description of the test topics. Dividing and listing the sections will help your team focus on these areas and will help to identify skill gaps in training at a later date.

Example sections:

- vision and strategy;
- product features and benefits;
- merchandising standards;
- store guidelines;

TABLE 6.1 Example test passing score

Example sections	No of questions	% of example
Vision and strategy	15	15
Product features and benefits	15	15
Merchandising standards	20	20
Store guidelines	15	15
Task duration estimate	20	20
Directives and planograms	15	15
Total	*100*	*100*

- task duration estimate;
- directives and planograms.

Test passing score

What is considered a passing score? It can be a tricky question to answer. It is important for your team to know all the material presented before being deployed, but some areas may be more important than others. To address this concern, determine which sections hold the most value and make them worth a higher percentage of the final grade. It would also be beneficial to create additional questions in these areas as well. An example is provided in Table 6.1.

Frequently asked questions

On the blueprint, try to anticipate questions the team may have about taking the test. This will be very helpful to the team and may also eliminate the need for numerous phone calls or e-mails to answer common questions.

Provide answers to these types of questions:

- How quickly will I get my test results?
- Who will administer the test?

- How much time will I have to complete the test?
- Will I be able to retake the test if I do not make a passing grade?
- How can I find out if I answered a specific question correctly?
- What score do I need to make in order to pass the test?
- What if I don't agree with my final score? Can I appeal it?
- Are there specific dates on which the test will be given?
- Can I request my score be re-evaluated?
- Who will be responsible for evaluating the test?

Designing the evaluation test

Designing the test involves determining two very important items:

- question format;
- the type of questions to be asked.

Question format

Questions on a training evaluation test should be structured in a way to ascertain if the team member has the comprehensive understanding needed to succeed as a field merchandiser for the brand.

Questions can be true or false, multiple choice or whatever format works to obtain positive outcomes. Be sure to ask questions that will retrieve answers to support the assumption that the field merchandiser has the knowledge and understanding to become a valuable member of the team. Remember: when each member of the team has a clear understanding of the objectives and knows what part they play in making the vision a reality, they acquire a sense of direction and become more dedicated and confident when they are fully trained. In addition, they take ownership of their job.

When determining what question format to use for a particular section of the test, be sure to offer an explanation of the format along with instructions that explain the requirements for answering the questions.

Type of questions to consider

Let's look at three types of formats along with an explanation and instructions on how to answer the questions. It may be necessary to use illustrations when developing questions to ensure the information is clear to understand. (The correct responses to these queries are offered).

Example of true or false question format: Section 3 – Merchandising standards

This section comprises true or false statements that may include an illustration to explain the merchandising standard.

Read the questions and view the illustrations to determine if the statements are true or false.

1 When sizing apparel that is side hung, should apparel be sized with the smallest on the left and largest on the right?

FIGURE 6.6 Sizing hanging apparel: Side hung

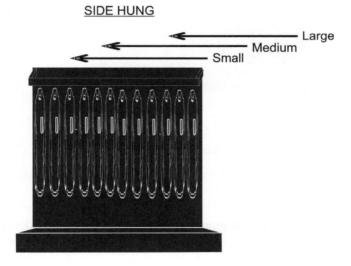

A. True   B. False

(*The answer to this question is A*)

2 When sizing apparel that is faced out, should apparel be sized with largest at the front and smallest at the back?

FIGURE 6.7 Sizing hanging apparel: Faced out

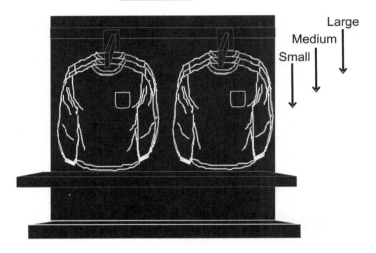

FACED OUT

Large
Medium
Small

A. True   B. False
(*The answer to this question is B*)

Example of multiple choice question format: Section 5 – Task Duration Estimate

This section consists of multiple choice questions, which may offer one or more potential correct answers.

Read the questions and make your selection from the list of answers provided.

1 The task duration estimate is a document utilized by field visual merchandisers for what purpose?

A To estimate the time it takes to fold T-shirts using a folding board.

B To estimate the time it should take to complete the in-store survey after a store visit.

C To provide directions along with estimated times for completion of multiple tasks for each store visit.

(*The answer to this question is C*)

2 Which of the following tasks are not found on a task duration estimate? (Select two)

A Final walk through.
B Place order for signage.
C Visual assessment.
D A photo of the store front.
E Work product from backroom to sales floor.

(*The answers to this question are B and D*)

Example of complete sentence question format: Section 6 – Directives and planograms

This format enables you to ensure the merchandisers have understood the purpose of all the elements in the directives and planograms.

Read the question and select the best answer to complete the sentence.

1 Planograms provide _____ directions showing the fixture, the product with style numbers and how the product is to be merchandised.

A Written
B Visual
C Recorded

(*The answer to this question is B*)

Administering the evaluation test

The best way to administer the test would be to work with the MSO to upload the test to their website. Merchandisers will be able to complete the test after all other training has been concluded.

Administering the training programme

Once all training materials have been created and reviewed, the next step should be to allocate the sum of time needed for each area of training. The goal is to be certain each field visual merchandiser has adequate time to complete the training and pass the certification test prior to being deployed. Keep in mind there is a training cost associated with this undertaking.

When determining time frames for each section during your training, it is recommended that you go through your material as often as possible to determine the length of time it takes to review the information. Furthermore, organize the training in sequence and list the order in which it should be accomplished. The training programme works best when it flows smoothly from one topic to another. For example, the merchandising standards and visit guidelines section could precede the task duration estimates section, and the programme could conclude with the evaluation test.

If the material is taught in sequence, the field visual merchandiser will have adequate information and explanations to support his or her learning process, especially when demonstrations are given to ensure a clear under-standing of the objective. For instance, if someone is teaching about the many ways to fold a shirt, it would be much more effective for the team member to complete the task if the trainer provided a demonstration beforehand on completing that same task.

Your training schedule should be similar to the following:

1 Merchandising standards manual (1 hour)

2 Understanding store visit guidelines (1 hour)

3 Understanding and using the task duration estimate (1 hour)

4 Interpreting directives and planograms (1 hour)

5 Product features and benefits (catalogues) (1.5 hours)

6 Merchandising standards training and certification (2 hours)

7 Complete and pass 'training evaluation test' (1 hour)

Be sure to work with the MSO on the specifics involved in the training, such as the hours and materials needed to render the instructions. Therefore, it is wise to document this information, spelling out the requirements for the training programme and forwarding it to the MSO for confirmation.

Training programme requirements

It is wise to create a document to be distributed to the MSO that gives in-structions for the required training and calculates the cost associated with the programme (Table 6.2). The field merchandising training programme

TABLE 6.2 Field merchandising training programme requirements

Training hours allocation	Field merchandisers 8.5 hours		
Training time frame	21 days prior to deployment: from 17/5/12 to 6/6/12		
Training specifications	Field merchandiser training	1. Merchandising standards manual	1 hour
		2. Understanding 'store visit guidelines'	1 hour
		3. Knowing how to use 'the task duration estimate'	1 hour
		4. Interpreting merchandising directives and planograms	1 hour
		5. View product features and benefits	1.5 hours
		6. Merchandising standards training and certification	2 hours
		7. Training evaluation test	1 hour
	Field management training	1. Conduct one-on-one training in the field to ensure all field merchandisers are well trained prior to deployment	
		2. Administer the certification test	
	Training materials	1. Merchandising standards manual	
		2. Understanding store visit guidelines	
		3. Knowing how to use the task duration estimate	
		4. Interpreting merchandising directives and planograms	
		5. Merchandising standards training and certification	
		6. Product features and benefits manual (catalogues)	
		7. Training evaluation test	

requirements document should be distributed to your MSO with all training materials. Adequate time should be allocated for the MSO to review all training information and materials with their field management team and subsequent confirmation should be received of their willingness to comply.

Training log

Once all training materials and the evaluation test have been created, the next step is to develop a log to ascertain the skill set of the team. The training log is a document that can be used to record team members that have been trained and to identify skill gaps at a glance when visiting stores after the team has been deployed.

This training log can be developed using Microsoft Excel. To develop the log, review two documents that were previously developed: the 'Training Needs Assessment' and the 'Training Evaluation Test'. On the training log, create areas for each of the following (Figure 6.8):

- Names of every field merchandiser on the team.
- All training that must be performed and include the completion date.
- A breakdown of each section in the evaluation test to include the team members' scores and completion date.

Identifying skill gaps in the field

Once the programme is up and running, the leader should visit stores that are being serviced to monitor the execution of the strategy. The merchandiser's training log helps to identify top performers who can be selected for special projects at a later time. Let's look at some examples of how the merchandising training log can be used to identify skill gaps or excellence.

Example 1: Training skill gap

While visiting five stores serviced by field visual merchandiser Taylor Johnson, the presentation of folded T-shirts in each store does not meet the expectations established in the merchandising standards manual. After reviewing the task duration estimate, it has been confirmed that there is enough time allocated to complete the task according to the merchandising standards.

In the merchandising training log, Taylor was given a score of 15 out of 20 in the merchandising standards section. This score, along with the in-store observations, indicates that additional training on merchandising standards would benefit this team member.

FIGURE 6.8 Merchandiser's training log

FIELD VISUAL MERCHANDISERS TRAINING LOG	Cindy Jones	Pat Brown	Jack Allen	Taylor Johnson	Liz Wells	Tommy Horton						
TOTAL SCORE	97	100		94								
DIRECTIVES & PLANOGRAMS SCORE	15	15		15								
TASK DURATION ESTIMATE SCORE	20	20		20								
STORE GUIDELINES SCORE	12	15		14								
MERCHANDISING STANDARDS SCORE	20	20		15								
PRODUCT FEATURES & BENEFITS SCORE	15	15		15								
VISION & STRATEGY SCORE	15	15		15								
DATE COMPLETED	25-Jan	12-Jan		25-Jan								
EVALUATION TEST SCORES	X	X		X								
DATE COMPLETED	20-Jan	10-Jan		25-Jan								
TRAINING EVALUATING TEST	X	X		X								
PRODUCT TRAINING/CATALOGUES	X	X	X	X	X	X						
DATE COMPLETED	15-Jan	10-Jan		20-Jan		15-Jan						
MERCHANDISING CERTIFICATION TEST	X	X		X		X						
DATE COMPLETED	12-Jan	6-Jan	15-Jan	17-Jan		15-Jan						
MERCHANDISING DIRECTIVES & POG	X	X	X	X		X						
DATE COMPLETED	12-Jan	6-Jan	12-Jan	16-Jan		15-Jan						
TASK DURATION ESTIMATE	X	X	X	X		X						
DATE COMPLETED	12-Jan	6-Jan	14-Jan	16-Jan	12-Jan	12-Jan						
STORE VISIT GUIDELINES	X	X	X	X	X	X						

Example 2: Top performer needed for a special project

An account executive needs a field merchandiser to visit a particular store to ensure the company's product is well presented in preparation for a store visit by the Vice President of Sales. There are two field visual merchandisers servicing stores near this location.

It is determined that field merchandisers Jamie Jones and Sam Brown live near the store and both scored a perfect 20 on the merchandising standards section of the evaluation test. A closer look at the merchandising training log reveals that Sam Brown has been merchandising the company's product longer than Jamie and Sam's overall evaluation test score was 100. This is a very important store visit and only one field merchandiser is needed; thus, Sam Brown is selected for the project.

Chapter 6 checklist

- Am I equipped with a full understanding of how to access the training needs and do I possess the necessary skills to set training expectations for my field team or is additional training needed?

- Does my in-house management team know how to create a training programme in a field visual environment?

- Am I comfortable with developing a training needs assessment?

- Do I possess a full conception of the seven types of training materials presented to educate my field team?

- Will my company have concerns with providing each field visual merchandiser with a copy of the company's product catalogue for training on product features and benefits?

- Does my team have the cognitive comprehension and skill set to develop merchandising standards manual, or should this task be outsourced?

- Do I recognize the importance of developing a certification test?

- Do I have the knowledge to develop store visit guidelines once the supporting documents have been obtained from each retailer?

- Have I gained a full view of what a task duration estimate is and how it is used?

- Do I have a well-defined notion of how to develop a task duration estimate?

- Am I clear on why an evaluation test should be developed to guarantee every field visual merchandiser knows the objective of the strategy?

- Does the use of an evaluation test make sense to me?

- Do I understand the evaluation test format and how to prepare the exam?

- Do I agree that the best way to administer the test would be to work with the MSO to upload the test to their website?

- What are my views on why the training requirements document should be given out to my MSO along with all training materials?

- Do I know how to prepare a training log and why one is needed?

- Do I recognize how to use the training log to identify skill gaps in the field?

Tricks of the trade: 'The game of mix and match'

As leaders, we all have had occasions where hiring employees became necessary. The process is usually not extraordinarily painful, but at times it can be frustrating when you can't identify the necessary skills needed for new employees who will be placed in a creative role. Field visual merchandisers usually follow written directives and planograms that are very explanatory and provide specific directions. If you work in an environment where your field team may periodically have the responsibility for pulling outfits for window displays, it may be necessary to provide some sort of training. The question is what type of training?

Early in my career, I stumbled on a unique way to train visual merchandisers on pulling product for window displays. When I would visit stores, I would usually talk to sales personnel to get an idea of what product was selling. On one occasion, a sales manager was waiting for a customer to come in and pick up three suits that had been altered. The sales manager asked me if I would help him pull together a few shirts and ties that would match the three suits. He wanted to lay out a few tasteful combinations that would possibly stimulate an additional sale.

As we pulled a few ties, I ask him to pull a matching shirt. I noticed that he would only select solid colour shirts, so I ask him to pull shirts with a pattern, but stay within the same colour scheme of the pin-striped suits and the multi-coloured ties. He was a little uncomfortable with this process, so I began to tell him how to coordinate outfits using patterns in a different scale from each other. After he tried it a few times, he wanted to test my ability. He would pull a tie and ask me to pull an outfit together within the same colour scheme using all patterns. So the game was on; we played this game a few times until he got the hang of it. Then, I let him have it: as I selected a tie, I ask him to pull three outfits, one business, one business casual and one casual. The catch was once again staying within the colour scheme and using all patterns.

This game became a great way to develop a rapport with sales assistants whenever I travelled to stores. It was not until I needed to hire a district visual merchandising manager that I realized that this game would be a great way to identify a person's ability to coordinate clothing and select merchandise for visual presentations. So I started using the game in the interview process. I would tell the applicant that our company's mission was not only to sell menswear, but to educate our customers on how to become well dressed. I followed the procedure of selecting a tie, then asking the applicant to walk the store and select three coordinated outfits for a window presentation that would reflect the mission of our organization. Of course, this was not the deciding factor whether I hired a person or not, but it gave me an idea of where I needed to start in the training process if I hired a person who would have responsibility for selecting product for window and interior displays. This became a great addition to an interview process when conducted in a store environment, but I knew I would not always have the luxury of conducting this process in a retail store.

As I began to work with outsourced FVM teams, it became necessary to train the entire team on how to select merchandise for window displays. The process was tweaked and became a segment of a much larger training programme called 'The Game of Mix and Match'. Let's walk through the process of conducting this game.

For the instruction part of the game, I suggest using Chapter 3 of this book to discuss the following topics:

- merchandise presentation and visual merchandising skills;
- developing a high taste level;
- mannequin styling and clothing coordination;
- mixing patterns in clothing coordination;
- effects of colour in visual merchandising.

TABLE 6.3 The game of 'mix and match'

Objective	This exercise helps each team member improve the process of selecting merchandise for window displays
Group size	6–30 divided into teams
Time required	60 minutes, depending on the size of the group
Materials	Three handouts: 1. Store front document showing two window displays 2. Product catalogues, one per group 3. Effects of colour in visual merchandising
Procedure	1. Divide the group into small teams of 3–6 people 2. Give each group one each of the three handouts above 3. Direct each group to select merchandise from the catalogue provided for each of the two windows in the handout 4. Instruct the group to utilize the techniques discussed in the instruction part of the game 5. Have each group select a spokesperson to present their team's window presentations to the group 6. As the facilitator, walk the room and take note of how each team works together to select product and what techniques are applied in their window presentations

Effects of colour in visual merchandising

RED

Intense red: Danger, passion, love, excitement, conspicuousness.

Dark red: Wealth, power, sometimes evil.

Pink: Cheerfulness, youth, festivity.

Light or pastel pink: Femininity, innocence, relaxation, delicacy.

ORANGE

Orange: Friendliness, warmth, celebration, clarity.

Dark orange: Wealth, success, fame, rich depth.

Light or pastel orange: Stimulation (to the appetites), security, relaxed
  euphoria (sense of well-being).

YELLOW

Yellow: cheerful optimism, sunshine, springtime, renewal, intense,
  demanding, revealing, warmth, intellect, stimulation.

Golden yellow: Wealth, affluence, status, distinction, high esteem.

Middle to light yellow: Intelligence, wisdom, compassion, freshness,
  cheerfulness, optimism, goodness, clarity, cleanliness.

GREEN

Green: Nature, calmness, friendliness, integrity, practicality, frankness.

Dark green: Solidity, anchored, tenacity, security.

Blue–green: Sea and sky, cleanliness, nostalgia, calmness.

Yellow–green: Youthfulness, freshness, happiness.

BLUE

Blue: Loyalty, honesty, integrity, royalty, stimulation, restlessness.

Deep blue: Sincerity, conservatism, safety, peacefulness, kindness,
  compassion.

Light or pastel blue: Tentativeness, cleanliness, calm, expanded time and
  space, lack of security.

PURPLE OR VIOLET

Purple or violet: Optimism, imagination, royalty, dignity, poise, renewal,
  commitment.

Dark purple or violet: Depth, richness, security, sternness, soberness,
  sobriety, dullness.

Light or pastel purple: Freshness, springtime, flowers, imaginativeness,
  femininity, kindness, sensitivity.

FIGURE 6.9 Catalogue and store front with two windows

PRODUCT CATALOG

Bossman
2010 FALL

STORE FRONT WITH 2 WINDOWS

WINDOW 1

WINDOW 2

WINDOW 1
Mannequin 1

Mannequin 2

WINDOW 2
Mannequin 1

Mannequin 2

Planning your combat strategy

So far in Part Two, you have gained an understanding of the components associated with initiating your strategy, such as defining objectives, developing standards and analysing the battlefield. You have discovered the structure of an MSO, the ways in which you can prepare your strategy proposal, the steps to take when selecting an MSO and the ideas to keep in mind while training in the field environment. In Chapter 6, we discussed training documents utilized by the FVM team when visiting retail locations. In this chapter, we will address the manner in which the information in these documents will be gathered, the ways to disseminate the material, along with the data you will need to prepare the strategic plan. Prior to developing the strategic plan, it is essential to obtain the retailer's requirements before the field team is released to begin servicing stores. We must put mechanisms in place to help foster a cohesive relationship with the retailers.

Defining retailer requirements

Grave mistakes have been made when launching a field merchandising strategy with poor communications and which ignores the necessity to cultivate proper relations with the retailer. Retailers are the most important group in the development and execution process. If a field merchandising strategy is being launched in 100 retail locations and the manager on duty from each of these stores is not aware of the launch, you are destined for failure. Field visual merchandisers will not be welcomed if they show up at a retailer unannounced, claiming to have arrived to merchandise product. It is like showing up to a wedding without an invitation. Every retailer has guidelines for vendors who visit their stores. These guidelines may be different at each retailer. Therefore, before moving forward, the leader should provide each retailer with a strategy scope statement explaining the objectives of the strategy along with the details of the store visits.

Strategy scope statement

The strategy scope statement provides an overview of the strategy details and gives the retailer distinct insight about the work that will take place in their stores and describes the general objectives. Chapter 5 walked us through the process of producing a strategy proposal. In this document, 90 per cent of the data required to prepare a strategy scope statement can be found. Thus, it is not necessary to begin from scratch. The strategy scope statement should include the following information pulled from the strategy proposal:

1 Retail merchandising strategy overview.
2 Strategic objective.
3 Competitive advantage.
4 Strategy scope.
5 Merchandiser task duration estimates.
6 Strategy direction.

Once this has been completed for each retailer involved, it's time to identify a corporate contact from each retailer. The goal is to establish communication through the account executive who is ordinarily the most likely individual possessing a relationship with someone in the retailer's corporate office. Remember, the account executive is usually the sponsor who represents the brand and who has discussed and received approval to execute the strategy in specified retail locations. The leader's role is to provide the retailer with the strategy scope statement and work with the account executive to gain an understanding of the store visit guidelines.

In order to conform to these guidelines, it is imperative that one works with the retailer to define their requirements for store protocol. Clearly, the field team cannot succeed unless the retailer's requirements have been defined and met. Also, at times it may become necessary to communicate with all involved parties; this includes store personnel to ensure clarity on the brand's execution. Therefore, it is a good idea to obtain important contact information for key people in the retailer's organization.

Corporate retail contacts

When you are rolling out an FVM strategy in key retail accounts, usually the account executive has obtained approval from someone in the retailer's corporate office. This may be a buyer or a senior level executive who has the authority to grant this type of approval. This person may not be the right individual to provide detailed knowledge for the team, but should be able to recommend a contact person at the retail level who can supply additional information. It is a good idea to make contact once an individual has been identified.

When making this contact, be sure to offer the strategy scope statement which provides project knowledge. It would be in the best interests of all parties involved to maintain open lines of communication. Also, this is a great time to gather the contact information for the regional, district and store managers, just in case unforeseen issues arise. You will appreciate having secured sufficient contact information for everyone in the chain of command. At times, information can be fused with incorrect data at the store, causing mix-ups and delays to the implementation process. It would be wise to ask the retailer for a management contact list in the event miscommunication regarding the strategy occurs.

A case in point: if a merchandiser shows up to a retail store with a document stating they are to restock product and the team from the store is not aware of their visit, a quick call to the district or regional manager could eliminate this confusion. It is always advisable to engage in opportunities to develop a closer relationship with the retailer. The merchandiser is not an outside force and should be viewed as someone desiring to assist in escalating sales.

Retailer management contact list

When receiving the store list from the account executives, there is a chance it will contain contact information for management. If not, when requesting the list, be sure to ask for it in an Excel spreadsheet format. The information contained in this spreadsheet should include each store address, phone number, manager's name, and district and the regional managers' names and phone numbers.

Retailer letter of introduction

The retailer letter of introduction is a note from the retailer's corporate office addressed to store management, revealing upcoming events and announcing the rollout of the strategy. The goal of this letter is to introduce the launch details of the strategy and inform store management that an field visual merchandiser will perform merchandising services for a particular brand.

The leader should assume an active part in emphasizing to the corporate contact the importance of creating a letter of introduction; this will eliminate confusion when a merchandiser visits a store with the letter in hand. It is wise to ask the contact to forward the letter to all retail locations involved in the strategy.

The letter serves as a standard of respect and gets the relationship between the field visual merchandiser and the store's management team off to a secure beginning. Imagine answering your door one morning and the person standing there says, 'Hello, my name is Mickey and I am here to rearrange your furniture.' After your first response of being puzzled, you would probably say 'no thank you' and close the door. Respect is always important in this industry and should not be considered lightly. The managers on duty are very protective of their stores and do not allow random people to walk into their stockrooms and do whatever they desire. It only takes one manager on duty to call the corporate office and complain about an unpleasant experience with a field visual merchandiser, and the programme in all stores could be cancelled. A solid relationship with the retail manager is imperative.

The manager on duty should be aware of the execution, but occasionally there will be times when things are very busy in the retail store and the management team may not recall the details of the launch. This letter should be used to alleviate confusion and serve as a point of reference for the strategy. To facilitate this document and for the sake of simplicity, it would be wise to create a sample letter to the corporate contact outlining a few pertinent facts to be shared with the store's personnel.

The sample retailer letter of introduction (Figure 7.1) should include the following:

- name of the brand to receive the merchandising services;
- the merchandising organization responsible for the implementation;
- date services will begin;
- services performed;
- other important contact information.

Retailer store visit guidelines

The next step in defining retailer requirements is to request information pertaining to the process of entering each retail location and the general protocol when servicing the store. Many stores have an employee entrance

FIGURE 7.1 Sample retailer letter of introduction

M

Moors Department Stores
2145 W. Morris Street
Denver, CO 80203

To: Store Manager
From: Briar Hayden, Menswear Buyer
Date: 13/5/2012
Subject: Bossman Clothing Company, Field Visual Merchandising Services

Your store has been selected to be a part of a national field visual merchandising strategy in partnership with the Bossman brand and the Kick-Start Merchandising Organization. A Kick-Start merchandiser will begin servicing your store between the weeks of 3/10/2012 – 18/10/2012 and will continue thereafter, every two weeks.

The Kick-Start Merchandising representative's primary responsibilities will be updating the in-store presentations of the Bossman brand to ensure the product is restocked, resized, refolded and signage placed correctly. They are also required to take before and after photos of their work. Prior to the store visit, you will receive a call indicating the actual date of the visit.

On the day of the visit, the representative will sign in at the service desk and ask for a member of store management. Please provide support and access to your inventory so they can maximize sales in your store. Should you have any questions regarding the store visit, please contact Brook Adams at the Bossman Corporate Headquarters:

Brook Adams
Director of Field Visual Merchandising
123-456-7891
b.adams@bossman.com

Thank you in advance for your support.
Yours sincerely,

Briar Hayden
Menswear Buyer
198-765-4321
b.hayden@moors.com

and/or vendor sign-in sheet. It is important for the field merchandiser to be cognizant of the policies and procedures for entering the retail store. In addition, each retailer may have 'sales floor rules'. This may be a list of what is permissible and what has been deemed as an unacceptable practice. Each vendor must follow these guidelines when visiting the store; if not followed, the consequences could include a warning, up to being asked to leave the establishment.

A list of things that may be permitted or prohibited might include the following:

- It is required for vendors to be always professional and to practise common courtesy.
- No offensive or inappropriate language.
- Professional attire is needed at all times.
- Name tags must be visible during times of service.
- Cell phones must be turned off while on the sales floor.
- Visual merchandisers may *not* wear any of the store's clothing.
- Vendors should always be accompanied by a store employee to any stockroom area.
- No food or drink on the sales floor.
- Vendors are subject to bag checks.
- Merchandiser must be checked out by a manager before leaving.

Once you have obtained the entrance instructions, policies and procedures for each retailer, develop the store visit guidelines for the team. These guidelines should provide clear-cut directions for all aspects of the store visit with the list of the retailer's instructions attached.

The store visit guidelines should include the following:

- scheduling the visit with the store manager;
- instructions for the sign-in system at the retail store upon arrival;
- procedures after sign-in.

The store visit guidelines are primarily for the FVM team, but will likewise function as a guide to store management detailing the services to be performed during a particular visit. Showing this document to a manager in the stockroom will help explain why the merchandiser needs access to the store inventory.

Field visual merchandising strategy

Store visit guidelines for Moors Department Store

These guidelines have been developed to provide instructions on servicing this retailer. Prior to visiting the store, pack your task duration estimate, planograms, signage or any point of purchase materials required. In addition to the information below, please review the attached 'sales floor rules' and govern yourself accordingly.

Scheduling your visit with the store manager:

- It is mandatory that you call two weeks prior to servicing the store to confirm the visit with the manager on duty.

- Make inquiries for the location of the employee/vendor entrance.

- If the manager on duty is not available, be sure to obtain another contact person.

When you arrive at the store:

- Enter through the employee entrance.

- Sign in on the vendor log at the security or customer service desk. A vendor identification badge will be given and must be worn at all times during the visit.

- Locate the department area and determine where the priority of work should begin. This will help determine how to allocate time correctly based on the department needs.

Before you start merchandising:

- Review the task duration estimate to identify objectives.

- Locate store contact and check in with the appropriate individuals. Communicate with all involved parties the priority to help restock and restore the Bossman product presentation as the planogram dictates.

- Walk the department manager through the changes to be made to the Bossman presentation.

- Ask for assistance when locating the Bossman product in the stockroom, and find out where damaged product should be placed, if found on the floor while merchandising.

- Ask if the store has any special merchandising requests.

- Make sure to take photos before restoring the presentation.

Developing the strategic plan

In Chapter 1, we discussed thinking strategically and presented two instances where leaders developed a strategic plan document to launch new assortments in a department store. In Chapter 2, we discussed project management as a principal skill needed by the leader in order to create the details of the strategy. Having a comprehensive understanding of these two subjects will help one develop a flawless strategic plan. In this chapter, information will be presented with more in-depth understanding of the development process along with indicative factors showing how the elements of strategic thinking and project management collaborate.

A strategic plan defines all the details of the strategy. To communicate this direction, one must develop documents that can be forwarded to all parties involved to make certain everyone understands their role in carrying out the strategic plan. One of the most effective ways to communicate a strategic plan is by using a project management schedule (timeline). This document is crucial when developing and executing an FVM strategy. This timeline serves as the road map utilized by everyone involved to grasp where the execution is at any given point. The leader's task is to develop the strategic plan timeline and monitor it closely to make certain everything is moving in the right direction and on schedule. In addition, this document will clarify everyone's role in the implementation process, and depict the progression and flow as the strategy is carried out.

Phase progression

According to a well-known saying, you eat an elephant one bite at a time. A strategic plan is like an elephant; it is a large undertaking and the best way to execute it is to break it up into small manageable pieces called phases. If you place these phases in sequence to one another, you will have a natural progression from start to finish. To prepare the strategic plan document, one would use the traditional project management process. Traditionally, there are five basic phases in the project management process but all phases are not utilized every time. The traditional phases are:

1 Initiation.
2 Planning.
3 Execution.
4 Monitoring.
5 Completion.

To show the progression, each phase and goal should be added to the strategic plan timeline in chronological order. We will use only four of the traditional phases to develop the strategic plan: Initiation, Planning, Execution and Monitoring. We will not apply the fifth phase, completion, because a strategy of this magnitude is similar to a programme which extends indefinitely. Once the strategy launch has been implemented, very similar to a programme, merchandising services are continuously provided.

Goals

In order to accomplish each phase, one may need to complete numerous tasks referred to as goals. On the strategic plan timeline, goals are listed below each phase (Figure 7.2). A timeline also lists the number of days it should take to complete the task, the start and finish dates, and the person responsible for completing the task. When all phases and goals have been completed and added, the document can be forwarded to all parties to sign off before the launch. At that point, the strategic plan documented becomes a road map to implement the launch (Figure 7.2).

Initiation phase

The initiation phase is the first step in the process. It establishes the authorization and approval to execute the strategy by the retailers. It likewise serves as a guide to highlight what should be accomplished by each party involved and the time frame to complete the specified task. In this phase, the leader should contact each party involved to confirm their understanding of their role in the strategic plan and the estimated time frame required to complete the assigned task. It is important to obtain confirmation in writing to ensure there is no misunderstanding of the responsibilities to be accomplished and the expected execution date. An efficient manner to convey this message is by way of a document called a launch directive.

Launch directives

To obtain confirmation, the leader should send a 'launch directive' to each party detailing the task and estimated time of completion. Each party involved should analyse the estimated time frame they have been given to complete their task and confirm availability to meet the deadline. If the time frame is not realistic, request a more accurate completion time and update your records.

Each launch directive represents a goal that is documented and accomplished in a logical order, in a specified time and within a particular phase. Having a launch directive is advantageous when plotting a goal on the

FIGURE 7.2 Strategic plan: Phases, goals and timelines

Phase → Goal → Days to complete → Responsible party →

TASK NAME	DURATION	START	FINISH	RESOURCE
National Field Merchandising Strategy		Thu 2/2/12		
Initiation	**79 days**	**Thu 2/2/12**	**Tue 5/22/12**	
– Develop Strategy Scope Statement for Each Retailer and Forward	1 days	Thu 2/2/12	Thu 2/2/12	Brook Adams
– Provide Approval to Execute Strategy in Retail Stores	2 days	Thu 2/2/12	Fri 2/3/12	Retailer
– Provide Management Contact List to Brook Adams	7 days	Fri 2/3/12	Mon 2/13/12	Retailer
– Provide Retailer Letter of Introduction to Brook Adams and Store Managers	7 days	Tue 2/14/12	Wen 2/22/12	Retailer
– Provide Retailer Store Visit Guidelines to Brook Adams	5 days	Fri 3/23/12	Thu 3/29/12	Retailer
– Forward Letter of Introduction and Store Visit Guidelines to MSO for Approval	15 days	Fri 3/30/12	Thu 4/19/12	Brook Adams
– Forward and Review Training Materials with Printer for Production	1 day	Fri 4/20/12	Fri 4/20/12	Brook Adams
– Forward Training Programme Requirements to MSO for Approval	1 day	Mon 4/23/12	Mon 4/23/12	Brook Adams
– Provide Approval of Training Requirements/Visit Guidelines/Letter Intro	14 days	Tue 4/24/12	Fri 5/11/12	MSO
– Review/Approve and Sign Off on Strategy	7 days	Mon 5/14/12	Tue 5/22/12	Account Executives
Planning	**65 days**	**Wed 5/23/12**	**Tue 8/21/12**	
– Conduct Strategy Kick-off Meeting with Retailer, MSO and Account Executives	14 days	Wed 5/23/12	Mon 6/11/12	Brook Adams
– Produce Copies of Training Materials for Field Merchandisers	15 days	Tue 6/12/12	Mon 7/2/12	Color Block Printing

strategic plan timeline. It confirms the identities of the people responsible for each task, identifies the start and finish times, and ultimately assists in determining how long it will take to execute the strategy.

To offer more insight into developing a launch directive, let's look at an example. In Chapter 6, we discussed developing two training manuals: one called the Product Features and Benefits Manual (catalogues) and another called the Merchandising Standards Manual. It is necessary to produce and distribute these training manuals to the MSO and the visual merchandising team.

So, to get started, it is essential to allocate the appropriate time to have these manuals produced, packaged and shipped to the field team. Creating a launch directive for the copy centre, detailing the request and discussing the estimated time to produce the manuals must be considered in order to meet the deadlines that have been designated.

Although a launch directive can be nothing more than an e-mail, creating a document such as the example below can make it fast and trouble-free to identify the information needed to plot on the strategic plan document.

Field merchandising strategy launch directive for Color Block Printing

Objective:
We are launching our field merchandising strategy and developing the time frames for execution. Please review the information below and confirm that you will be able to meet the deadlines listed.

Resource name:	Bailey Anderson
Resource title:	Account Representative
Resource company:	Color Block Printing
Phone number:	224-222-2222
E-mail address:	**banderson@colorblockprinting.com**
Task name:	300 merchandising standard manuals
	300 product features and benefits manuals
Task description:	Produce, package and ship manuals to merchandising service organization, address listed on the original cost estimate.
Duration:	15 days to produce manuals
	3 days to package manuals
	12 days to ship manuals

Now that you are clear on launch directives, let's get back to our initiation phase. At the start of this chapter, we discussed three main documents to be obtained from the corporate retail contact that will assist in completing the initiation phase of the strategic plan. If you have received these materials prior to this point of the development, have them on hand for review. If not, forward a launch directive to request these documents. It's important to go over this data once it is received and to cross reference the dates and deliverables with your estimates to certify that all dates are realistic before plotting the info on the strategic plan timeline. Let's look at the documents previously discussed that should be received from the corporate retailers.

Documents from the retailers

1 Management contact list.

2 Retailer letter of introduction.

3 Store visit guidelines.

To ensure you do not have any setbacks at the beginning of your launch, ask the retailer to forward the three documents back to you by a specified date. This time frame should be plotted in the initiation phase.

Plotting the initiation phase

Once the launch directives have been received, the next step is to plot the initiation phase and determine the completion of this phase. Project management software is recommended, but if this software is not available, you could prepare the strategic plan timeline using MS Excel (Figure 7.3).

The first step is to create headings such as task name, duration, start, finish and resource. Below the headings, list the name of the strategy. The finish time and the duration cannot be confirmed at this time, so skip it for now and just add the start date. As an example, we will use Thursday 2 February 2012. It is not possible to determine the duration and finish time of the strategy until all other information has been added. Next, list the first phase of the strategy 'initiation' and begin by reviewing the launch directives and plotting each goal in sequence. Keep in mind that there are specific tasks the leader must accomplish, such as forwarding information to other parties, reviewing training materials with the copy centre's personnel and obtaining signatures for the training programme from the MSO. Additionally, these tasks should be plotted and placed in sequence.

FIGURE 7.3 Developing the launch plan: Initiation phase tasks

TASK NAME	DURATION	START	FINISH	RESOURCE
National Field Merchandising Strategy		Thu 2/2/12		
Initiation				
– Develop Strategy Scope Statement for Each Retailer				
– Provide Approval to execute Strategy in Retail Stores				
– Provide Management Contact List to Brook Adams				
– Provide Retailer Letter of Introduction to Brook Adams and Store Managers				
– Provide Retailer Store Visit Guidelines to Brook Adams				
– Forward Letter of Introduction and Store Visit Guidelines to MSO for Approval				
– Forward and Review Training Materials with Printer for Production				
– Forward Training Programme Requirements to MSO for Approval				
– Provide Approval of Training Requirements/Visit Guidelines/Letter Intro				
– Review/Approve and Sign Off on Strategy				

Next, list the start and finish times for each goal under the initiation phase (Figure 7.4). Be sure to list the resource for each goal as well. The resource is the person or company responsible for completing the goal. This document will be extremely useful if it notes accurate duration, start and finish times. Review this information closely. If project management software is not being utilized, it is highly recommended to use a calendar to confirm correct dates.

When determining dates, only place deadlines on weekdays, not weekends. This will certify that adequate time is given and no task is due on a day when team members are not working. Once all goals in the initiation phase have been documented, determine the phase duration and its start and finish times by looking at the start date of the first goal and the end date of the last goal. Using the calendar, count the days required to complete the phase and plot this information on the form. If calculated properly, it will require 79 days to complete the initiation phase in the example below.

Once this phase is completed, start over and review each detail for accuracy. In Chapter 1, we discussed five essential steps of thinking strategically. These five steps were researching, identifying risk, developing a road map, field communication and coordinating the execution with the FVM team. Using these five steps, review the details to be certain the road map is leading everyone in the same direction and no two goals are out of sequence or interfering with each other. Once these steps have been reviewed and all is well, move along to the planning phase.

Planning phase

Now that you have completed the initiation phase of your strategy, it is time to focus on the planning phase. This phase will require you to coordinate all materials that are to be produced, shipped and reviewed. The first step in this phase is to conduct a strategy kick-off meeting with the account executives, your MSO and each retailer separately. This encounter is essential as the leader will bring together all parties involved in the strategy to discuss the execution details. The meeting can be conducted face to face or on a conference call. The significance of this meeting is to affirm that everyone involved possesses a well-defined understanding of their role, the planning required to take place within their teams and the manner in which it will be executed going forward. Before setting up the encounters, convene with the MSO and develop an agenda. It is best to keep the appointment with each retailer separate. Try to concentrate on one merchant at a time and give each retailer an opportunity to ask questions that pertain to their stores specifically.

FIGURE 7.4 Developing the launch plan: Initiation phase timeline

TASK NAME	DURATION	START	FINISH	RESOURCE
National Field Merchandising Strategy		Thu 2/2/12		
Initiation	**79 days**	**Thu 2/2/12**	**Tue 5/22/12**	
– Develop Strategy Scope Statement for Each Retailer	1 days	Thu 2/2/12	Thu 2/2/12	Brook Adams
– Provide Approval to Execute Strategy in Retail Stores	2 days	Thu 2/2/12	Fri 2/3/12	Retailer
– Provide Management Contact List to Brook Adams	5 days	Fri 2/3/12	Thu 2/9/12	Retailer
– Provide Retailer Letter of Introduction to Brook Adams and Store Managers	7 days	Tue 2/14/12	Wed 2/22/12	Retailer
– Provide Retailer Store Visit Guidelines to Brook Adams	5 days	Fri 3/23/12	Thu 3/29/12	Retailer
– Forward Letter of Introduction and Store Visit Guidelines to MSO for Approval	15 days	Fri 3/30/12	Thu 4/19/12	Brook Adams
– Forward and Review Training Materials with Printer for Production	1 day	Fri 4/20/12	Fri 4 20/12	Brook Adams
– Forward Training Programme Requirements to MSO for Approval	1 day	Mon 4/23/12	Mon 4/23/12	Brook Adams
– Provide Approval of Training Requirements/Visit Guidelines/Letter Intro	14 days	Tue 4/24/12	Fri 5/11/12	MSO
– Review/Approve and Sign Off on Strategy	7 days	Mon 5/14/12	Tue 5/22/12	Account Executives

Kick-off meeting agenda

This agenda should be created to help streamline the meeting with topics covering pertinent information and to keep all parties focused on implementation. Likewise, when an agenda is provided prior to the meeting, it gives each participant an opportunity to review the subjects to be discussed and formulate questions.

Strategy kick-off meeting

Date/Time: 1:00 pm
Conference call dial-in number: 216-405-0270
Participant code: 126459#

Meeting Agenda

1 Vision of the strategy

2 Strategy scope

3 Number of stores to be serviced

4 Store visit schedule

5 Responsibilities of each party

6 Risk

7 Execution phase

8 Monitoring phase

9 Milestones

10 Ongoing communication

11 Strategy updates

12 Questions

Agenda topics

Although these topics may have been communicated previously, the participants in the meeting may have a desire to discuss these topics to gain further knowledge of processes. Let's review and highlight the importance of each topic:

- **The vision of the strategy**: We all recognize the benefits for the brand, but in this meeting, everyone involved should comprehend the vision and recognize how the strategy would benefit the retailer.

- **Strategy scope**: The scope reveals the work to be performed to fulfil the objectives of the strategy.

- **Number of stores to be serviced**: It is essential for everyone involved to have clear insight on the number of stores to be serviced on a regular basis.

- **Store visit schedule**: The store visit schedule gives the retailer knowledge on the visit rotation. Your visit rotation may consist of store visits twice a month, once a month or twice a quarter. Whatever the case, this information must be provided to the retailer.

- **Responsibilities of each party**: This is where the leader reviews the details of everyone's responsibility and answers questions.

- **Risk**: When reviewing the possible risk associated with the strategy, discuss processes that have been put into place to address potential issues. In addition, ask your attendees to offer input and feedback on other concerns that may not have been addressed that could affect the outcome of your attempts to meet the strategic objective.

- **Execution phase**: This is the time to discuss how the strategy will roll out.

- **Monitoring phase**: Go through what will be done to monitor the strategy on an ongoing basis during and after the launch.

- **Milestones**: Discuss the key significant points in the execution. Completion of these milestones will signify the fact that the group is making progress in the correct direction.

- **Ongoing communication**: Encourage the group to review the strategic plan documents as they will function as a road map to help everyone to stay abreast of the execution at any given point.

- **Strategy updates**: Notify the group that periodic updates will be given to keep everyone informed of major changes.

- **Questions**: This is the time to answer any inquiries or requests for additional information.

At the close of the call, don't forget to verify that all questions were answered and all have the same opinion regarding the direction of the strategy. Make sure to let each person know that additional questions can be entertained at a later date if necessary.

Plotting the planning phase

Now it is time to add the planning phase to the strategic plan document. Follow the same procedure as listed under 'Plotting the initiation phase' on page 173. Begin by plotting the strategy kick-off meeting. Although the meeting has taken place, the group will be able to view the strategic plan document and locate where the strategy is at any given point in the process. Next, review the launch directives and plot each goal in sequence, list the start and finish times for each goal under the planning phase section (Figure 7.5) and be sure to list the resource for each goal.

Remember it is crucial that you include accurate time information. Review this information closely, and again, use a calendar to ensure your dates are correct. When determining the important dates, select only from the working weekdays, as previously stated. This will confirm that adequate time is given and no task is due on a weekend. When all goals in this phase have been documented, determine the duration, start and finish time for this phase by looking at the start date of the first goal and the end date of the last goal. Using your calendar, count the days it would take to complete this phase and plot this information. The planning phase in the figure below will take 65 days to complete.

Execution phase

In this phase, your strategy is ready to launch. Everything described and developed in the planning, the strategy proposal, the MSO selection, the training plans and the production of all training materials is set to be implemented. This is usually the longest phase in the life cycle of the strategy. With launch directives in hand, it's time to start reviewing every detail of the execution to confirm dates, times and sequences to verify that each part will flow as planned. In this specific strategy, there are three retailers. So, it is best to launch your strategy in three phases starting with one retailer in phase one, the second retailer in phase two and the third in phase three. This process gives you the opportunity to identify obstacles in the first phase, and then develop a plan to eliminate these situations in the following phases.

FIGURE 7.5 Developing the launch plan: Planning phase timeline

TASK NAME	DURATION	START	FINISH	RESOURCE
National Field Merchandising Strategy		Thu 2/2/12		
Initiation	**79 days**	**Thu 2/2/12**	**Tue 5/22/12**	
– Develop Strategy Scope Statement for Each Retailer and Forward	1 days	Thu 2/2/12	Thu 2/2/12	Brook Adams
– Provide Approval to Execute Strategy in Retail Stores	2 days	Thu 2/2/12	Fri 2/3/12	Retailer
– Provide Management Contact List to Brook Adams	7 days	Fri 2/3/12	Mon 2/13/12	Retailer
– Provide Retailer Letter of Introduction to Brook Adams and Store Managers	7 days	Tue 2/14/12	Wed 2/22/12	Retailer
– Provide Retailer Store Visit Guidelines to Brook Adams	5 days	Fri 3/23/12	Thu 3/29/12	Retailer
– Forward Letter of Introduction and Store Visit Guidelines to MSO for Approval	15 days	Fri 3/30/12	Thu 4/19/12	Brook Adams
– Forward and Review Training Materials with Printer for Production	1 day	Fri 4/20/12	Fri 4/20/12	Brook Adams
– Forward Training Programme Requirements to MSO for Approval	1 day	Mon 4/23/12	Mon 4/23/12	Brook Adams
– Provide Approval of Training Requirements/Visit Guidelines/Letter Intro	14 days	Tue 4/24/12	Fri 5/11/12	MSO
– Review/Approve and Sign Off on Strategy	7 days	Mon 5/14/12	Tue 5/22/12	Account Executives
Planning	**65 days**	**Wed 5/23/12**	**Tue 8/21/12**	
– Conduct Strategy Kick-off Meeting with Retailer, MSO and Account Executives	14 days	Wed 5/23/12	Mon 6/11/12	Brook Adams
– Produce Copies of Training Materials for Field Merchandisers	15 days	Tue 6/12/12	Mon 7/2/12	Color Block Printing
– Package Training Materials to be Shipped to MSO	3 days	Tue 7/3/12	Thu 7/5/12	Color Block Printing
– Ship Training Materials to MSO	12 days	Fri 7/6/12	Mon 7/23/12	Color Block Printing
– Review and Approve Training Materials	7 days	Tue 7/24/12	Wed 8/1/12	MSO
– Forward Training Materials to MSO Field Management	14 days	Thu 8/2/12	Tue 8/21/12	MSO

Plotting the execution phase

It is vital for the strategy to be executed with a systematic approach. Therefore, it is necessary to review the dates and times on the launch directives
and all documents involved to determine what goals should follow after the
planning phase. The last goal in the planning phase is to 'forward training
materials to MSO field management' (Figure 7.6). The group responsible for
this goal is the MSO. In Chapter 6, we discussed preparing a document called
'field merchandising training programme requirements'. This document is
to be forwarded to the MSO along with the training materials. This document also provides details on the number of days it should take to train the
field team. Reviewing this document will show the time needed to train
the team is 21 days. Let's discuss the parts of the plotting process:

- When reviewing the last goal in the planning phase, it is noted that
  all training materials should be received by Tuesday, August 21 2012.
  Therefore, the first goal to plot under the execution phase should be,
  'conduct FVM training' (Figure 7.6). Under the 'Duration' heading
  for this goal, list the time frame for training, which is 21 days.

- Training should start the day after the training materials have been
  received. Therefore, under the 'Start' heading for this goal, list
  Wednesday, August 22 2012 (Figure 7.6). Using your calendar, count
  21 days from Wednesday, August 22 omitting any weekend days and
  this will show you the finish date of September 19 2012. Plot this
  date under the 'Finish' heading (Figure 7.6)

- In Chapter 6 we discussed 'store visit guidelines'. These guidelines
  provide direction to the field team for specific procedures when
  visiting stores. In these guidelines, the field visual merchandisers are
  directed to call the department manager two weeks prior to visiting
  a store in order to schedule their visit. Therefore, the next goal in the
  execution phase should be 'conduct pre-calls to each retail store
  manager to schedule the first visit'. Using your calendar and the
  procedures discussed, plot the duration, start and finish times for this
  goal (Figure 7.6).

Your next step in plotting the execution is to list each phase of the launch.
If all pre-calls are to be finished by Tuesday, February 10 2012, your next
step should be to plot phase one launch. Previously in this chapter, we
discussed the 'retailer letter of introduction'. This letter is produced by
the retailer and forwarded to each store that is being serviced by the FVM
team to provide details of the execution. This letter should also be forwarded

FIGURE 7.6 Developing the launch plan: Execution phase timeline

TASK NAME	DURATION	START	FINISH	RESOURCE
National Field Merchandising Strategy	252 days	Thu 2/2/12	Fri 1/18/13	
Initiation	79 days	Thu 2/2/12	Tue 5/22/12	
– Develop Strategy Scope Statement for Each Retailer and Forward	1 days	Thu 2/2/12	Thu 2/2/12	Brook Adams
– Provide Approval to Execute Strategy in Retail Stores	2 days	Thu 2/2/12	Fri 2/3/12	Retailer
– Provide Management Contact List to Brook Adams	7 days	Fri 2/3/12	Mon 2/13/12	Retailer
– Provide Retailer Letter of Introduction to Brook Adams and Store Managers	7 days	Tue 2/14/12	Wed 2/22/12	Retailer
– Provide Retailer Store Visit Guidelines to Brook Adams	5 days	Fri 3/23/12	Thu 3/29/12	Retailer
– Forward Letter of Introduction and Store Visit Guidelines to MSO for Approval	15 days	Fri 3/30/12	Thu 4/19/12	Brook Adams
– Forward and Review Training Materials with Printer for Production	1 day	Fri 4/20/12	Fri 4/20/12	Brook Adams
– Forward Training Programme Requirements to MSO for Approval	1 day	Mon 4/23/12	Mon 4/23/12	Brook Adams
– Provide Approval of Training Requirements/Visit Guidelines/Letter Intro	14 days	Tue 4/24/12	Fri 5/11/12	MSO
– Review/Approve and Sign Off on Strategy	7 days	Mon 5/14/12	Tue 5/22/12	Account Executives

FIGURE 7.6 *continued*

TASK NAME	DURATION	START	FINISH	RESOURCE
Planning	**65 days**	**Wed 5/23/12**	**Tue 8/21/12**	
– Conduct Strategy Kick-off Meeting with Retailer, MSO and Account Executives	14 days	Wed 5/23/12	Mon 6/11/12	Brook Adams
– Produce Copies of Training Materials for Field Merchandisers	15 days	Tue 6/12/12	Mon 7/2/12	Color Block Printing
– Package Training Materials to be Shipped to MSO	3 days	Tue 7/3/12	Thu 7/5/12	Color Block Printing
– Ship Training Materials to MSO	12 days	Fri 7/6/12	Mon 7/23/12	Color Block Printing
– Review and Approve Training Materials	7 days	Tue 7/24/12	Wed 8/1/12	MSO
– Forward Training Materials to MSO Field Management	14 days	Thu 8/2/12	Tue 8/21/12	MSO
Execution	**82 days**	**Wed 8/22/12**	**Thu 12/13/12**	
– Conduct Field Visual Merchandising Training	21 days	Wed 8/22/12	Wed 9/19/12	MSO
– Conduct Pre-Calls to Each Retail Store Manager to Schedule First Visit	9 days	Thu 9/20/12	Tue 10/2/12	Field Visual Merchandisers
Launch Phase 1 – Start In-Store Rotation in Retailer 1/200 Stores	12 days	Wed 10/3/12	Thu 10/18/12	Brook Adams, MSO
– Forward Phase 1 Weekly Store Visit Report	1 day	Fri 10/19/12	Fri 10/19/12	MSO
– Review Phase 1 Weekly Store Visit Report and forwad to Account Executives	4 day	Mon 10/22/12	Thu 10/25/12	Brook Adams
Launch Phase 2 – Start In-Store Rotation in Retailer 2/200 Stores	12 days	Fri 10/26/22	Mon 11/12/12	Brook Adams, MSO
– Forward Phase 2 Weekly Store Visit Report	1 day	Mon 11/12/12	Mon 11/12/12	MSO
– Review Phase 2 Weekly Store Visit Report and Forwad to Account Executives	3 day	Tue 11/13/12	Thu 11/15/12	Brook Adams
Launch Phase 3 – Start In-Store Rotation in Retailer 3/200 Stores	12 days	Fri 11/16/12	Mon 12/3/12	Brook Adams, MSO
– Forward Phase 3 Weekly Store Visit Report	1 day	Tue 12/4/12	Tue 12/4/12	MSO
– Review Phase 3 Weekly Store Visit Report and Forwad to Account Executives	7 day	Wed 12/5/12	Thu 12/13/12	Brook Adams

to district managers and regional managers to guarantee those involved are aware of the strategy and times of the execution.

After the letter has been forwarded, each retail store will be expecting the launch to be executed on the dates listed in the letter which is Wednesday, October 3 – Thursday, October 18 2012 (Figure 7.7). If you use the calendar and count the days, you will see that phase one launch will take 12 days, the launch start date will be October 3 and the finish date will be October 18 2012. This information can now be plotted (Figure 7.7).

After each launch, the MSO should provide a weekly store visit report providing details of each store visit including photos. The time frame to receive these reports is determined by the MSO. For this strategy, we will state that the reports will be received on the day following the launch. Therefore, if launch one ended Thursday, October 18 2012, your phase one report would be received on Friday, October 19 and the duration would be one day. It is now time to plot this information (Figure 7.7).

Once you have reviewed the report and the photos and confirmed the execution is proceeding in the right direction, this information should be forwarded to the respective account executive responsible for the retailer. It is essential that one estimates the length of time required to review this report in order to supply the duration and finish date. Remember, the report was received on Friday, October 19 and the start date should follow that date. But, because the following day falls on a Saturday, you would skip the weekend days. Therefore, the actual start date will be Monday, October 22 (Figure 7.7). As always with plotting dates, review all dates and deliverables and make certain all information is correct before moving forward to plotting phase two and phase three launches of the execution.

Review the dates and times for accuracy and proceed to the monitoring phase. Again, the execution phase is usually the longest phase within the strategy. Therefore, it is important that your dates are correct. If one date is incorrect, it will have a domino effect and all of the following dates will be inaccurate.

Monitoring phase

The monitoring phase involves focusing on the details of the execution after the launch has taken place. It involves a list of duties that are the sole responsibility of the leader. In order to plot this phase, one must have a thorough understanding of what needs to take place.

By this time, the strategy should be moving towards the objective, but to be certain, it is necessary to review and analyse the procedures that have

FIGURE 7.7 Developing the launch plan: Timeline detail checked

TASK NAME	DURATION	START	FINISH	RESOURCE
National Field Merchandising Strategy	**252 days**	**Thu 2/2/12**	**Fri 1/18/13**	
Initiation	**79 days**	**Thu 2/2/12**	**Tue 5/22/12**	
– Develop Strategy Scope Statement for Each Retailer and Forward	1 days	Thu 2/2/12	Thu 2/2/12	Brook Adams
– Provide Approval to execute Strategy in Retail Stores	2 days	Thu 2/2/12	Fri 2/3/12	Retailer
– Provide Management Contact List to Brook Adams	7 days	Fri 2/3/12	Mon 2/13/12	Retailer
– Provide Retailer Letter of Introduction to Brook Adams and Store Managers	7 days	Tue 2/14/12	Wed 2/22/12	Retailer
– Provide Retailer Store Visit Guidelines to Brook Adams	5 days	Fri 3/23/12	Thu 3/29/12	Retailer
– Forward Letter of Introduction and Store Visit Guidelines to MSO for Approval	15 days	Fri 3/30/12	Thu 4/19/12	Brook Adams
– Forward and Review Training Materials with Printer for Production	1 day	Fri 4/20/12	Fri 4/20/12	Brook Adams
– Forward Training Programme Requirements to MSO for Approval	1 day	Mon 4/23/12	Mon 4/23/12	Brook Adams
– Provide Approval of Training Requirements/Visit Guidelines/Letter Intro	14 days	Tue 4/24/12	Fri 5/11/12	MSO
– Review/Approve and Sign Off on Strategy	7 days	Mon 5/14/12	Tue 5/22/12	Account Executives
Planning	**65 days**	**Wed 5/23/12**	**Tue 8/21/12**	
– Conduct Strategy Kick-off Meeting with Retailer, MSO and Account Executives	14 days	Wed 5/23/12	Mon 6/11/12	Brook Adams
– Produce Copies of Training Materials for Field Merchandisers	15 days	Tue 6/12/12	Mon 7/2/12	Color Block Printing
– Package Training Materials to be Shipped to MSO	3 days	Tue 7/3/12	Thu 7/5/12	Color Block Printing
– Ship Training Materials to MSO	12 days	Fri 7/6/12	Mon 7/23/12	Color Block Printing
– Review and Approve Training Materials	7 days	Tue 7/24/12	Wed 8/1/12	MSO
– Forward Training Materials to MSO Field Management	14 days	Thu 8/2/12	Tue 8/21/12	MSO

FIGURE 7.7 *continued*

TASK NAME	DURATION	START	FINISH	RESOURCE
Execution	**82 days**	**Wed 8/22/12**	**Thu 12/13/12**	
– Conduct Field Visual Merchandising Training	21 days	Wed 8/22/12	Wed 9/19/12	MSO
– Conduct Pre-Calls to Each Retail Store Manager to Schedule First Visit	9 days	Thu 9/20/12	Tue 10/2/12	Field Visual Merchandisers
Launch Phase 1 – Start In-Store Rotation in Retailer 1/ 200 Stores	**12 days**	**Wed 10/3/12**	**Thu 10/18/12**	**Brook Adams, MSO**
– Forward Phase 1 Weekly Store Visit Report	1 day	Fri 10/19/12	Fri 10/19/12	MSO
– Review Phase 1 Weekly Store Visit Report and forwad to Account Executives	4 day	Mon 10/22/12	Thu 10/25/12	Brook Adams
Launch Phase 2 – Start In-Store Rotation in Retailer 2/ 200 Stores	**12 days**	**Fri 10/26/22**	**Mon 11/12/12**	**Brook Adams, MSO**
– Forward Phase 2 Weekly Store Visit Report	1 day	Mon 11/12/12	Mon 11/12/12	MSO
– Review Phase 2 Weekly Store Visit Report and Forward to Account Executives	3 day	Tue 11/13/12	Thu 11/15/12	Brook Adams
Launch Phase 3 – Start In-Store Rotation in Retailer 3/ 200 Stores	**12 days**	**Fri 11/16/12**	**Mon 12/3/12**	**Brook Adams, MSO**
– Forward Phase 3 Weekly Store Visit Report	1 day	Tue 12/4/12	Tue 12/4/12	MSO
– Review Phase 3 Weekly Store Visit Report and Forward to Account Executives	7 day	Wed 12/5/12	Thu 12/13/12	Brook Adams

been performed. There are six goals that one should plot in the monitoring phase of the strategy:

1 Monitor store visit rotation against plan for accuracy.

2 Monitor task duration estimates for accuracy.

3 Review merchandisers in-store survey to identify issues and concerns.

4 Review merchandisers before and after photos to identify training gaps.

5 Review MSO reports for accuracy, successes, concerns and issues.

6 Identify corrective actions to be addressed and any issues with each launch.

Monitor store visit rotation against plan for accuracy

Within this strategy there are three retailers, each with 200 stores on your store visit rotation. In Chapter 4, we discussed the account executives and their expectations. We looked at their request for the following visual merchandising services. One retailer will receive visual merchandising services once a month while the other two will receive services twice a month. As the leader of this strategy, your role is to make certain these store visit rotations are being executed as directed by the account executives. Therefore, in the monitoring phase, work with the MSO on a weekly basis to confirm the store visit rotations are meeting the objective of the account executives.

Monitor task duration estimates for accuracy

In Chapter 4 we discussed task duration estimates. The task duration estimate is the document that field visual merchandisers will use at the store visit to provide step-by-step directions for essential assignments to be completed. This document is an estimate because all stores will not be the same size. Therefore, the estimates may require adjusting so that all tasks on each store visit are accomplished within the time frame allotted. In the monitoring phase, the leader should review these estimates and make adjustments where needed, while at the same time staying within the allotted budget for the strategy.

Review merchandisers' in-store survey to identify issues and concerns

At each store visit, the field visual merchandisers will complete an in-store survey. This survey provides information on the accomplished task, needed product and any other feedback requested by the leader and the account executives. In the monitoring phase, the leader should review these surveys for accuracy, missing information and excessive unnecessary data on a given subject. At times you may want to streamline the feedback or perhaps modify the questions to obtain more helpful information.

Review merchandisers' before and after photos to identify training gaps

In addition, each survey will include 'before' photos of what the area looked like prior to merchandising and 'after' photos to show what was accomplished. In the monitoring phase, you also want to use these photos to identify training gaps to determine if anyone on the field team requires additional training on merchandising standards or clothing coordination.

Review MSO reports for accuracy, successes, issues and concerns

The MSO management team will forward weekly and monthly reports that present valuable information. In the monitoring phase, analyse these reports and make adjustments if needed or change the structure of the report to meet the needs of the account executives. Make sure to glean as much necessary information as possible to assist with the success of the strategy.

Corrective actions and pending issues

Within each launch you may identify issues that should be corrected. There are many things that can happen at the beginning of launching a strategy of this nature. For example, one of the store managers may not be particularly fond of the field visual merchandiser who services a certain store. Therefore, the leader may advise the MSO of the issue and the only decision may be to switch the merchandiser to another store to keep the strategy on schedule.

Now that you have insight into what the monitoring phase entails, let's plot the dates and times for completing these goals. It is strongly suggested that you aim to achieve all these goals simultaneously. Review each goal daily throughout the monitoring phase and identify issues that may require correction.

To plot this time frame, one will need to determine how much time is desired for the monitoring. For this strategy we will select 26 days. Be sure to monitor all six goals and use the same start, finish and duration times for each goal. The monitoring phase should start the day after the last goal on the execution phase. Thus, the beginning date will be Friday, December 14 2012 (Figure 7.8).

FIGURE 7.8 Developing the launch plan: Monitoring phase timeline

TASK NAME	DURATION	START	FINISH	RESOURCE
National Field Merchandising Strategy	252 days	Thu 2/2/12	Fri 1/18/13	
Initiation	79 days	Thu 2/2/12	Tue 5/22/12	
– Develop Strategy Scope Statement for Each Retailer and Forward	1 days	Thu 2/2/12	Thu 2/2/12	Brook Adams
– Provide Approval to Execute Strategy in Retail Stores	2 days	Thu 2/2/12	Fri 2/3/12	Retailer
– Provide Management Contact List to Brook Adams	7 days	Fri 2/3/12	Mon 2/13/12	Retailer
– Provide Retailer Letter of Introduction to Brook Adams and Store Managers	7 days	Tue 2/14/12	Wed 2/22/12	Retailer
– Provide Retailer Store Visit Guidelines to Brook Adams	5 days	Fri 3/23/12	Thu 3/29/12	Retailer
– Forward Letter of Introduction and Store Visit Guidelines to MSO for Approval	15 days	Fri 3/30/12	Thu 4/19/12	Brook Adams
– Forward and Review Training Materials with Printer for Production	1 day	Fri 4/20/12	Fri 4/20/12	Brook Adams
– Forward Training Programme Requirements to MSO for Approval	1 day	Mon 4/23/12	Mon 4/23/12	Brook Adams
– Provide Approval of Training Requirements/Visit Guidelines/Letter Intro	14 days	Tue 4/24/12	Fri 5/11/12	MSO
– Review/Approve and Sign Off on Strategy	7 days	Mon 5/14/12	Tue 5/22/12	Account Executives
Planning	65 days	Wed 5/23/12	Tue 8/21/12	
– Conduct Strategy Kick-off Meeting with Retailer, MSO and Account Executives	14 days	Wed 5/23/12	Mon 6/11/12	Brook Adams
– Produce Copies of Training Materials for Field Merchandisers	15 days	Tue 6/12/12	Mon 7/2/12	Color Block Printing
– Package Training Materials to be Shipped to MSO	3 days	Tue 7/3/12	Thu 7/5/12	Color Block Printing
– Ship Training Materials to MSO	12 days	Fri 7/6/12	Mon 7/23/12	Color Block Printing
– Review and Approve Training Materials	7 days	Tue 7/24/12	Wed 8/1/12	MSO
– Forward Training Materials to MSO Field Management	14 days	Thu 8/2/12	Tue 8/21/12	MSO

FIGURE 7.8 *continued*

TASK NAME	DURATION	START	FINISH	RESOURCE
Execution	**82 days**	**Wed 8/22/12**	**Thu 12/13/12**	
– Conduct Field Visual Merchandising Training	21 days	Wed 8/22/12	Wed 9/19/12	MSO
– Conduct Pre-Calls to Each Retail Store Manager to Schedule First Visit	9 days	Thu 9/20/12	Tue 10/2/12	Field Merchandisers
Launch Phase 1 – Start In-Store Rotation in Retailer 1/ 200 Stores	12 days	Wed 10/3/12	Thu 10/18/12	Brook Adams, MSO
– Forward Phase 1 Weekly Store Visit Summary	1 day	Fri 10/19/12	Fri 10/19/12	MSO
– Review Phase 1 Weekly Store Visit Summary and Forward to Account Executives	4 day	Mon 10/22/12	Thu10/25/12	Brook Adams
Launch Phase 2 – Start In-Store Rotation in Retailer 2/ 200 Stores	12 days	Fri 10/26/22	Mon 11/12/12	Brook Adams, MSO
– Forward Phase 2 Weekly Store Visit Summary	1 day	Mon 11/12/12	Mon 11/12/12	MSO
– Review Phase 2 Weekly Store Visit Summary and Forward to Account Executives	3 day	Tue 11/13/12	Thu 11/15/12	Brook Adams
Launch Phase 3 – Start In-Store Rotation in Retailer 3/ 200 Stores	12 days	Fri 11/16/12	Mon 12/3/12	Brook Adams, MSO
– Forward Phase 3 Weekly Store Visit Summary	1 day	Tue 12/4/12	Tue 12/4/12	MSO
– Review Phase 3 Weekly Store Visit Summary and Forward to Account Executives	7 day	Wed 12/5/12	Thu12/13/12	Brook Adams
Monitoring	**26 days**	**Fri 12/14/12**	**Fri 1/18/13**	
– Monitor Store Visit Rotation Against Plan for Accuracy	26 days	Fri 12/14/12	Fri 1/18/13	Brook Adams
– Monitor Task Duration Estimates for Accuracy	26 days	Fri 12/14/12	Fri 1/18/13	Brook Adams
– Review Merchandisers In-Store Survey to Identify Issues and Concerns	26 days	Fri 12/14/12	Fri 1/18/13	Brook Adams
– Review Merchandisers Before and After Photos to Identify Training Gaps	26 days	Fri 12/14/12	Fri 1/18/13	Brook Adams
– Review MSO Reports for Issues, Concerns and Accuracy	26 days	Fri 12/14/12	Fri 1/18/13	Brook Adams
– Identify Corrective Actions Needed to Address Any Issues in Each Launch	26 days	Fri 12/14/12	Fri 1/18/13	Brook Adams

Real-world situation No 2

Issues with documenting your strategic plan timeline

Background information

When preparing a strategic plan timeline, an important facet of this process is making certain the correct dates and times have been documented as planned. If one incorrect date is logged, the subsequent dates will be inaccurate as well.

Situation

All launch directives have been received and all information has been plotted. You assume everything is complete until you receive a call from the copy centre stating they need five additional days to produce the training manuals due to a major storm hitting the area (Figure 7.9).

As the leader, you realize the best course of action is to update the planning phase of the document to reflect these changes before moving to the execution phase.

The challenge

Under the planning phase, the goal that should be updated is 'produce copies of training materials for field merchandisers'. The resource for this goal is your printer 'Color Block Printing'.

The challenge is to make changes to this goal and determine a new 'duration' date and a new 'finish' date for the planning phase. Remember: in order to ensure all dates are correct, every date following the change will need to be amended (Figure 7.10).

After you have determined the new duration and finish dates, answer the follow questions:

1 What is the new start date for the goal 'ship training materials to MSO?'

   A July 11 2014

   B July 15 2014

   C July 13 2014

2 What is the new finish date for the goal: 'review and approve training materials?'

   A August 4 2012

   B August 8 2012

   C August 10 2012

FIGURE 7.9 The launch plan: Amending the timeline

TASK NAME	DURATION	START	FINISH	RESOURCE
National Field Merchandising Strategy		Thu 2/2/12		
Initiation	**79 days**	**Thu 2/2/12**	**Tue 5/22/12**	
– Develop Strategy Scope Statement for Each Retailer and Forward	1 days	Thu 2/2/12	Thu 2/2/12	Brook Adams
– Provide Approval to Execute Strategy in Retail Stores	2 days	Thu 2/2/12	Fri 2/3/12	Retailer
– Provide Management Contact List to Brook Adams	7 days	Fri 2/3/12	Mon 2/13/12	Retailer
– Provide Retailer Letter of Introduction to Brook Adams and Store Managers	7 days	Tue 2/14/12	Wed 2/22/12	Retailer
– Provide Retailer Store Visit Guidelines to Brook Adams	5 days	Fri 3/23/12	Thu 3/29/12	Retailer
– Forward Letter of Introduction and Store Visit Guidelines to MSO for Approval	15 days	Fri 3/30/12	Thu 4/19/12	Brook Adams
– Forward and Review Training Materials with Printer for Production	1 day	Fri 4/20/12	Fri 4/20/12	Brook Adams
– Forward Training Programme Requirements to MSO for Approval	1 day	Mon 4/23/12	Mon 4/23/12	Brook Adams
– Provide Approval of Training Requirements/Visit Guidelines/Letter Intro	14 days	Tue 4/24/12	Fri 5/11/12	MSO
– Review/Approve and Sign Off on Strategy	7 days	Mon 5/14/12	Tue 5/22/12	Account Executives
Planning	**65 days**	**Wed 5/23/12**	**Tue 8/21/12**	
– Conduct Strategy Kick-off Meeting with Retailer, MSO and Account Executives	14 days	Wed 5/23/12	Mon 6/11/12	Brook Adams
– Produce Copies of Training Materials for Field Merchandisers	15 days	Tue 6/12/12	Mon 7/2/12	Color Block Printing
– Package Training Materials to Be Shipped to MSO	3 days	Tue 7/3/12	Thu 7/5/12	Color Block Printing
– Ship Training Materials to MSO	12 days	Fri 7/6/12	Mon 7/23/12	Color Block Printing
– Review and Approve Training Materials	7 days	Tue 7/24/12	Wed 8/1/12	MSO
– Forward Training Materials to MSO Field Management	14 days	Thu 8/2/12	Tue 8/21/12	MSO

FIGURE 7.10 Revised launch plan

TASK NAME	DURATION	START	FINISH	RESOURCE
National Field Merchandising Strategy		Thu 2/2/12		
Initiation	**79 days**	**Thu 2/2/12**	**Tue 5/22/12**	
– Develop Strategy Scope Statement for Each Retailer and forward	1 days	Thu 2/2/12	Thu 2/2/12	Brook Adams
– Provide Approval to execute Strategy in Retail Stores	2 days	Thu 2/2/12	Fri 2/3/12	Retailer
– Provide Management Contact List to Brook Adams	7 days	Fri 2/3/12	Mon 2/13/12	Retailer
– Provide Retailer Letter of Introduction to Brook Adams and Store Managers	7 days	Tue 2/14/12	Wed 2/22/12	Retailer
– Provide Retailer Store Visit Guidelines to Brook Adams	5 days	Fri 3/23/12	Thu 3/29/12	Retailer
– Forward Letter of Introduction and Store Visit Guidelines to MSO for Approval	15 days	Fri 3/30/12	Thu 4/19/12	Brook Adams
– Forward and Review Training Materials with Printer for Production	1 day	Fri 4/20/12	Fri 4/20/12	Brook Adams
– Forward Training Programme Requirements to MSO for Approval	1 day	Mon 4/23/12	Mon 4/23/12	Brook Adams
– Provide Approval of Training Requirements/Visit Guidelines/Letter Intro	14 days	Tue 4/24/12	Fri 5/11/12	MSO
– Review/Approve and Sign Off on Strategy	7 days	Mon 5/14/12	Tue 5/22/12	Account Executives
Planning	**70 days**	**Wed 5/23/12**	**Tue 8/28/12**	
– Conduct Strategy Kick-off Meeting with Retailer, MSO and Account Executives	14 days	Wed 5/23/12	Mon 6/11/12	Brook Adams
– Produce Copies of Training Materials for Field Merchandisers	20 days	Tue 6/12/12	Mon 7/9/12	Color Block Printing
– Package Training Materials to be Shipped to MSO	3 days	Tue 7/10/12	Thu 7/12/12	Color Block Printing
– Ship Training Materials to MSO	12 days	Fri 7/13/12	Mon 7/30/12	Color Block Printing
– Review and Approve Training Materials	7 days	Tue 7/31/12	Wed 8/8/12	MSO
– Forward Training Materials to Field Management for Training	14 days	Thu 8/9/12	Tue 8/28/12	MSO

Chapter 7 checklist

- Am I aware that a strategy scope statement provides retailers with a clear understanding of what will take place in their stores and gives insight into the overall objectives?

- Should I review the strategy scope area to obtain a clear understanding?

- Do I understand that a strategy scope statement describes the details of an objective?

- Do I have a grasp of the store visit guidelines and understand how this sets the tone for the relationship with the retailers?

- In order to communicate my strategic plan, do I know how to develop a project management timeline?

- Does my company use project management software or will I need to complete my strategic plan in MS Excel?

- Do I possess a solid awareness of the four phases that are used in preparing the project management timeline?

- Am I clear on the manner in which to plot each phase and goal on a project management timeline?

- Do I understand the reason behind having a strategy kick-off meeting?

Tricks of the trade: 'What's your standard?'

We briefly discussed merchandising standards in Chapters 4 and 6, but I cannot express how essential it is to have a merchandising standards manual when executing a field visual merchandising strategy. I'm sure you have eaten at your favourite fast food restaurant. Although the service and the food may not be exceptional in each location, each fast food chain tries to duplicate themselves by developing a standard and repeating it over and over again in as many stores as possible. If you eat at McDonald's in one location, you have a good idea what to expect when you go to a McDonald's in another location. Although each store may not be the same size, however, they all have the golden arches and similar menus. This is why many customers frequent the restaurant.

The same process applies when you are a retailer with 600 stores or a clothing manufacturer with 300 brand shops placed in department stores. The goal is to increase customer loyalty and what is a better way to do this than to create a shopping experience that flows with ease? You want to stimulate a mood, create an image, and duplicate it in every location. When it comes to product presentation, this too should be duplicated in every store. To guarantee your product presentation is consistent in all locations, it is wise to develop a training booklet such as a merchandising standards manual to be given to store personnel or field visual merchandisers. If your team duplicates the standards presented in the manual, a consistent product presentation and company image will be presented to the customers. The product will be on the retail floor presented as set forth in the standards manual, in a manner to stimulate sales.

Let's walk through a scenario of developing a basic merchandising standards manual.

The scenario

Your company is a specialty retailer with 900 retail stores throughout the country. The company is launching a new line of private label product in all stores with a designated area in each location where the product will be presented. You have developed a 3D rendering of the space with fixturing, signage and product showing the intended look after the presentation is set (Figure 7.11).

Due to the importance of this product, senior management has asked you to outsource an FVM company to service these small departments in each account on a regular basis as opposed to hiring additional sales assistants in each store. To guarantee the product presentation stays consistent in each location, you have also been asked to develop a merchandising standards manual to distribute to all stores and the FVM team.

Step 1

Before beginning, the goal is to eliminate any confusion on product presentation. In other words, every item in the shop should have a merchandising standard. This implies that if a product is to be folded, a standard about proper folding techniques should be in the manual. If that same product is to be placed on hangers at a different store or under another set of circumstances, there should be a standard on proper hanging techniques when using hangers. This may seem basic, but if employees from two separate stores are folding shirts using different guidelines, and a new employee works at both stores periodically, the employee may ask about which method to use.

Your first step should be to look at each item in the shop, from tops and bottoms to signage and determine how each should be presented. Example:

FIGURE 7.11 Developing a merchandising standards manual: 3D rendering

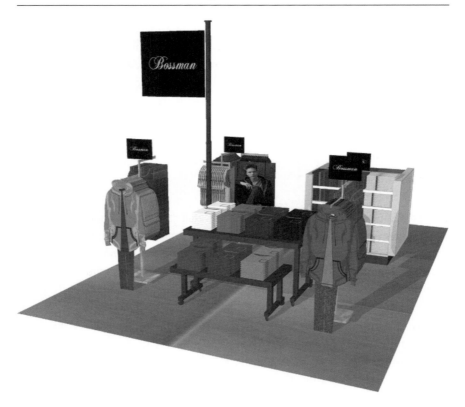

There will be three different styles of tops to be merchandised in the shop and they are T-shirts, polo shirts and hooded sweatshirts.

If it is determined that each item can be hung and sized in the same manner, one standard for sizing hanging tops can be acceptable for all. It would be wise to use mind-mapping techniques to visualize every step in the process of sizing the product to be certain every detail is communicated. It is also a good idea to walk through the process using your directions to confirm the information is clear and understandable.

Step 2

To communicate this standard, develop written directions and reinforce the information by creating a visual aid to clearly explain the task from a pictorial viewpoint (Figure 7.12).

FIGURE 7.12 Developing a merchandising standards manual:
Sizing instructions

SIZING APPAREL

When apparel is sized and a full size run is offered, the customer has a great
shopping experience. The customer can easily locate their size and move to the
payment point or fitting room. The following sizing instructions will help you
create and maintain this atmosphere for your customers.

Apparel should be sized left to right, small to large or front to back,
small to large.

SIDE HUNG

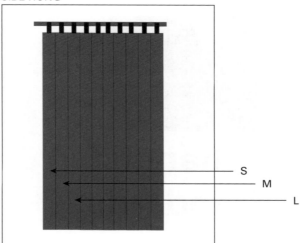

FACED OUT

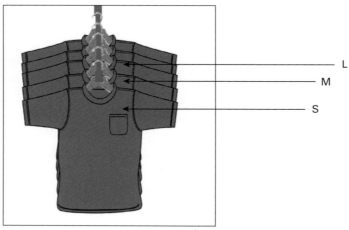

This procedure should continue until you have addressed every item in the shop. Don't forget to also include directions on placing signage.

Step 3

This step includes developing a cover page for the manual and laying out each page to determine the flow of material from one page to the next (Figures 7.13.1–7.13.6).

FIGURE 7.13.1 The completed merchandising standards manual

FIGURE 7.13.2

PRESENTING OUTFITS

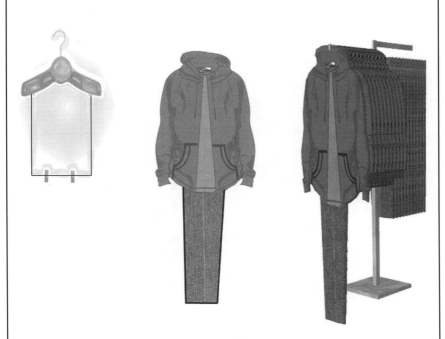

When presenting outfits, product should be layered on the display hanger and placed as the first item on the fixture. Be sure that when presenting outfits, the product is adjacent to the presentation.

FIGURE 7.13.3

FOLDING APPAREL

SHIRTS

To maintain clean and well-presented displays involving folded tops, the use of folding boards is recommended.

Centre the folding board vertically on the top of the shirt

Fold the right sleeve over the folding board

Fold the left side the same way

Fold the bottom of the shirt over the sleeves

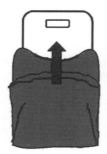

Remove the folding board

Turn the shirt over

FIGURE 7.13.4

SIZING APPAREL

When apparel is sized and a full size run is offered, the customer has a great shopping experience. The customer can easily locate their size and move to the payment point or fitting room. The following sizing instructions will help you create and maintain this atmosphere for your customers.

Apparel should be sized left to right, small to large or front to back, small to large.

SIDE HUNG

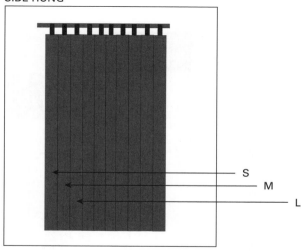

FACED OUT

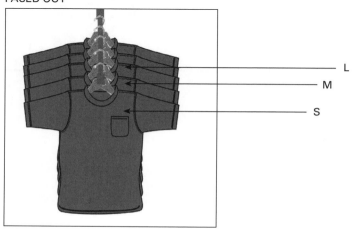

FIGURE 7.13.5

SIGNAGE

FIGURE 7.13.6

FOLDING APPAREL

JEANS

Jeans should be folded in uniform manner with information tag facing the customer.

Fold jeans inward placing legs together and back pockets facing outwards

Place jeans flat on surface with legs together and information tag face down

Keeping legs together, fold in approximately 18 inches

Fold over once again

Flip over and you now have perfectly folded jeans

Review every page closely to confirm the information is well defined and in the proper order. Once this is completed, add page numbers.

Step 4

It is always a good idea to add a table of contents in the manual to provide a list of headings along with page numbers for each topic. This provides the reader with a quick point of reference to utilize when locating a specific topic to gather needed instructions. In addition, it is recommended to add a checklist in the back of the book. This checklist should provide directions on a final walk-through of the department to confirm every item meets the criteria presented in the manual.

As a final test to confirm the ease of locating each topic in the manual, review the 3D rendering with the manual in hand, identify a particular item from the rendering, and then try locating a topic in the manual that pertains to the merchandising standard for that particular product (Figure 7.14).

FIGURE 7.14   Reviewing the manual: 3D rendering vs instructions

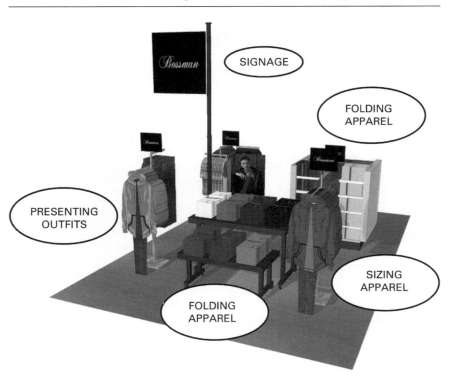

Step 5

The last step would entail adding a final page that provides contact information with phone numbers in case someone has additional questions about merchandising standards. When all is complete, pull together all pertinent documents and prepare to forward to the copy centre for printing. These manuals should be produced and shipped to each of the retail store locations and field visual merchandisers. In addition, the manual should also be available electronically to forward by e-mail if needed.

PART THREE
Executing the strategy

So you have prepared for the battle by developing your management team and learning the fundamentals. You've planned your strategy, hired the right MSO and trained your team of field visual merchandisers. Now it's time to execute your strategy.

In Chapter 2, we discussed field communications, noting the methods and the appropriate times for communication in an FVM environment. This last part will take you through the final stage of applying these methods of communication and bringing your strategy to life. We will end by presenting ways to enhance your strategy with numerous types of tactics and special projects.

PART THREE
Executing
Crosstegy

Communicating and monitoring the strategic plan

Effective communication is the key to success as you execute the strategy. Whatever the management team communicates must be clear, concise and easily understood. Every party involved should have a comprehensive understanding of the direction of the strategy. We have laid out the responsibilities of all parties involved and the time frame allocated to complete those tasks. As the leader, your role is to be sure there is no misunderstanding relating to the objectives and to communicate all details in a timely manner.

In this process, the leader and the management team will be communicating internally to the sponsors and externally to the MSO management team, the FVM team, and to all vendors involved in the implementation of the strategy. In addition, the leader will be the person to receive communication back from all parties to include questions, details and reports.

The manner in which information is released and the appropriate time to expedite communication should be considered when relaying effective messages. In order to communicate effectively, one must determine a format to use, such as e-mail, visual directives, planograms or via a conference call. If the team is communicating with a small group and the discussion includes concerns or issues about the execution process, it might be advantageous to connect via conference call or schedule a face-to-face meeting whenever possible; the leader can always forward everyone the timeline and other documents pertaining to the meeting. This gives everyone an opportunity to exchange dialogue, ask questions, discuss risks, and part in full agreement to resume the implementation of the strategy.

Communicating by e-mail is great if you keep the information brief and to the point. Additionally, it provides an avenue to receive attachments quickly when forwarded. Also, keep in mind that recipients cannot hear your tone. Therefore, use your words carefully. Remove ambiguous language. If you use the word 'whatever', for example, your recipient could take this term to have negative or positive implications.

Avoid using ALL CAPITAL LETTERS when communicating because all caps gives the impression that the sender is yelling. Last but not least, don't use an e-mail to avoid making a phone call or speaking to someone face to face. With that said, don't forsake following up in writing if the conversation pertains to information such as dates, times and responsibilities in the strategy execution process.

Distribution of the strategic plan timeline

Now that you and your team have gone through the process of developing the strategic plan timeline, the next step will be to distribute it to all parties involved in executing the strategy. Remember, this timeline serves as the road map for everyone to use in identifying where the strategy is at any given time in the execution process. It also provides direction to signify who is responsible for each goal listed under each phase of the plan.

If this is the first time you are executing a strategy using this format, be sure to explain to all parties involved the manner in which the strategic plan timeline is to be used. At times, when sending this document out to a team that is not accustomed to executing a strategy in this manner, it is reviewed and then put aside or saved to a file for future references. Therefore, as the strategy is being executed, numerous calls and e-mails are received asking for the status of the execution and where we are in the process of next steps. In this situation, the leader is challenged with the task of referring those that enquire after the document has been sent out to the strategic plan timeline for direction, reiterating the convenience of utilizing this document to stay abreast of current and future progress. Remind those involved to refer to this document often; it will usually answer a lot of questions that may arise during the implementation. Assure them this document will be updated and all parties will be notified of any changes to dates and responsibilities.

This process will help steer all involved parties back to the document rather than to constant phone calls or e-mails. To some, it is a good idea to print the strategic plan timeline and keep it near to review dates and responsibilities as the strategy progresses. In addition, be available to answer any questions about dates and deliverables until everyone gets on the same page of reviewing this document regularly.

Monitoring the execution

Although your strategy may be well planned and everyone involved may appear to have clear direction on the step-by-step process in the execution, challenging situations may still occur. The purpose of monitoring is to be aware of the details of the execution and to review, analyse and identify any risk that may present problems with meeting the strategic objective.

Major milestones

One task of monitoring the execution is identifying major milestones. These milestones are physical accomplishments within the execution to signify the FVM strategy is moving in the right direction to meet the objective. These milestones are events that show progress, such as the completion of phase one. If you have three retailers and you are launching your strategy in three phases, the completion of the first phase is a major milestone.

Once the strategy has reached a major milestone, it should be communicated to the entire group. The purpose of the communication is to confirm the goal has been achieved and to identify successful processes that should be used going forward, or to identify unsuccessful processes that may require replacements. It would be wise to schedule a conference call with the group at each major milestone to discuss the good, the bad and the ugly.

SWOT analysis

As you monitor the progress of the strategy, you should conduct a SWOT analysis. The acronym stands for strengths, weaknesses, opportunities and threats. The purpose of completing a SWOT analysis is to gain an understanding of what your FVM team is doing well, what are its weaknesses, opportunities for improvement and to identify any threats that need to be addressed. It would be wise to conduct the SWOT analysis as your FVM team is in the middle of completing the first phase of the launch. By this time you will have enough information to conduct the analysis and time to make changes before the team starts the phase two process. The first step in conducting a SWOT analysis is to develop a list of questions to ask yourself as you monitor the execution.

Once you have developed a list of questions, create a chart to record your answers for each group of questions (Table 8.1).

TABLE 8.1   SWOT analysis chart

Question	Answer
Strengths	
1 What is my field visual merchandising team doing well?	
2 As the leader, what do I see as strengths of the team?	
3 What do the retailers say about the service and the team's strength?	
4 What do my sponsors say about the team's strengths?	
5 What do the vendors do well?	
Weaknesses	
1 What does my field team need to improve upon?	
2 What do my vendors need to improve?	
3 What weaknesses has the retailer identified?	
4 What weaknesses have the sponsors identified?	
Opportunities	
1 Can I identify anything that could potentially enhance our effectiveness?	
2 Are there opportunities to gain more floor fixtures for the brand?	
3 Are there opportunities to add more stores to the rotation due to the success of this execution?	
4 Are there any new trends that can be incorporated?	
Threats	
1 Is the team developing relationships with the manager on duty?	
2 Are task duration estimates being utilized by the team?	
3 Are stores being visited on a consistent basis?	
4 Are the vendors meeting deadlines?	

Resource needs assessment

Once the leader has conducted a SWOT analysis and has identified what the team should do to improve, conduct a needs assessment to determine what resources are required to get the strategy back on track. In Chapter 6, we discussed conducting a training needs assessment to identify the skill set the field team needed to be successful. The resource needs assessment utilizes similar processes.

The purpose of this assessment is to identify the resources required to correct a problem at hand. Once you have identified a problem and determined a solution, there may be cost associated with correcting the problem. Personnel may be needed and a time frame may be associated as well. There are 10 steps to conducting a resource needs assessment:

1 Gather information: The first step is to gather as much information on the problem as possible.

2 Analyse the details: Often we may believe we have an understanding of the problem until we do a thorough investigation.

3 Identify the problem to be corrected: The leader may have to dig a little deeper to ascertain the root cause (not simply a symptom) of the problem.

4 Gain a consensus: Discuss the problem with the MSO and sponsors to gather their input and gain a consensus on the problem. It is best to conclude on an area requiring improvement with the collaboration of your team.

5 Brainstorm to identify the best possible solution: In Chapter 2, we discussed brainstorming techniques. This is the perfect time to utilize these techniques to identify the best possible solution to the problem. It is wise to conduct a brainstorming meeting with your management team and MSO to develop the best solution.

6 Resources: Now that the problem has been identified, determine the resources needed to implement the solution.

7 Time analysis: To implement the solution, you may need to establish a time frame to complete the process.

8 Personnel analysis to execute the implementation: The leader should determine if the right people are involved or if additional individuals should participate.

9 Cost analysis: Often,when modifications are made, the cost associated will increase. Determine if potential costs are associated with solving the situation. This may be the cost of additional materials and the cost of additional personnel.

10 Obtain signatures: Before moving forward, obtain necessary signatures from your sponsors and senior management for their support of the findings and all details involved with the solution. If the leader does not have budgetary controls to agree on the necessary spending, this area must be addressed to those with this authority to sign off on the increase. If modifications require additional expenses, the additional cost must be given serious consideration because this may require reworking processes to accommodate the new item added to the budget.

Communication with sponsors

In Chapter 4, we discussed the sponsors of the strategy. These account sponsors are usually senior level executives and communication to this group is very important. As you probably know, these individuals are very busy and although they are part of the reason your strategy exists, pinning them down can be difficult at times.

Before you give up, take the time to understand senior management and how to communicate with this group. There are five points to keep in mind when communicating with sponsors:

1 **Don't waste their time:** These senior level executives have a limited amount of time to spend on the project. Some would prefer you do not waste their time with all the details and the intricate information before making the decision. Learn your senior executive team and the communication styles they prefer. Do they want to know every detail or just enough to maintain a broad understanding of the project? Most prefer you to send a mildly informative e-mail to refer to at a time convenient for them. Be sure to provide information on the major or important aspect of the strategy with the supporting documentation for your findings.

2 **Financial aspects of the strategy:** Your communication should be very focused on the financial aspect of increasing sales. The bottom line for the strategy is to increase sales and brand awareness while adhering to the company standard as set forward. Your strategy exists because they see the possibility of increasing sales of the company's products by deploying a service of this magnitude. If you want to discuss an issue pertaining to additional training, you must demonstrate how the additional training will ultimately increase sales.

3 **What do you want to achieve?** Before communicating, have a clear understanding of your objective. In other words, know what you are trying to achieve through this communication. Gather all supporting

documents to strengthen your view. If the leader has access to sales analysis, this can be a great supporter of factual information. Compare your supporting information with the opposite opinion to decide upon the best option for the organization at the time. Does your objective increase the company's market share, increase the bottom line and/or improve the organization over time?

4 **Consider their needs:** When communicating, consider the needs of the executive by providing information they can use to show the progress. Often they want to provide their accounts with information to show how the strategy is progressing. Therefore, be sure the information you are providing is accurate and can be forwarded to a retail account.

5 **Understand their objectives:** Senior executives have objectives for the strategy you are executing. Therefore, you should have a complete understanding of what those objectives are and keep this information in mind when communicating to this group. When considering your relationship, you can think of yourself as a partner watching out for their back. You will see ways to increase market share through your merchandising team's involvement. The merchandising team not only creates consistency throughout the region, but also sets the mood for shoppers and entices customers to make multiple purchases. They provide invaluable feedback on what is selling and what is not. They keep the executive aware of the amount of product retrieved from the back room to the sales floor and give essential updates on the competitors' promotions.

Most senior level executives are results-oriented: they see the strategy as a means of increasing sales. When you speak their language they want to hear what you have to say.

Status and progress reports

Status and progress reports are important to your account executives. These reports provide information gathered from your FVM team and give feedback on what is happening in all the stores your team services. Although your MSO will provide comprehensive reports, as the leader it is your job to know the information best suited for your sponsors.

In Chapter 4, we discussed evaluating your sponsor's expectations and developing an account profile to list key information about the type of visual merchandising services needed for each account. It is a good idea to review these profiles and add additional information about the needs of the sponsors, as it pertains to receiving status reports.

When adding additional information to the profile, ask yourself the following questions and add the answers to the account profile. If you cannot answer all the questions, you should meet with your account executive to obtain the answers.

Questions pertaining to status reports:

- What type of information would they like to see on the status reports?
- How do they want to receive the status reports? Should you forward the information in an e-mail or would they like to review the reports in scheduled meetings or a conference call?
- When would they like to receive the reports? Once a week or twice a month?
- Do they want the details of each store visit, or just an overview?

Once you have answered the questions, you should work with your MSO on developing status reports to meet the sponsor's objectives. It is a good idea to ask your MSO to provide a sample report for everyone to review. We will discuss MSO reports in more detail in this chapter.

Communicating with your MSO

Usually, MSOs have a communication platform already in place. In Chapter 4, we discussed the role of the account or programme manager. The contact person could be the VP of Sales, but he or she will most likely be an account manager. This person will be the point of contact for everything within the MSO. Communicating with this individual on a weekly basis is highly recommended.

Whenever directives are to be communicated or any information is to be sent to the FVM team, it should go through the account manager. The account manager passes the information to the field team, which includes the FVM team and all levels of field management. Information should flow from the field to the MSO account manager and then to the leader. It is recommended that you follow the same procedure in your organization so all information flows from account executives to the leader who forwards the information to the account manager who in turn forwards the information to the field.

The purpose of this procedure is to minimize confusion. As the leader, one should be aware of every situation and all information being communicated to the field team. It is best to have one person giving direction to the MSO and taking responsibility for executing the strategy. That individual (who is usually the leader) has often been responsible for keeping the services within budget and is accountable for the success or failure of the strategy. If the leader is out of the loop on any communication or task, he or she cannot certify that assignments are being executed. This procedure should be communicated to everyone in your organization involved in executing the strategy.

Weekly conference calls

Having a weekly conference call with your account manager keeps you aware and up-to-date on all activities being executed in the field. Prior to each conference call, start an agenda by developing a list of topics throughout the week to discuss while on the call. It is a good idea to ask your account manager to do the same. On your call, each of you can review your list and discuss the issues. After the call, both should communicate with your respective organizations, gather information needed and follow the procedure of flowing information to and from your FVM team.

Quarterly face-to-face meetings

In addition to communicating through weekly conference calls with the account manager, it is recommended that you have a quarterly face-to-face meeting with your MSO management team to review the progress of the strategy. This progress should include reviewing the budget and determining if everything is up-to-date and not over budget, training of your field team and any additional training needs, and anything pertaining to in-store activities.

This meeting should be planned and the location for the meeting should be established. In addition, an agenda should be created along with a request for any presentation equipment required to be on-hand. Periodically, the leader may want to invite sponsors to these meetings for introduction purposes to the MSO management team along with a presentation of feedback on what the retail accounts are saying about the execution of the strategy. The sponsors would also provide communication about the report format and whether or not this data provides necessary information to glean an adequate overview or snapshot of their business.

In addition to providing information to both parties, this is an opportunity for the sponsor to get more acquainted with, to provide one-on-one dialogue with, and to foster a solid working relationship with the MSO.

After this meeting, resume the consistent procedure of flowing communication through the leader to the account manager and then to the field.

Merchandising service reports

Once the strategy is launched, the FVM team will become your eyes and ears in the field. On a daily basis they will travel from store to store, merchandising product and gathering important information that will be communicated to the leader and the sponsors.

The MSO will most likely have a secure state-of-the-art web-based reporting system where the field team will complete online reports pertaining to each store visit within 24 hours. These reporting systems vary by MSO and each offers numerous reporting packages that can provide as much information as needed. Normally, the MSO field management team and the account managers review the information provided by the field visual merchandisers and develop a report format that specifically meets the needs of the leader. As stated, there are numerous reporting packages, but we will review a few of the standard reports that one may encounter. Having access to this much information is great, but if it is not reviewed and analysed regularly, you and your sponsors will miss the most important opportunity to make a difference at retail.

In-store service schedule

The in-store service schedule is a spreadsheet that provides dates of each field visual merchandiser's store visit. Your MSO can provide this document every two weeks, or they can provide a spreadsheet that shows a rotation frequency showing the dates of store visits that will take place every two weeks on the same days. Depending upon the programme, the rotation may vary and you may have a retailer that has store visits every two weeks, once a week or once a month. The information in this document is usually presented in columns that provide the retailer name, store address, dates or frequency of store visits, the team member's name and the field manager's name (Figure 8.1).

How to use the in-store service schedule

This document keeps you informed on when store visits will take place and could help you and your sponsors in the planning process. For example,

FIGURE 8.1 In-store service schedule

GOLD STAR
MERCHANDISING

Bossman Merchandising Service Schedule - September 2010

Account	Location/Mall	Door #	Door Address	Door City	Door State	Door Zip	Visit Status	Frequency	Planned Hours
Moors	Anchorage	11	1000 East Northern Lights Blvd.	Anchorage	AK	99508	Confirmed	2x monthly	2.00
Moors	Anchorage - 99504	18	7701 Debarr Road	Anchorage	AK	99504	Confirmed	2x monthly	2.00
Macys	Brooklyn - Pennsylvania Ave	33	1000 Pennsylvania Ave	Brooklyn	NY	11207	Confirmed	2x monthly	2.00
Moors	Burlington	24	920 South Burlington Blvd.	Burlington	WA	98233	Confirmed	2x monthly	2.00
Macys	Chicago - Elmwood Park	1090	1601 N Harlem Ave	Chicago	IL	60613	Confirmed	2x monthly	2.00
Macys	Costa Mesa	1388	3333 Bristol St	Costa Mesa	CA	92626	Confirmed	2x monthly	2.00
Macys	Dearborn	1700	18900 Michigan Ave STE 1001 Fairlane Town Center	Dearborn	MI	48126	Confirmed	2x monthly	2.00
Macys	Deptford Mall	1464	1750 Deptford Cener Rd	Deptford	NJ	8096	Confirmed	2x monthly	2.00
Empires	Glendale Galleria	6999	333 W. Colorado St.	Glendale	CA	91210	Confirmed	2x monthly	2.00
Empires	Herald Square	109	1293 Broadway	New York	NY	10001	Confirmed	2x monthly	1.00
Macys	Lincoln Park - MI	1250	2100 Southfield Rd	Lincoln Park	MI	48146	Confirmed	2x monthly	2.00
Macys	Metro Center	1588	10001 N Metro Pkwy W	Phoenix	AZ	85051	Confirmed	2x monthly	2.00
Macys	North Riverside	1212	7503 Cermak Rd	North Riverside	IL	60546	Confirmed	2x monthly	2.00
Modell's	NYC - West 181 St	98	606 West 181 St	New York	NY	10033	Confirmed	2x monthly	2.00
Empires	Penn Station	7749	250 West 34th Street	New York	NY	10019	Confirmed	3x monthly	1.00
Moors	Salt Lake City	0	455 South 500 East	Salt Lake City	UT	84102	Confirmed	2x monthly	2.00
Macys	Sunrise Mall - CA	1538	5900 Sunrise Mall	Citrus Heights	CA	95610	Confirmed	2x monthly	2.00
Empires	Washington - DC	108	1518 Bennings Rd	Washington	DC	20002	Confirmed	2x monthly	2.00
Empires	Brooklyn - Fulton II	158	464 Fulton St. Brooklyn	Brooklyn	NY	11201	Confirmed	2x monthly	2.00
Empires	Brooklyn - Fulton Street	7	360 Fulton Street	Brooklyn	NY	11021	Confirmed	2x monthly	2.00
Empires	Galleria at Tyler	19604	3605 Galleria at Tyler	Riverside	CA	92503	Confirmed	2x monthly	2.00
Empires	Green Acres Mall	19	1002 Green Acres Mall	Valley Stream	NY	11580	Confirmed	2x monthly	2.00
Empires	Hamilton Mall	1554	4409 Black Horse Pike	Mays Landing	NJ	8330	Confirmed	2x monthly	2.00
Empires	Livonia	1460	29500 7 Mile Rd	Livonia	MI	48152	Confirmed	2x monthly	2.00
Empires	Bronx - 3rd Ave	20	2929 3rd Ave	Bronx	NY	10455	Confirmed	2x monthly	2.00
Zacs	Montebello	1998	1401 N Montebello Blvd.	Montebello	CA	90640	Confirmed	2x monthly	2.00
Zacs	Montebello Towne Center	21725	1600 Town Center	Montebello	CA	90640	Confirmed	2x monthly	2.00
Zacs	Parkway Plaza - CA	1438	575 Fletcher Parkway	El Cajon	CA	92020	Confirmed	2x monthly	2.00
Zacs	Rego Park	1544	9605 Queens Blvd	Rego Park	NY	11374	Confirmed	2x monthly	2.00
Zacs	Brooklyn - Church Ave	124	2101 Church Ave	Brooklyn	NY	11212	Confirmed	2x monthly	2.00
Zacs	Brooklyn - Flatbush Ave	104	140 Flatbush Avenue	Brooklyn	NY	11217	Confirmed	2x monthly	2.00
Zacs	Brooklyn - Graham Ave	153	4 Graham Avenue	Brooklyn	NY	11206	Confirmed	2x monthly	2.00
Zacs	Chicago Ridge Mall	1840	6501 95th St	Chicago Ridge	IL	60415	Confirmed	2x monthly	2.00
Zacs	Chula Vista	1358	565 Broadway	Chula Vista	CA	91910	Confirmed	2x monthly	2.00
Empires	Coronado Center	24349	6600 Menaul Blvd. NE	Albuquerque	NM	87110	Confirmed	2x monthly	2.00
Empires	Fairfield - CA	1159	1544 Travis Blvd	Fairfield	CA	94533	Confirmed	2x monthly	2.00
Empires	Fort Smith	0	1401 Highway 71 S	Fort Smith	AR	72901	Confirmed	2x monthly	2.00
Empires	Hillsdale Shopping Center	0	40 Hillsdale Mall	San Mateo	CA	94403	Confirmed	2x monthly	2.00
Moors	Juneau	0	8181 Old Glacier Hwy	Juneau	AK	99801	Confirmed	2x monthly	2.00
Empires	Mall del Norte	2247	5300 San Dario Avenue	Laredo	TX	78041	Confirmed	2x monthly	2.00
Empires	Mayaguez Mall	1935	975 HOSTOS AVE STE 110	Mayaguez	PR	680	Confirmed	2x monthly	2.00
Empires	Meadowood	4788	5200 Meadowood Mall Circle	Reno	NV	89502	Confirmed	2x monthly	2.00
Empires	Meadowood	1978	5400 Meadowood Mall	Reno	NV	89502	Confirmed	2x monthly	2.00
Empires	Owasso	0	11510 N Garnett Rd.	Owasso	OK	74055	Confirmed	2x monthly	2.00

if your company is planning a promotion in a specific retailer and new signage is being shipped to each store, the shipping and installation of the signage can be coordinated with the field team's store visits to ensure all signage is up prior to the promotion. In addition, if new product is being shipped, the field visual merchandisers can be instructed to look for the product on their next store visit.

In-store survey

As your field team visits each store on their rotation, they will complete an in-store survey. The in-store survey provides details of what was accomplished on the store visit. The survey is completed while the team members are in the store and maybe a written document that's filled out and uploaded to a website at the end of the day. The merchandiser could also have a hand-held device or smartphone where the information is uploaded instantly.

At the start of the programme, it is advantageous to work with the MSO to construct this document. If you or your sponsors want specific information on a regular basis, questions can be placed in the survey to obtain the information requested. The survey usually reflects the name of the retailer, location, date of service, store contact, a list of questions the leader (keeping in mind the objectives of the sponsors) and the MSO have developed and, last but not least, before and after photos of the merchandising task completed (Figure 8.2).

Each in-store survey is usually not forwarded to you individually, but compiled into a weekly store visit summary.

Weekly store visit summary

Once in-store surveys are completed, they are reviewed by the MSO's field management team and your account manager. The account manager develops a detailed weekly store visit summary containing all information pulled from the in-store surveys. This spreadsheet is the most important document that you will receive on a weekly basis and provides you and the sponsors with a high level view of what was executed in each retail store.

This spreadsheet usually presents information in columns so you can scroll down the page and view answers to store visit question at a glance. The document will list the name of the retailer, store service dates and questions that were answered (Figure 8.3).

In addition, you will usually have a link that will give you the option to view each in-store survey in detail. You will also have the option to view the before and after photos from each store visit.

Before and after photos

Once you have selected the link to the in-store survey, you may have the option to view the before and after photos of the task completed at the store visit. These photos paint a clear picture of what was completed in each retail location and how the product was presented and displayed. It is imperative that you, as the leader, review these photos with a keen eye because the product presentation will reflect the manner in which the merchandising standards are executed in each retail store.

Alert/red flag issues and concerns

There will be times when issues or concerns may arise in the retail store that may require immediate attention. These situations may demand fast

FIGURE 8.2 In-store survey

GOLD STAR
MERCHANDISING

Bossman Merchandising Account Visit Recap

Report #:	300987			
Account:	Moors		**Merchandiser:**	Jorden Brown
Location	Concord Mall, 4709 State St, Wilmington, DE 19721		**Region:**	Northeast
Market:	North , DE		**Purpose of Visit:**	Monthly Rotation
Channel of Distribution:	Department Store		**Date of Visit:**	6/3/2010
Consumer:	Men's		**Time In/ Out:**	10am
Store Contact:	Robert Jones		**Date of Last Visit:**	5/4/2010

Before Photo:
Photos required for each department visited

After Photo:
Photos required for each department visited

Urgent Issues/ Follow Up Requested: None
please list who made the request and the
timeline

Product

Visit Rating		men's	women's	kids'	accessories
please rate the condition of the space	1- disaster				
upon arrival	2- poorly maintained				
	3- store in good condition	3			
	4- store looks great				

Level of Product		men's	women's	kids'	accessories
please rate how full the fixtures are on	1- empty				
selling floor	2- could use more	2			
	3- full				
	4- unshoppable				

FIGURE 8.3   Weekly store visit summary

GOLD STAR MERCHANDISING

Weekly Store Visit Summary

store	Store #	City	State	Start Date	Hours	In-store contact	Contact's Title	Product Location	Condition of Department	Back Stock	Merchandising Standards	Units Brought Sales Floor	Fixtures Gained	Changes in Position	Location of Product	Missing Signage Types	# of Units Sold	Comments	Next Service Date
Moors	178	Aurora	IL	2/25/2010	2.5	Bob Jay	Team Lead Fashion's	Middle of Department	Fair presentation- Some product available on sales floor	10	Yes	10		No			2	The department looks good. I talked to the team lead about the upcoming planogram changes. After service the department looks good.	3/12/2010
Moors	169	Bolingbrook	IL	2/25/2010	2	Sandy White	Team Lead Fashions	Middle of Department	Fair presentation- Some product available on sales floor	10	Yes	10		No			2	The department looks good. Most clearance has been sold. The Department Manager is getting ready for the upcoming floor change. After service the department looks good.	3/12/2010
Moors	215	Bolingbrook	IL	2/25/2010	2.5	Alycia Brown	Team Lead Fashion's	Middle of Department	Fair presentation- Some product available on sales floor	10	Yes	10		No			1	A customer in the store needed a size of Bossman jeans that the store did not have. I called another store for her and had the store hold it for the customer. She was very happy and thanked me for taking the time to find what she needed.	3/11/2010
Moors	204	Camby	IN	/2/25/2010	2.5	Sharon Sanders	Fashions Team Leader	Middle of Department	Fair presentation- Some product available on sales floor	0	Yes	0		No			0	This location is not offering any promotions on the Bossman men's merchandise at this time. This location is out of the following products: Bossman Jeans Stone Wash 34x30 slim fit Jeans Brown Wash 34x34 Bossman T-shirt 40x30	3/11/2013
Moors	130	Carmel	IN	2/25/2010	2.5	Kathy Russ	Fashions Team Leader	Middle of Department	Fair presentation- Some product available on sales floor	0	Yes	0		No			0	This location is in need of gray long SL shirts in long sleeved and all colours of the single T-shirts.	3/14/2013
Moors	243	Clinton Twp	IL	2/26/2010	2.5	Stacy Simon	Associate	Middle of Department	Good- Some product available on sales floor/Some merchandising assistance is needed	0	Yes	0		No			0	This store shares a fixture with Jazz. The top 2 shelves are Bossman jeans and the bottom 2 shelves are Jazz.	3/13/2013
Moors	104	Columbus	IL	2/26/2010	3	Bill Jackson	SLTL	Middle of Department	Good- Some product available on sales floor/Some merchandising assistance is needed	0	Yes	0		No			2	This store has good stock levels and good size runs. They have work shirts and T-shirts that need new packaging. They are folded on the trousers table.	3/12/2013
Moors	249	Delaware	IL	2/26/2010	3	Mike York	CSTL	Middle of Department	Good- Some product available on sales floor/Some merchandising assistance is needed	0	Yes	0		No			2	This store has good stock levels and good size runs. All of their stock is on the floor. They have not received the shorts programme yet.	3/13/2010
Moors	58	Dublin	IL	2/26/2010	3	Andy Cliton	Department Lead	Middle of Department	Good- Some product available on sales floor/Some merchandising assistance is needed	0	Yes	0		No			0	This store has good stock levels and good size runs. All of their stock is on the floor. They have sweatshirts and T-shirts that need new packaging. They are folded on the trousers table. It would be great if I could get packaging for the shirts.	3/12/2013

solutions or might introduce obstacles hindering the implementation of the strategy. These issues could serve as notification of sold-out product to the sponsor or require advice regarding product placement changes. These alerts or red flag concerns should be addressed as soon as possible. In these situations, the MSO account manager may be notified by a field manager with issues requiring an answer rather quickly. A form may be created or a simple e-mail may relay the message of the immediate need. The leader should address these concerns immediately or if necessary forward to the account executive for approval or further evaluation.

Quarterly reviews

Quarterly reviews are top-line reports that are usually broken down by retailer. These reports provide a review of what happened in each retail chain quarterly. It may provide information such as a percentage of how many store visits were completed and any concerns such as the number of stores without signage or product shortages.

Quarterly reviews may also provide information on product requested by field team members who service numerous store locations that need the same items. This is a very important concern because your sponsors may receive sales analysis stating that specific products sold well in stores, but their numbers do not reflect their true potential.

For example, field merchandisers visited 20 stores in a specific retail chain in a particular quarter and store assistants stated that customers continually asked for a particular shirt in size XL but each store only received two XLs in each shipment. This information may have been listed on each field merchandiser's in-store survey every quarter, but you and the sponsor did not realize how often these sizes were requested. The quarterly review may reflect the shirt in size XL was requested 18 times in 15 stores, but the sponsors report only shows that size XL sold well along with the other sizes.

Report distribution

For your strategy to succeed, the sponsors should identify and address the needs and issues in each retail store location. This information is contained in the numerous reports discussed. Therefore, it is vital that you distribute these reports as soon as possible and follow up with sponsors to ensure they have a clear-cut understanding of what is occurring in the stores. This is a great time to certify the combined objectives are being met. In order to outsmart the competition, the sponsors should know what is going on at the retail level and address each issue as it arises.

Monitoring field visual merchandisers' performance

Although the FVM team is outsourced, monitoring their performance is vital. An evaluation of each person's performance is necessary to maintain a high standard of excellence. The field team is an extension of your brand and as a result, they understand the features and benefits of your company's products. They know the company strategies that are being executed and have developed strong relationships with the manager on duty and their staff. In order to evaluate each person's performance, a review of several aspects of responsibilities should be investigated. There are six key areas that should be examined:

- adherence to merchandising standards;
- in-store surveys;
- sales analysis per market;
- planogram compliance;
- retailer feedback;
- market tours.

1 **Adherence to merchandising standards**: How product is presented at retail is a reflection of your brand. Well merchandised product stimulates sales and attracts target consumers. Consistency is the key and every store serviced by a field visual merchandiser should reflect your brand's image. This means that if five stores are serviced in one week by the same team member, the merchandising standards should be consistent in all five stores. To confirm each team member meets the expectations, it is necessary to review photos from their in-store surveys and visit a few of their stores on a regular basis to certify the presentation consistency. The leader should also make certain the team member is adhering to and meeting the standards presented in the merchandising standards manual.

2 **In-store surveys**: As the leader, every week your MSO account manager will forward a weekly store visit summary that contains in-store surveys from a previous week. These surveys should be reviewed to identify what activities took place during the store visit. As the leader, you want to confirm that no information was omitted, all questions were answered, all answers made sense and all details were clear and explained.

3 Sales analysis per market: One key way to evaluate a field visual merchandiser's performance is to review sales analysis for stores serviced by a team member. The sponsor should have access to sales reports that reflect the product sales by a specific retailer, possibly per store. By comparing sales figures for stores that are not serviced with sales figures of stores that are serviced, you can gain insight on how much of a sales increase took place due to the team member's merchandising expertise.

4 Planogram compliance: If planograms were presented to the field team for execution, before and after photos would have been taken and forwarded to the leader by the MSO account manager. These photos reveal compliance with the planogram; when reviewing the photos, compare them to the planogram to ascertain if directions were followed and if the presentation is identical. By comparing the two, you will confirm the team member is consistent with planogram compliance.

5 Retailer feedback: By contacting the management team at the retail stores regularly serviced by a particular field visual merchandiser, you should try to obtain feedback on how well the team member was able to develop relationships with sales personnel. Management may be willing to provide insight on the team member's performance during implementation. When your team is doing a great job it is always exciting to obtain this kind of feedback.

6 Market tours: One of the most effective ways to evaluate the field visual merchandiser's performance is to conduct market tours. In a market tour, one would visit a group of stores serviced by a field visual merchandiser to gain insight on consistency in meeting the merchandising standards and developing relationships with the retailer. It is a good idea to travel to different stores throughout the year and not wait until the end of the year to visit all markets.

In addition to the six key areas to examine, each field visual merchandiser should be evaluated on the following six attributes:

- communication skills;
- dependability;
- creativity;
- attitude;
- enthusiasm;
- cooperation.

FIGURE 8.4   Field visual merchandiser performance evaluation chart

FIELD VISUAL MERCHANDISER PERFORMANCE EVALUATION				
NAME:_____				
DATE:_____	EXCELLENT	GOOD	FAIR	POOR
Merchandising Standards				
In-Store Surveys				
Sales Analysis per Market				
Planogram Compliance				
Retailer Feedback				
Market Tour Review				
Communication Skills				
Dependability				
Creativity				
Attitude				
Enthusiasm				
Cooperation				

Once you have evaluated each team member, develop a basic performance evaluation chart (Figure 8.4) and record this information. Keeping a performance record of each field visual merchandiser on your team will help the leader and the MSO understand and rate the strategy as a whole. In addition, the performance evaluation chart provides valuable information on how well the employee is performing based on their expertise and attributes. This is a time-consuming task, but worth the effort to maintain a high standard of excellence.

Real-world situation No 3

New retailer needing FVM services

Background information:

You have just been informed that your company has a new retail account that needs FVM services. The retailer has 100 stores and each store will stock your company's line of long-sleeve T-shirts. Each store will receive a total of 120 long-sleeve T-shirts to be presented on the back wall of the young men's department in a folded presentation.

In order to obtain a budget for this service, you have been asked to provide the cost of servicing this account twice a month to maintain the presentation. To determine the cost of these services, you must determine how long each store visit will take in order to accomplish the set objectives. Therefore, you will have to develop a 'task duration estimate'.

Your department has developed a planogram showing how the presentation should be presented on the back wall with two displays and a sign (Figure 8.5).

FIGURE 8.5   T-shirts planogram

Situation

In addition to having the planogram, you travel to one of the retailer's stores to gain an understanding of the store layout. After speaking to the account executive responsible for this retail account, you learn the stockroom in each store is located in the basement and the department where your product will be presented is on the second floor. Once you arrive at the store, you determine that to get from the young men's department to the stockroom, you will need to take the freight elevator. You estimate that it will take 20 minutes to gather the product and signs, load onto a cart and transport these items to the sales floor where the presentation is to be presented in the department.

Using your merchandising standards manual and a folding board, you determine that it takes around 21 seconds to fold a shirt. To allocate enough time to fold 120 shirts, you adjust the time to 30 seconds per shirt. In addition, you allocate 20 minutes for the two displays and sign placement. Each store visit has several additional tasks to be calculated before you can determine the estimated time frame for each store visit. Therefore, you allocate 5 minutes each for 'visual assessment of area' and 'final walk through'. To determine the length of each store visit, your task duration estimate should reflect the time it will take to complete the following task:

TABLE 8.2   Task duration estimate

Task	Estimated duration
Visual assessment of area	
Work product from stockroom to sales floor	
Merchandising area to include two displays and sign	
Final walk through	

The challenge

Your challenge is to determine how much time should be allocated for each store visit. If your estimates are too low, your team will not be able to complete all the tasks necessary to provide the retailer with the proper FVM service. If your estimates are too high, more money will be allocated than needed, raising the cost unnecessarily and making it unrealistic to get the budget approved to launch the service in this account.

After reviewing the calculations, determine if each store visit should take:

A 1 hour

B 1.5 hours

C 2 hours

If this were a real-world situation, your next step would be to contact your MSO to confirm coverage in all 100 stores and the hourly rate of service based on your task duration estimate. Once the cost has been determined, inform the account executive or whoever has the budget for this execution.

Chapter 8 checklist

- Am I aware that the strategic plan timeline will serve as the road map for everyone to use to identify where the strategy is at any given time in the execution process?

- When monitoring the strategy execution, do I understand the importance of identifying major milestones?

- Have I gained the knowledge on how to conduct a SWOT analysis?

- After I have identified a problem, am I aware of how to conduct a needs assessment to determine what resources are required to get the strategy back on track?

- Do I know the most effective method of communicating with my sponsors and the appropriate time?

- Do I know the five points to keep in mind when communicating with sponsors?

- Am I aware of what to expect from status and progress reports?

- Do I understand the role of the MSO account manager and do I realize this person will be the point of contact for my dealings with the MSO?

- Do I understand the importance of having a weekly conference call with my MSO account manager?

- Am I aware of why I should have quarterly face-to-face meetings with my MSO management team?

- Do I know the purpose of an in-store service schedule?

- Do I know how to use the in-store service schedule?

- Do I know how to utilize the details of the in-store survey?

- Am I aware of what information a weekly store visit summary provides?

- Do I understand why before and after photos are taken at each store visit?

- Do I understand the usefulness of alert or red flag issues?

- Do I recognize the importance of quarterly strategy review reports?

- Am I aware that I can evaluate a field visual merchandiser's performance by obtaining a sales analysis report?

- Do I know how to develop a field visual merchandiser performance evaluation chart?

Tricks of the trade: Where's Waldo?

Are you familiar with the children's book *Where's Waldo?* (known in the UK as *Where's Wally?*). It was created by British illustrator Martin Handford and featured illustrations of crowd scenes filled with 3,000 to 4,000 tiny images. Waldo was the main character and wore a red and white striped hat with a matching shirt, blue trousers and big, round eye glasses. The objective was to find Waldo in the large crowd. Kids would spend hours trying to locate the little guy in the red and white. The key in the process was to know how to recognize Waldo.

As the leader, you and your team may not have the luxury of visiting each store location on a regular basis to ensure the visual presentation of the company's product meets your expectations. Therefore, the leader and the team should view and analyse in-store surveys regularly, including photos and providing feedback to the MSO on any issues or concerns as quickly as possible. It's a lot like looking for Waldo, because the key is to know what to look for. Let's walk through the process:

The scenario

You and your team have just launched a national FVM strategy that provides services to 600 stores. Your FVM team has been visiting stores for three weeks when you receive your first weekly store visit summary. As the leader, you want to guarantee that the training you and your management team developed is off to a good start. Therefore, everyone on your management team is reviewing a number of the in-store surveys before you forward the summary to your sponsors.

Step 1

In this first round of reviewing in-store surveys, you want to provide your management team with a few guidelines. To start, you instruct each manager to focus on one specific market. Each manager should select six in-store surveys from their chosen market. If possible, select six stores that are serviced by the same field visual merchandiser or split it by selecting three stores each from two field team members. Also, if possible, select stores from two different retailers.

Example

Six in-store surveys from two markets:

TABLE 8.3   Store selection

South-east market	Taylor Johnson	Macy's (3 stores)
		Vandyck's (3 stores)
North-west market	Pat Brown	Bob's Menswear (3 stores)
	Tommy Horton	Moors Department Store (3 stores)

Step 2

After the store selection process, provide information on the materials needed in the review process, which are:

- merchandising standards manual;
- task duration estimates for each account;
- planograms or store layouts for each shop;
- six in-store surveys from the market.

FIGURE 8.6 Review process: Materials needed

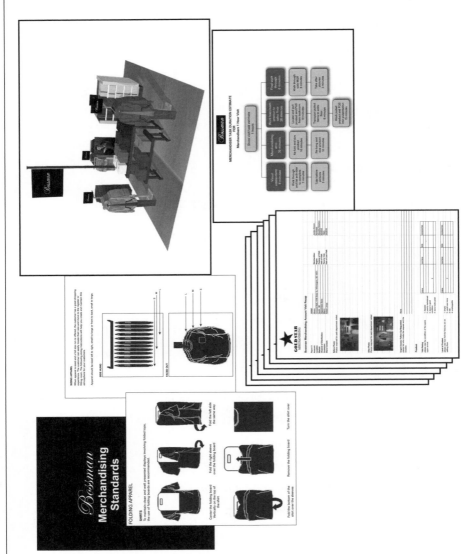

Step 3

Process for reviewing in-store surveys:

You and your team will most likely review in-store surveys from the MSO's secure website and not be able to review all six reports in a given market side by side. Therefore, it would be wise to develop a checklist indicating what to look for in each report. In *Where's Waldo?* you can't find Waldo if you don't know what he looks like. Your checklist should provide questions that direct your managers seeking specific answers. Let's look at an example of a few questions on a basic checklist:

TABLE 8.4   Store visit report checklist

Question	Comment
☐ Was the store visit completed within the time listed on the task duration estimate?	
The report will probably indicate how much time was spent on the store visit. The answer to this question will help you determine if more time is needed to service this store.	
☐ How many units were brought to the sales floor from the stockroom?	
If this question is on the store visit report, it may provide an explanation of why the store visit took longer than anticipated.	
☐ Since your last visit, was the product maintained according to merchandising standards?	
If this question is on the store visit report, it will help you determine if you should increase the number of store visits, or possibly have the field visual merchandiser provide sales associates with training on merchandising standards.	

Step 4

The process for reviewing before and after photos. One of the most effective ways to review and analyse before and after photos is to use the following procedures:

1 Obtain a copy of your merchandising standards manual and your task duration estimates.

2 Review the before and after photos of all stores serviced by one specific merchandiser at a time.

3 When viewing the after photos, use the merchandising standards manual as a guide to determine if the FVM is consistently presenting product in the same manner stated in the manual. Look for inconsistencies such as product not being folded correctly in two out of three stores.

4 Review the before photos and the task duration estimate and determine if the time allotted for each task looks sufficient.

This process will also help you determine whether or not the field merchandiser needs additional training or if the time to complete each task in a specific store needs to be increased. You may not have time to view all in-store surveys. Therefore, by randomly selecting a few in-store surveys from a specific field merchandiser and asking your management team to do the same, you will be able to identify skill gaps and see if objectives are being met in each account. If the leader and the team document findings and submit together a snapshot of the individual, this could be utilized as feedback of visual merchandising services to be reviewed with your MSO account manager. Your MSO will be eager to conduct additional training to ensure your standards are met.

If you determined that the time allocations of visits in specific stores need to be increased on the task duration estimate, make adjustments to estimate and review with your MSO account manager. Keep in mind that you may need to decrease the visit times in other store locations to accommodate the increase in the stores with time estimate issues.

Planning and executing tactics and special projects

Now that you have gained a better understanding of the ways to communicate and monitor your strategic plan, it's time to obtain information on the numerous types of tactics used in the execution of the strategic plan. It doesn't matter if you are a retailer or a manufacturer: understanding how and when to use the following tactics will help your organization gain and maintain an advantage over your competitors. Let's look at the current strategic plan timeline and determine the type of execution tactic we have in place (Figure 9.1).

Under the execution phase, there are 600 stores that will receive field visual merchandising services. In Chapter 7, we discussed launching this strategy in three phases (see page 179) starting with one retailer in phase 1, the second retailer in phase 2 and the third in phase 3. Executing a launch in this manner is one type of field visual merchandising tactic we will examine.

Field visual merchandising tactics

Different types of tactics are used for specific reasons and are sometimes used simultaneously or consecutively. Let's look at six types of tactics that could be used in the execution process of launching your strategy and then used again once your strategy is up and running.

FIGURE 9.1 Strategic plan timeline: Snail tactic

TASK NAME	DURATION	START	FINISH	RESOURCE
National Field Merchandising Strategy	252 days	Thu 2/2/12	Fri 1/18/13	
Initiation	79 days	Thu 2/2/12	Tue 5/22/12	
– Develop Strategy Scope Statement for Each Retailer and Forward	1 days	Thu 2/2/12	Thu 2/2/12	Brook Adams
– Provide Approval to Execute Strategy in Retail Stores	2 days	Thu 2/2/12	Fri 2/3/12	Retailer
– Provide Management Contact List to Brook Adams	7 days	Fri 2/3/12	Mon 2/13/12	Retailer
– Provide Retailer Letter of Introduction to Brook Adams and Store Managers	7 days	Tue 2/14/12	Wed 2/22/12	Retailer
– Provide Retailer Store Visit Guidelines to Brook Adams	5 days	Fri 3/23/12	Thu 3/29/12	Retailer
– Forward Letter of Introduction and Store Visit Guidelines to MSO for Approval	15 days	Fri 3/30/12	Thu 4/19/12	Brook Adams
– Forward and Review Training Materials with Printer for Production	1 day	Fri 4/20/12	Fri 4/20/12	Brook Adams
– Forward Training Programme Requirements to MSO for Approval	1 day	Mon 4/23/12	Mon 4/23/12	Brook Adams
– Provide Approval of Training Requirements/Visit Guidelines/Letter Intro	14 days	Tue 4/24/12	Fri 5/11/12	MSO
– Review/Approve and Sign Off on Strategy	7 days	Mon 5/14/12	Tue 5/22/12	Account Executives
Planning	65 days	Wed 5/23/12	Tue 8/21/12	
– Conduct Strategy Kick-off Meeting with Retailer, MSO and Account Executives	14 days	Wed 5/23/12	Mon 6/11/12	Brook Adams
– Produce Copies of Training Materials for Field Merchandisers	15 days	Tue 6/12/12	Mon 7/2/12	Color Block Printing
– Package Training Materials to be Shipped to MSO	3 days	Tue 7/3/12	Thu 7/5/12	Color Block Printing
– Ship Training Materials to MSO	12 days	Fri 7/6/12	Mon 7/23/12	Color Block Printing
– Review and Approve Training Materials	7 days	Tue 7/24/12	Wed 8/1/12	MSO
– Forward Training Materials to MSO Field Management	14 days	Thu 8/2/12	Tue 8/21/12	MSO

FIGURE 9.1 *continued*

TASK NAME	DURATION	START	FINISH	RESOURCE
Execution	**82 days**	**Wed 8/22/12**	**Thu 12/13/12**	
- Conduct Field Visual Merchandising Training	21 days	Wed 8/22/12	Wed 9/19/12	MSO
- Conduct Pre-Calls to Each Retail Store Manager to Schedule First Visit	9 days	Thu 9/20/12	Tue 10/2/12	Field Merchandisers
Launch Phase 1 – Start In-Store Rotation in Retailer 1/ 200 Stores	**12 days**	**Wed 10/3/12**	**Thu 10/18/12**	**Brook Adams, MSO**
- Forward Phase 1 Weekly Store Visit Summary	1 day	Fri 10/19/12	Fri 10/19/12	MSO
- Review Phase 1 Weekly Store Visit Summary and Forward to Account Executives	4 day	Mon 10/22/12	Thu 10/25/12	Brook Adams
Launch Phase 2 – Start In-Store Rotation in Retailer 2/ 200 Stores	**12 days**	**Fri 10/26/22**	**Mon 11/12/12**	**Brook Adams, MSO**
- Forward Phase 2 Weekly Store Visit Summary	1 day	Mon 11/12/12	Mon 11/12/12	MSO
- Review Phase 2 Weekly Store Visit Summary and Forward to Account Executives	3 day	Tue 11/13/12	Thu 11/15/12	Brook Adams
Launch Phase 3 – Start In-Store Rotation in Retailer 3/ 200 Stores	**12 days**	**Fri 11/16/12**	**Mon 12/3/12**	**Brook Adams, MSO**
- Forward Phase 3 Weekly Store Visit Summary	1 day	Tue 12/4/12	Tue 12/4/12	MSO
- Review Phase 3 Weekly Store Visit Summary and Forward to Account Executives	7 day	Wed 12/5/12	Thu 12/13/12	Brook Adams
Monitoring	**26 days**	**Fri 12/14/12**	**Fri 1/18/13**	
- Monitor Store Visit Rotation Against Plan for Accuracy	26 days	Fri 12/14/12	Fri 1/18/13	Brook Adams
- Monitor Task Duration Estimates for Accuracy	26 days	Fri 12/14/12	Fri 1/18/13	Brook Adams
- Review Merchandisers In-Store Survey to Identify Issues and Concerns	26 days	Fri 12/14/12	Fri 1/18/13	Brook Adams
- Review Merchandisers Before and After Photos to Identify Training Gaps	26 days	Fri 12/14/12	Fri 1/18/13	Brook Adams
- Review MSO Reports for Issues, Concerns and Accuracy	26 days	Fri 12/14/12	Fri 1/18/13	Brook Adams
- Identify Corrective Actions Needed to Address Any Issues in Each Launch	26 days	Fri 12/14/12	Fri 1/18/13	Brook Adams

Snail tactics

The execution tactic used in Figure 9.1 is called the snail tactic. This process gives the leader the opportunity to identify obstacles in the first phase and information to formulate a plan to eliminate those same obstacles from occurring again in the subsequent phases. In Figure 9.1 there are three phases of the execution; however, one can have as many phases as necessary when using this tactic. There are numerous ways to utilize snail tactics. Let's look at a few quick examples.

Example 1

Your company is a clothing manufacturer launching a field visual merchandising strategy in three retail accounts with 100 stores each. One retail account has 20 stores in a major market where your competition has a strong presence. Your goal is to present your brand as a leader in this area where the competition has a strong hold. Your plan is to carry out your strategy using a snail tactic with four phases.

In the first phase of the snail tactic you and your team will ensure your product presentation is well planned and flawless in the 20 stores located in your competitor's market. In the second phase you will do the same for the 80 additional stores with this retailer and the last two phases will focus on the other 200 stores in the remaining two retail accounts. This tactic allows you to roll out the strategy in a slower process, but with a more concentrated effort to address this key market.

Example 2

Your company is a retailer that uses an outsourced field visual merchandising team to carry out their in-store strategies. Your company has developed a new window display concept to be rolled out to 300 stores in time for a major promotion. This is a very important execution, so you decide to use a snail tactic to set the window displays in 40 stores distributed across four markets before rolling out to the remaining 260 stores. This course of action allows you to analyse the execution process with your chosen vendors, evaluate the window display presentation to ensure consistency in all 40 stores and work out any errors that may have surfaced during this process. This is also a perfect time to calculate all associated costs and examine any budget issues before you roll out the presentation to other stores.

Programme blitz tactics

The next tactic is a programme blitz, which involves utilizing the field visual merchandisers to service identified stores once or twice a week for a month in order to get the shops or areas up to standard. After that, the team would begin its regular service schedule of twice a month. This execution process may be applied when a particular retail account has stores in a very busy market. Due to high traffic, your product presentation would require weekly servicing to keep it up to standard. Subsequently, the field team would service the account on a regular two-week rotation cycle. This type of tactic works well, but extra funding will be required to double the service at the kick-off of the launch. Let's look at two examples of how this approach can be applied.

Example 1

As a retailer, your company has 80 stores nationally and 30 of those stores are in popular tourist regions. The sales increase in these 30 stores is almost double what it was last year. As you develop your field visual merchandising strategy, you plan to use a programme blitz tactic at the beginning of your launch to gain control over the product presentation in these 30 stores, while all other stores receive service on a regular two-week rotation.

Example 2

This tactic can also be applied at the beginning stage of a launch to acquire control over the product presentation and train the stores' sales assistants. Example, you are launching a field visual merchandising strategy in one retail account with 50 stores. As the leader, you choose a programme blitz tactic for the beginning month of the launch by utilizing your field team to service these 50 stores once a week for four weeks before moving to a two-week rotation. This tactic increases your store visits by adding two additional visits at the beginning of the launch. With the two additional store visits, your field team will offer product knowledge training to sales assistants at one visit and train on merchandising standards at the second visit. Therefore, when your field visual merchandising team switches to the regular two-week rotation, all sales assistants in this account will be trained on the company's merchandising standards and product knowledge. This helps to instil the standards you will require when going forward and will impart valuable knowledge to the sales assistants to aid in increasing the sales of your product.

Swarm tactics

Swarms are designed to saturate a market or a group of stores with one targeted objective to make sure the product presentation is superb prior to a major event. In this tactic, a launch begins with all merchandisers visiting stores on the same date. This can be used in conjunction with a national product launch and simultaneously with other tactics, but it must be well planned in advance. Let's look at two examples.

Example 1

As a retailer your company has opened 50 stores in a new market and is now preparing to launch a major advertising campaign. This campaign will announce the date of your company's grand opening of those 50 stores to attract your target consumers and simultaneously introduce your stores to new customers. As the leader, you work closely with all departments and vendors to coordinate product, fixture deliveries and signage to ensure all is received in each store and confirmed prior to the launch date. Your objective is to have the field visual merchandising team service each of these 50 stores the day before the grand opening to make sure each store's product presentation is fresh and well coordinated prior to the grand opening. So, you use a swarm tactic to accomplish this strategy.

Example 2

In the same scenario, your company is a clothing manufacturer that has been approached by the retailer above. The retailer is requesting that your brand participate in this campaign by providing field visual merchandising services to these 50 stores on the day before the grand opening to ensure your product presentation is in tip-top condition. As the leader, you utilize a swarm tactic to make it all come together.

In the planning process, you decide to combine the swarm tactic with a programme blitz tactic to showcase the brand in these 50 stores. Therefore, in addition to the field team providing visual merchandising services to these 50 stores on the day before the grand opening, you add two additional store visits. These additional visits will be used for educating sales personnel on product knowledge during one visit and training on merchandising standards on the other. So if the store's grand opening is on May 10, and the retailer requested you to provide visual merchandising services on May 9, on May 7 and 8 the field team will provide product knowledge training followed by training on merchandising standards.

Wave tactics

Stores that are not serviced on a regular basis can be visited by the field visual merchandising team in waves. Once a quarter, the field team may visit a group of stores once a week for one month, and then three months later in the next quarter those same stores may be serviced again. This process extends throughout the strategy.

Example 1

The budget for the strategy has already been allocated and you are gearing up for the launch. Prior to launching the strategy, one of your sponsors has a concern. This sponsor wants to add an additional retail account to the list of stores to receive services, but the sponsor has limited financing for this undertaking. To accommodate the sponsor's request, you recommend using a wave tactic to save on the cost of service. If this tactic meets the objectives of the sponsor, obtain a quote from your MSO to make sure this tactic will work within the sponsor's budget.

Example 2

Wave tactics are also used to service stores in rural areas. If your company is a retailer that has a few stores in a small rural market, your MSO may not have trained field visual merchandisers living in that market. It would therefore be wise to use a wave tactic to provide services to these stores. Keep in mind that, when using this tactic, you will incur travel expenses for members of your field team to travel to this market once a quarter. Take, for example, the following:

Your strategy is up and running and the sponsors are pleased with the type of field visual merchandising services that are being provided by the MSO team. A sponsor informs you of one retailer's intent to open five additional stores in a new market and wants to know the cost of adding these stores to the visit rotation schedule for routine monthly services. After receiving the store addresses for the five new locations, you discuss the possibility of servicing theses stores with your MSO account manager. You both realize all five stores are in a rural market where your MSO does not have trained field visual merchandisers. Due to the fact that the five stores are very far apart from each other, it would not be cost effective for you to pay one person to service all five of these stores. The travel expenses would be too costly. If you decided to hire one person in each location to service the stores, there would not be enough work to keep the person employed. Therefore, the best option would be to use a wave tactic to service these locations.

When using this tactic, you could utilize the field visual merchandisers who reside close to the nearest markets in order to service these stores once a quarter. Therefore, you would pay the cost of the normal store visit along with the travel cost per quarter. In addition, the chosen field visual merchandisers servicing these accounts would already be trained and aware of your brand standards and promotions. This tactic would minimize additional cost and alleviate the downtime associated with new team member training.

Shock tactics

At times a retailer is sceptical about brands using an outsourced field visual merchandising team to service their stores. It has been stated that some individuals employed by MSOs lack training in visual merchandising and in-store strategy implementation. Shock tactics are intended to deliver a significant impact and to amaze your retailers, while stunning your competition. This manoeuvre is accomplished when four or more well-trained field visual merchandisers visit a store in uniform, with visual directives, a planogram and detailed plans to execute a selected strategy. This truly will turn heads when the team visits a store at a time when the retailer's executives are present and your competitors are taking note. It is commonly done in small implementations, but may also be mixed with wave tactics. You may be wondering about the benefits of this tactic, so let's look at an example.

One of your sponsors approaches you about providing a team of field visual merchandisers to assist with installing a new brand shop in a major retail account. Your sponsor has negotiated with the retailer to place this shop in one of their new store locations opening in six weeks. Your sponsor has high hopes of rolling out an additional 50 shops in this account and having all shops serviced by your field team on a regular basis. The retail account has approved this shop installation, but is sceptical about moving forward with additional shops using a field visual MSO. In addition, your company and your competitor are both trying to secure floor space in this retailer's new locations, which will be opening in the following eight months. If successful, these 50 shops would have a major increase in sales for your company's product.

As the leader, you realize that a shock tactic could be useful to change the retailer's outlook on giving your brand the allocated space for 50 brand shops in their new stores. At the same time, it could increase your chances of providing ongoing services if the field team has a well-planned, turnkey shop execution process that leaves your brand shop looking exceptional and, most of all, attracts buying consumers. In addition, when the FVM team shows up in uniforms bearing your company's logo, it presents a positive image to the retailers.

Sneak attack tactics

Merchandisers are visiting retailers all the time and relationships are constantly being harnessed. These relationships will help to leverage the brand's power while helping the retailer increase its profits. Remember: the FVMs are your eyes and ears in the marketplace. Therefore, your merchandisers are tasked with identifying opportunities to increase your brand's floor space. When the competitor's merchandise is adjacent to your company's product and it appears their sales are low due to a lack of product being presented on their fixtures, a sneak attack tactic may be useful to secure additional floor space for your company's product. This method is somewhat unconventional, but it will allow you to outflank your competitors. To implement this tactic, a field visual merchandiser is directed by the leader to negotiate with the store management team to add one additional floor fixture to your company's floor space due to the competitor's lack of sales. This process will gain more 'real estate' for your brand. If the tactic works, details are communicated to the MSO account manager and the leader.

All other field visual merchandisers who service the same retailer in other locations will be directed to try the same process to gain additional space for one floor fixture if the competitor is losing sales due to a lack of product. To take advantage of the competitor's position, the account executive will try to sell in more product to maintain the additional space acquired by the FVM team. This is a strategic move because if one additional floor fixture that houses 120 units is added to 300 stores and the account executive is able to sell in merchandise to be presented on these fixtures, this would cause an increase of 36,000 units in this retail account alone.

In-store tactics

In-store tactics are executed on the sales floor. These tactics are used to educate your target consumers, provide ease of access to your merchandise and introduce new product. In addition, these tactics work together simultaneously to sell your company's merchandise. Let's look at each of these tactics and how they work together to create a great shopping experience for your customers.

Product knowledge seminars

Providing product knowledge information works hand in hand with your visual merchandising presentation. Many people believe that outsourced field team should not conduct product knowledge training, but in this environment, the sales assistant in a retail store may only see a field visual merchandiser. This individual becomes the brand advocate that provides product knowledge to the store.

Training sales assistants on the features and benefits of specific products is ordinarily conducted in a seminar format that takes place prior to the store opening and sometimes after the store closes. There are many ways these seminars are presented, but the key is to educate sales assistants on the products sold in the store to equip them to relay information to the customer. Many brands train their field visual merchandisers on the features and benefits of their products and how to present a 30–40 minute training seminar. The value of conducting these training seminars cannot be stated often enough. Take for example the following:

At a new store opening, the field visual team does an exceptional job completing the shop layout, presenting the merchandise and ensuring product is sized, folded correctly and placed with the appropriate signage. The next step is to walk through the floor layout with the store management team to explain the product presentation. During this walk-through, the field visual merchandiser expresses the importance of training the store sales assistants on the features and benefits of the product. The management team agrees this is a very good idea and the field team member discusses an appropriate time to conduct the training. To coordinate the training, the FVM leaves a sign-up sheet for sales assistants to list their names if they plan to attend.

On the day of training, the field visual merchandiser presents the product line that is housed in that particular store. The features and benefits of all key items are discussed, questions are answered and the sales assistants participate in a game of role play. In this game, one assistant selects an item and the other tries to sell that item to the co-worker explaining the product features and benefits. Once the training is over, the FVM continues to train assistants one-on-one at each store visit. So the question is: how does this all work together with the visual presentation?

For example, a customer walks into the store and is attracted by the well-coordinated visual merchandise presentation of your company's product. A sales assistant walks over to assist the customer and is immediately asked questions about the product. The sales associate begins to answer all the product knowledge questions asked by that customer. The customer is impressed and makes a decision to purchase a few items after hearing about the features and benefits. While searching for these items, the customer is pleased at how easy it is to locate the appropriate size. The customer purchases the items and while leaving the store, thanks the sales assistant for a wonderful shopping experience.

In this scenario above, the visual presentation attracted the customer, the sales assistant educated the consumer on the product features and benefits, and the merchandise presentation was sized and easily accessible for the customer to locate the correct size. All elements worked together to provide a great shopping experience for the consumer.

Merchandising standards seminars

We have discussed merchandising standards many times throughout this book. As stated, these standards should be presented in a manner that can be easily understood. The FVM team should be experts on your company's merchandising standards and be able to present a 30–40 minute seminar on how to present product using these standards. Providing training seminars on your company's merchandising standards is another way of ensuring your target consumers receive the best shopping experience possible.

Keep in mind that the FVM team will be servicing stores on a rotation. They may be in a particular store twice a month, once a month or once a quarter. Therefore, it would be wise to train sales assistants on merchandising standards in order to maintain the product presentation between the merchandiser's store visits. In addition, it is recommended that the field team leave a copy of your company's merchandising standards manual at each store. This will provide the sales assistants with a document to refer back to if they have questions on how a particular product should be presented. It is essential for the retail store and the brand to have a solid relationship in order to facilitate continued success.

Together, both are working to satisfy the customer's demands, and as the leader in this environment, your role is to maintain a strong partnership with the retailers.

Special projects

Once your strategy is up and running, your team may be asked to execute special projects. These projects have a start and finish time and will require the field team to be on schedule and on budget. If your sponsors present a request for the team to take on a special project, whenever possible, be certain the request entails stores already serviced by the field team. If not, additional funding will be needed to fulfil the request. Special projects are included in addition to the services that you and the field team are already providing. To execute, there are a few standards of operation that a leader should be mindful of before moving forward. When a special project is requested, it would be advantageous to obtain answers to the following questions:

1 What is the scope of the project?

2 What is the time frame for accomplishing the project?

3 When should I expect to obtain a store address list for these particular locations?

4 Are these stores currently being serviced by our FVM team?

5 If not, do you have financial backing for this project?

6 Do I need to obtain a quote for the project?

7 If signage is involved, should it be shipped to the stores or to our field team?

8 Would the retail account provide a letter of introduction to be distributed to all stores involved, making them aware of the execution? When should I expect a copy?

9 Who will be the contact to provide additional information if needed?

10 Are there any special instructions for the field team?

Let's look at a few types of special projects one may encounter.

Hit-and-run special project

A hit-and-run project usually involves a short, quick visit to a large number of stores in order to create a consistent product presentation in all locations. This is often a one-time visit to put up signage or pull product from back room to the sales floor.

Example

One of your sponsors has signage being delivered to 500 stores in a retail account, some of which are serviced by your FVM team. After a thorough check you realize your field team services only 200 of these stores. The sponsor wants the field team to perform a one-time store visit to put up all the signage and take pictures to confirm all were completed correctly. To execute this project, the leader should adopt these guidelines:

1 Obtain the store list for all 500 stores.

2 Review the store list with the MSO account manager.

3 Determine if the MSO has representatives in locations that can cover the additional 300 stores.

4 Estimate the time it should take to set the signage and take pictures of this one-time store visit.

5 Obtain a quote from the MSO on providing the one-time visit for the additional 300 stores.

6 Review the quote and discuss with the sponsor.

7 If all parties agree, obtain a sign-off and move forward.

8 Once all agree, request a letter of introduction for the 300 stores.

9 Obtain the creative, showing what the signage looks like.

10 Obtain tracking information after signage ships.

11 Develop a directive that provides instructions on placing the signage.

12 Forward directive and tracking information to the MSO account manager.

13 Confirm delivery date of reports and photos from the MSO account manager.

14 Review the progression of the project until completion.

15 Upon completion, review the reports and photos for accuracy, then forward to the sponsor.

SWAT project

SWAT is an acronym for 'special weapons and tactics' and is a law enforcement term used to identify a special squad that uses military manoeuvres to accomplish its missions. In the FVM environment, it is used to signify that a well-trained team is required to execute a specific project. Within a SWAT project, three or more highly organized and qualified field visual merchandisers in a team swiftly visit two or more stores in a short time span to ensure product is presented properly prior to a promotion or special event. In this situation, each field team member performs a specific role in the execution process.

One field team member may be responsible for styling, which consists of selecting well-coordinated outfits for displays or window presentations. The other field team member may have the responsibility for quickly locating product in the retailer's stockroom and transporting all items to the sales floor to complete the merchandise presentation.

The last field team member may be responsible for guaranteeing product is presented in compliance with the merchandising standards. This would include sizing product, folding product on the tables and shelving and setting signage. This team works in concert with each other and usually has a set time for completion. Often a SWAT project is combined with a shock tactic.

Example

Your company is a retailer with three flagship stores in different cities. A senior executive in your company is conducting a market visit in each of these cities within one week, accompanied by investors. It is imperative for these flagship stores to look their best for these visits. As the leader, you have a short period of time to select the right FVMs to execute this project and submit a travel request. For this project, the leader should follow these guidelines:

1 Contact the MSO account manager and identify the field visual merchandisers with the skill set to execute this project within the time frame required.

2 Determine the order in which each store will be serviced.

3 Inform the MSO account manager that it is time to move forward with making travel arrangements.

4 Develop a list of in-store tasks selected to be accomplished in order to complete the project.

5 Develop task duration estimates for each field team member's responsibility.

6 Develop directives, planograms and a detailed timeline for all three stores.

7 Forward all documents to the field team.

8 Conduct a conference call with the SWAT team to ensure everyone is clear on the objectives and answer any questions presented.

9 Contact store managers in all three locations to inform and provide details of the execution.

10 Monitor the progress during the execution of each store visit.

Reconnaissance project

A reconnaissance project is used as a fact-finding mission to identify and locate an item that is not selling. This project may be completed in conjunction with regular store visits or stores that are not serviced by a field visual merchandising team. Let's look at an example:

Your sponsor gives you a call with an issue about a product that is not selling well in 300 stores. Your sponsor states the sales report indicates very few of the sports coats in style number BB8459BK have sold in 1–3 stores and none have been sold in the other 297 stores. The sponsor has requested the field team visit these 300 stores to locate the sports coats to determine why they are not selling. To execute this project, the leader follows these guidelines:

1 Develop a directive indicating the style number of the sports coats with a description and a photo to indicate what the coat looks like.

2 Obtain a store list of the 300 stores.

3 Develop a list of questions that will help to determine the status of the sports coats for the field team to review, answer and then document on their store visit summary.

4 Provide the directive and the time frame for execution to your MSO account manager.

5 Once reports have been received and answers have been explored, forward the findings to the sponsor.

Shop installations

When your company has negotiated with a retailer to place a brand shop in one of their locations, what takes place is a shop installation. Retailers from time to time decide to remodel, update, change the layout of specific locations or move to another location. This could be due to expansion, a new location, an upcoming event or the process of incorporating a new manufacturer or brand. When a company is installing new fixturing in a department or in a new store, this too would be considered as a shop installation. In this type of project, a number of FVMs may be requested to assist with the installation to merchandise the product on new fixturing and displays. Example:

Your company is a retailer that is opening a new store and you have been contacted to provide FVMs to assist with a shop installation in the men's department prior to the opening. To plan for this project the leader should follow these guidelines:

1 Obtain the store address and the date of the installation.

2 Obtain the blueprint for the floor layout. If a planogram has not been developed, meet with the appropriate people and gather the details to develop one.

3 Using your merchandising standards manual and the planogram, calculate how long it should take to merchandise the product and the number of FVMs needed to complete the installation.

4 Develop a task duration estimate to fine-tune your calculations.

5 Develop a directive that would include the time, the date, the planogram and other pertinent details associated with the installation.

6 Forward all documents to the MSO account manager along with the name of the contact person that will be present at the installation.

7 Once the MSO account manager has confirmed the availability for the requested number of FVMs, contact the store to inform the management team of your intent to deploy the field team to assist with the installation and the expected time of arrival.

Chapter 9 checklist

- Do I understand the difference between a tactic and a project?
- Am I clear on the six types of tactics that can be applied in the implementation process for launching the strategy?
- Am I aware of the numerous ways in which snail tactics can be applied when launching a strategy?
- Do I know which tactics will require additional funding?
- Is my knowledge on a swarm tactic detailed enough to be used in a strategy execution?
- Do I possess an adequate understanding of how and when to use a wave tactic?
- Am I clear on why shock tactics are used?
- When implementing a sneak attack have I done any investigative work to ascertain if this is the right tactic?
- Do I see the need to implement in-store tactics to complement my company's visual presentations?

- Do I believe that providing product knowledge seminars to sales assistants will work hand in hand with the visual merchandising presentations?

- Should merchandising standards seminars be provided to sales assistants? If so, why?

- Do I know the standards of operation that a leader should be mindful of before moving forward with a special project?

- Do I understand why a hit-and-run project is used?

- In a SWAT project, do I understand the roles of each field visual merchandiser?

- Do I know what tactic to use as a fact-finding mission to identify and locate an item that is not selling?

- Do I know how to determine the time needed to complete a shop installation?

Tricks of the trade: 'The flawless floor set'

We have discussed many special projects, but the largest and most notorious is the floor set. A floor set takes place when a retailer is opening a new store and the entire layout needs to be completed in a specific time frame. Although manufacturers may participate in a retailer's store set by installing a brand shop, often a retailer wants all products to be merchandised on their fixturing rather than on custom fixturing provided by a clothing manufacturer. In addition, the retailer may require each brand to provide staff to assist with the floor set. The key to developing a flawless floor set is to ensure all details are meticulously planned. Let's review a procedure that will make this process move smoothly with minimal chaos.

Before we proceed, we must discuss the departments and people who should be involved. Keep in mind that some store floor sets are larger than others and may require different duties to be accomplished by specific individuals. Let's look at who they are and their respective responsibilities:

- The **store opener** is responsible for:
    - pre-set preparations with the store manager;
    - all operations dealing with the entire flow of the work process;
    - ensuring that the placement of staff will correspond with the workload;

- answering questions and making decisions that pertain to the store set process;
- controlling all breaks and lunches;
- ensuring consistency;
- giving the signal to begin unpacking boxes.

● The **store manager:**
- will be available to answer any operational questions concerning the store;
- is responsible for pre-set preparations with the store opener;
- assists the store opener as needed.

● **Zone captains** are responsible for:
- productivity and the completion of the product set within their zone;
- maintaining quality standards;
- assigning team members to a specific fixture;
- informing the stockroom team about merchandise that needs to be transported to the stockroom.

● The **stockroom captain:**
- ensures merchandise is neatly organized in the stockroom;
- maintains quality standards;
- facilitates movement of merchandise from the sales floor to the stockroom as directed by the zone captains.

● The **zone field visual merchandiser:**
- places the boxes with the corresponding fixture number in their zone;
- unpacks the merchandise when directed to do so by the store opener;
- places product on the fixture as outlined in the planogram in accordance with merchandising standards;
- reports missing items and other needs to the zone captain.

● **Stockroom team members:**
- organize merchandise in the designated location within the stockroom;
- transport merchandise to the stockroom as directed by the zone captains.

- **Truck team members:**
  - unload the truck and transport the boxes to the store.
- **Maintenance crew:**
  - will properly dispose of all empty boxes and rubbish
  - confirm refuse disposal locations with the store opener.
- **Hardware crew:**
  - distribute hardware as needed;
  - ensure the hardware remains neat and organized.
- **Visual merchandising team:**
  - gives direction and input on product placement to all team members;
  - ensures compliance with merchandising standards.
- **Distribution centre team:**
  - orders merchandise by fixture.
- **Warehouse team:**
  - will pick the merchandise and box it by fixture.

The planning process

The planning process takes place well in advance of the execution. This process will include developing a floor layout to include fixture numbers and planograms, selecting the appropriate merchandise for each planogram, separating the layout into zones, ordering merchandise by fixture and picking and boxing product by the fixture number. This process is not for the faint at heart: it's a turnkey system using a detailed plan to be executed flawlessly. If everyone cooperates and agrees to do their part, it can be amazing. So let's get to it.

Step 1

The first step in the process is to develop the floor layout. At the end of Chapter 5, you were presented with a trick of the trade called 'You gotta have options'. Options are the things that can be pre-planned and used over and over again to save time. The type of options we discussed were merchandising options that would provide different ways of presenting product on a fixture that would include product capacity. Having these merchandising options on hand makes the process of planning the floor layout process move smoothly and accurately.

Also in 'You gotta have options', we discussed the importance of gaining an understanding of the different types of fixtures that will be used in the store layout. In addition, it's important to know the dimensions of each fixture you plan to use. Knowing this information will help you to lay out the store accurately once you have the dimensions of the space. Let's look at an example of how the process works.

Your company is a specialty clothing retailer chain preparing to open a new store in a shopping mall. Your company selected a great location in the mall, but the store is much smaller than your other locations. The store management has a stockroom crew, but has not hired a full team of sales assistants. Therefore, senior management has asked you to plan the store layout and use your outsourced FVM team to assist with completing the floor set. You have a full team from the warehouse and the distribution centre and everyone is waiting for your direction.

To create the floor layout, you need the dimensions of the space and the only thing you have been given is the square footage, which is 1,024 sq ft. Therefore, you travel to the retail space with a tape measure in hand to draw the dimensions. The space is 32ft × 32ft – a perfect square.

Step 2

At this point, you have everything required to complete the floor layout, such as the store dimensions, the type of fixturing to be used, their measurements and the product capacity of each fixture. This information is available from the merchandising options that your team created. Your goal now is to use MockShop visual retailing software to create the layout in order to communicate clear direction to your team. The process starts with reviewing the store measurements and the dimensions of the fixtures you are using (Figure 9.2).

Begin laying out the back wall, and move to the floor fixtures last. I have discovered that it is easier to finish the back wall first because the floor fixtures are not yet in the way. This will enable you to sustain a clear perspective of the wall presentation.

Next, start at the front of the store, positioning fixtures in a grid format in order to create aisles and walkways. From the front of the store, start with two-way fixtures; follow with 4-ways, rounders, and finally the gondolas. If something does not look pleasing, rework the floor layout until you are satisfied with the presentation. Be sure to leave at least 3ft between fixtures, creating a clear space for passage and traffic.

FIGURE 9.2 Store measurements and fixture dimensions

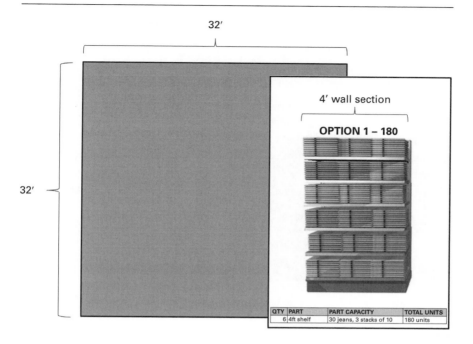

Step 3

So now you have a complete layout of the store with the product capacity of each fixture. Your next step should be to give each fixture a specific number that distinguishes it from the others on the floor layout (Figure 9.3).

Now that each wall and floor fixture has an individual number, let's place a group in a specific zone. This system will make the execution run smoothly on the day of the floor set (Figure 9.4).

Now each fixture has an individual number and is placed in a specific zone with others. Therefore, the first fixture on the floor would be fixture 1A. This indicates that fixture number 1 is located in zone A.

Step 4

In Step 4, your goal is to create a document for each fixture that includes its location. These documents will be used to determine product placement. Once these documents are ready, the next step would be to work with the merchandise buyers to select the product for each fixture. These documents will then become your planograms (Figure 9.5).

FIGURE 9.3   Numbering fixtures

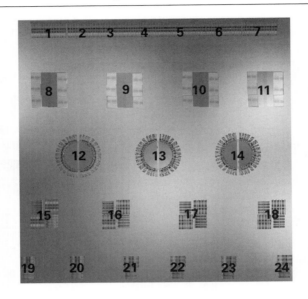

FIGURE 9.4   Zoning groups

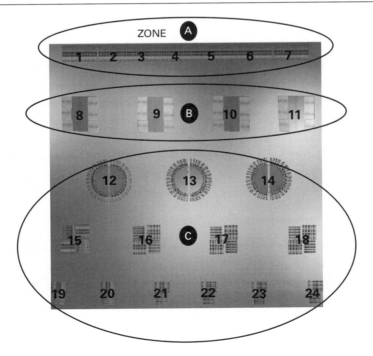

FIGURE 9.5   Planograms of fixtures

FIXTURE 1A
OPTION 1 – 180

FIXTURE #	BOSSMAN #	COLOUR	DESCRIPTION	TOTAL UNITS
1	BS7083	BK	BOSSMAN DENIM	60
1	BS7083	NY	BOSSMAN DENIM	60
1	BS7083	NY/WSH	BOSSMAN DENIM	60
				TOTAL UNITS 180

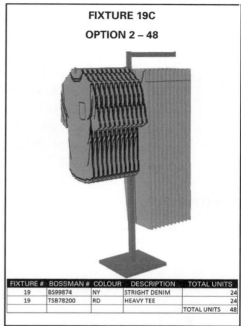

FIXTURE 19C
OPTION 2 – 48

FIXTURE #	BOSSMAN #	COLOUR	DESCRIPTION	TOTAL UNITS
19	BS99874	NY	STRIGHT DENIM	24
19	TSB78200	RD	HEAVY TEE	24
				TOTAL UNITS 48

Step 5

Your next step is to determine how long it will take to execute the floor set. This is critical because your FVM team is paid at an hourly rate and you are required to develop a budget for the floor set. To determine the time, you should obtain the following items:

- the merchandising standards manual;
- planograms for fixtures in the floor layout;
- stopwatch.

In Chapter 4, we discussed how to conduct a time study to determine how long it should take for an field visual merchandiser to complete all tasks associated with a store visit. Using the time study, we developed a document called the task duration estimate. We will use the same process to determine how long it should take to merchandise each fixture in a manner that complies with the merchandising standards.

Example

When looking at the planogram for fixture 1A (Figure 9.6), you realize there are 180 pairs of trousers. Review the standard for presenting folded trousers in the merchandising standards manual. If you know how long it takes to fold one pair, then you are half way there. If not, you will need to locate a pair and time yourself folding them in a manner that conforms to the merchandising standards. Let's say you have determined that it takes 10 seconds to fold the product to meet the standard. Multiplying the 10 seconds by 180 pairs, it should take 30 minutes to fold 180 pairs. The merchandising standards also call for the product to be sized small to large, from top to bottom and all size stickers to line up.

FIGURE 9.6   Merchandising times for one fixture

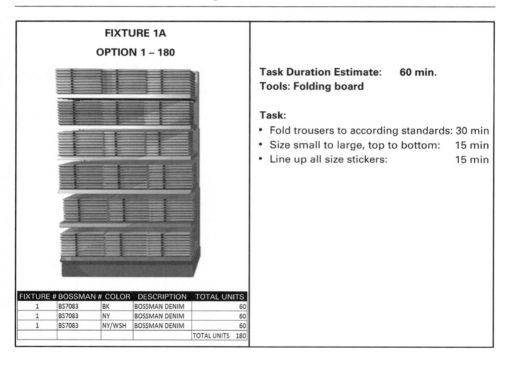

FIXTURE 1A

OPTION 1 – 180

Task Duration Estimate: 60 min.
Tools: Folding board

Task:
- Fold trousers to according standards: 30 min
- Size small to large, top to bottom: 15 min
- Line up all size stickers: 15 min

FIXTURE #	BOSSMAN #	COLOR	DESCRIPTION	TOTAL UNITS
1	BS7083	BK	BOSSMAN DENIM	60
1	BS7083	NY	BOSSMAN DENIM	60
1	BS7083	NY/WSH	BOSSMAN DENIM	60
				TOTAL UNITS 180

This document now becomes a planogram that also provides the estimated time it should take to merchandise this fixture.

Once a planogram has been created for every fixture, you should have the time frames you need to calculate how long the floor set should take (Figure 9.7).

FIGURE 9.7   Time frames for complete floor set

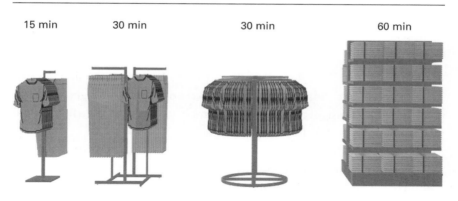

15 min   30 min   30 min   60 min

Step 6

So far, you have three zones with a group of fixtures in each. It is necessary for you to estimate how long it would take to merchandise each fixture. At this point, you should begin by determining how long it would take to merchandise each zone. To make these calculations, let's look at Figure 9.8.

FIGURE 9.8   Calculating merchandising time

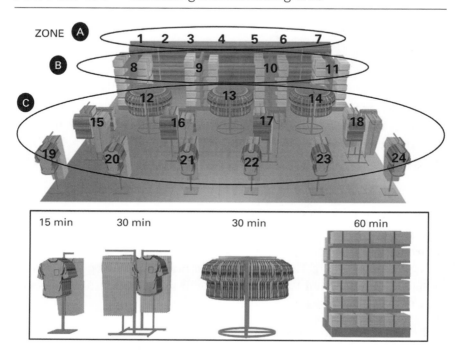

Zone A has seven 4ft wall sections with each fixture taking 60 minutes to complete. Therefore, it would take one person seven hours to merchandise this back wall. If you were to assign two field visual merchandisers, it should not take more than four hours.

Zone B has four 2-sided gondolas, each side holding the same quantity of product as a back wall section. Therefore, each gondola would take two hours to complete. So, zone B should take no more than eight hours to complete. If you assigned two field visual merchandisers to zone B, it should take no more than four hours to complete.

The last area is zone C which has six 2-way fixtures, four 4-way fixtures and three rounders. This zone should take no more than five hours to complete for one field visual merchandiser. Your calculations should look like the following:

TABLE 9.1 Calculating merchandising time

Zone	Time to complete	Number of field team needed
A	4 hours	2
B	4 hours	2
C	5 hours	1

Based on these calculations, if all five field visual merchandisers started merchandising the fixtures at the same time, it should not take more than five hours to complete. It is always wise to add a little extra time to be on the safe side. Therefore, you would need to budget for five field visual merchandisers for five to six hours.

Step 7

Several days prior to the store set you should work with your distribution department to order the merchandise by fixture. This process should be rather simple since the previously developed planograms have all the necessary information. This process should include providing direction on pulling the product and labelling boxes with the correct fixture numbers. Let's look at the process:

1 Orders are placed using the planograms that indicate the quantity of each item to be pulled and packed. Once orders are placed, the

warehouse will pull the merchandise and box all items by fixture. Each box will be marked with the zone and fixture number at the warehouse. The warehouse will then load the truck and deliver the merchandise prior to store set.

2 On the day of the floor set, the zone captain will place the corresponding planogram on the correct fixture and conduct a short meeting with the field visual team, explaining the procedures and answering any last-minute questions before the merchandise arrives. The goal is to make certain everyone knows how to interpret the planograms, how to check-in the shipment and how to merchandise the product in compliance with the merchandising standards. When all information is clear, no one is to start until the store opener gives the signal, indicating it is time to begin.

3 After the zone captain explains the procedures for merchandising the product, the FVMs are given a tour of the stockroom and the dock where the truck will deliver the merchandise. They are introduced to the stockroom captain who will facilitate movement of merchandise from the sales floor to the stockroom as directed by the zone captains.

4 When the shipment arrives, the truck captain verifies the box count as three people unload the truck. Three people from the stockroom team simultaneously transport the boxes to the store.

5 The boxes are delivered to an area where the zone captains determine in which zone the boxes should be placed, based on the store layout. The FVM team will then deliver the boxes to the correct fixture as directed by the zone captains.

6 As the boxes are being delivered to the corresponding fixture, the zone captains are walking the sales floor ensuring each box is placed in the correct location with the correct planogram.

7 After all boxes are unloaded and placed in the correct location, the zone captains inform the store opener that everything is in place and the team is ready to start. Before the store opener gives the signal to start, he or she takes a final walk through to ensure everything is in place and all stockroom personnel, field visual merchandisers and zone captains are in their correct location in case anyone has questions. The store opener gives the signal and each field visual merchandiser begins to check their shipment and merchandise their fixture in accordance with the merchandising standards, based on the direction from the planogram.

REFERENCES AND FURTHER READING

References

Bailey, S and Baker, J (2014) *Visual Merchandising for Fashion*, Bloomsbury Publishing, London

Bell, J and Ternus, K (2012) *Silent Selling: Best practices and effective strategies in visual merchandising* (4th edn), Fairchild Books, London

Bloomberg News, *Wal-Mart Customers Complain Bare Shelves Are Widespread*, www.bloomberg.com/news/2013-04-02/wal-mart-customers-complain-bare-shelves-are-widespread.html [accessed 3 June 2014]

BusinessDictionary.com, www.businessdictionary.com/definition/strategic-thinking.html [accessed 12 June 2014]

Flusser, A (2002) *Dressing the Man: Mastering the art of permanent fashion*, HarperCollins Publishers Inc, New York

Forbes.com, '5 Lessons For Mastering Your Mission', www.forbes.com/sites/lawrencesiff/2013/05/28/5-lessons-for-mastering-your-mission/ [accessed 10 June 2014]

Forbes.com, 'Visual merchandising culture', http://smallbusiness.chron.com/visual-merchandising-culture-67140.html [accessed 14 June 2014]

Gorman, GM (1998, 1996) *Visual Merchandising and Store Design Workbook*, St Publications Inc, Cincinnati, OH

Horwath, R (2009) *Deep Dive: The proven method for building strategy, focusing your resources and taking smart action*, Greenleaf

Hunter, M (2006) white paper, *Partners For Growth: The new role of merchandising service organizations*, MJH & Associates

Management Innovations, 'Tactical Planning vs Strategic Planning', http://managementinnovations.wordpress.com/2008/12/10/tactical-planning-vs-strategic-planning/ [accessed 12 June 2014]

MockShop [a PDF produced by www.visualretailing.com]

Nielson, KJ and Taylor, D (1990, 1994) *Interiors: An introduction* (2nd edn), McGraw-Hill

Nike.com, 'Nike Mission Statement', http://nikeinc.com/pages/about-nike-inc [accessed 10 June 2014]

Oxforddictionaries.com, www.oxforddictionaries.com/us/definition/american_english

Pegler, MM (2011) *Visual Merchandising and Display*, Fairchild Books

Pmi.org, Certifications, www.pmi.org/Certification/What-are-PMI-Certifications.aspx [accessed 12 June 2014]

RMIT University, Study & Learning Centre, 'Mind mapping', www.dlsweb.rmit.edu.au/lsu/content/1_StudySkills/study_tuts/mindmapping_LL/step1.html [accessed 23 June 2014]

Further reading

Allen, J (1986) *Showing Your Colors: A designer's guide to coordinating your wardrobe*, Chronicle Books, San Francisco, CA

Balanced Scorecard Institute, Strategy Management Group, 'What is a Strategic Plan', http://balancedscorecard.org/Resources/StrategicPlanningBasics/tabid/459/Default.aspx [accessed 12 June 2014]

Blumenthal, LA (1995) *Successful Business Writing*, The Putnam Publishing Group, Kirkwood, NY

Dymer, C, 'How to run a brainstorming session that works', www.brillianceactivator.com/wp-content/uploads/brainstorming-session.pdf [accessed 1 July 2014]

Forbes.com, 'Do you know your brand's DNA', www.forbes.com/sites/theyec/2012/12/14/do-you-know-your-brands-dna/ [accessed 14 June 2014]

Heldman, K, Baca, CM and Jansen, PM (2005) *PMP Project Management Professional Study Guide* (3rd edn), Wiley Publishing Inc, Hoboken, NJ

Monsef, DA (2011) *Color Inspirations: More than 3,000 innovative palettes from the colourlovers.com community*, HOW Books, Cincinnati, OH

Nielsen, L (Demand Media) *Houston Chronicle*, 'Example of Tactical Planning in Business', http://smallbusiness.chron.com/example-tactical-planning-business-5102.html [accessed 12 June 2014]

Retailminded.com, 'Do Designers need "Look Books"?', http://retailminded.com/do-designers-need-look-books/ [accessed 12 June 2014]

Today I Found Out, 'The Origin of *Where's Waldo*', www.todayifoundout.com/index.php/2013/08/the-history-of-wheres-waldo/ [accessed 24 July 2014]

INDEX

(*italics* indicate a table or figure in the text)

account managers   90, 106, 216, 217, 229

Bailey, S   34–35
Baker, J   34–35
Bell, Judy   10
brand   1, 88
    building   7
    presentation   2
    understanding DNA   9–10, 27
brainstorming   43, *44*, 50, 70, 73
    example   *75, 76*

clothing co-ordination   61–63, 72
    example   65, 67
    hooded sweatshirt   66
    mixing patterns   63–68
colour   68–70, 73, 159–60
    moods and   69–70
communication   28–41, 50, 209–11
    e-mail   209–10
    leader's role   2019
    methods   209
    MSO and   216–18
    sponsors and   214–16
    strategic plan timeline   210
    'tricks of the trade'   83
    see also monitoring
competitive advantage   113
concept board   *71, 75*
    Tuscan villa example   *76, 77*
concept shop   xv, 30, 112, 249
    example scenario   73–84
    instructions   81–82
    Nike   13
customers
    loyalty   194
    shopping experience   1

design concepts   70–72, 73
    example   *71*
    tricks of the trade   73–84
directives   11, 32–34
    cover page   *143*
    evaluation test directive   146–48
    floor layout   *143*
    examples   33, 34, 80

launch   170, 172–73, 179
    training   133, 140–44
distribution centre team   253

evaluation test   145–46, *147*
    administering   151–56
    designing   148–51
    example questions   *149, 150*, 151
    see also training

field visual merchandisers   2, 261
    apparel brand ambassadors   91, 92
    apparel field visual merchandisers
        91, 92
    attributes   225
    compared to visual merchandisers   7–8
    identifying skills gaps   154–56
    monitoring performance of   224–25,
        226
    role of   8, 88
    task breakdown evaluation   104
    task duration estimates   105, *106*,
        107–11
    task list   *101, 102, 103*
    training   130–61
    types   91–92, 107
field visual merchandising management team
        28–54, 74
    'bag of tricks'   51
    checklist   *50*
    communication   28–41
    problem-solving   42–46
    programme   18
    real-world situation   47–50
field visual merchandising (FVM) strategy
        xiii, 3, 5, 7, 13–14, 162–205
    checklist   27, 106–07
    components   87–111
    defining   12
    developing proposal   112–22
    example launch directive   172
    objectives   93–96
    sponsors   93–95
    standards   93–96
    thinking strategically   14–24
    see also strategic plan

fixturing 11, 57–60, 249
  accessories 126
  completed shop presentation 129
  custom 57
  presentation for 20ft wall 128
  presentation options for 4ft wall 127
  product capacities 126
  standard 57
  types 125
  wall 58, 59
floor set 251–61
  merchandising time 259
  numbering fixtures 256
  planning process 253–61
  planograms of fixtures 257
  roles 252–53
  store measurements 255
  time frames 259
  zoning groups 256
Flusser, Alan 10, 63
Forbes.com 12

Global Shop 10
Gorman, Greg 55–56

Handford, Martin 230
hardware crew 253
Horwath, Rich 10
high taste level 60
  developing 60–61

industry knowledge 10–12, 27, 60
in-store service schedule 218, 219
in-store survey 187–88, 219–20, 221, 224,
    233
interior presentations 11–12, 27

Kaufman, Steve 7

leadership of FVM 8–12, 93, 162, 165
  communication 209–10
  skills 9–12, 27
  sponsors and 93
look books 11, 39–41, 50
  examples 40, 41

maintenance crew 253
mannequin styling 61–63
market tours 225
master store list 97–100, 107, 112
McDonald's 194
merchandise presentation 55–57
  basic 63
  checklist 72–73
  example 56, 129
  jeans 203

layered 64
product listing 144
schematic 144
shirts 200
skills 56
types of patterns 65
wall 62, 127, 128, 129
see also clothing co-ordination, fixturing,
    wall presentations, window displays
merchandiser task list
  chart 142
  example 141
merchandising services organizations (MSO)
    xiv, 88
  account/programme managers 90, 106,
    216, 217, 229
  budget 122
  certification 89
  communication with 216–18
  contracts 123
  directors 90
  district managers 90
  field training managers 90
  leader 8–12
  levels of management 90
  outsourcing xvi, 2–3, 88
  numbers of 3
  regional/field service managers 90
  rejection letter 123
  reporting system 218–23
  request for proposal (RFP) 119–22
  retailers' view of 3
  role 8
  scorecard 120, 121
  selecting 114
  structure 89–92, 106
  team leaders 90
merchandising standards 21, 96, 224,
    257
  folding 24, 99
  manual 97, 136, 194, 195, 196, 197,
    204, 245
  presenting outfits 199
  seminars 245, 251
  signage 202
  sizing 25, 98, 197, 201
  trainer's instructions 137
  training 133, 138
Merchandising Standards Manual 172
mind-mapping 44–46, 50, 73
  example 44, 45
mission statement 12–13, 27
monitoring 184–90
  alert/red flag issue 220, 223
  before and after photos 220
  execution of strategy 211–14

monitoring *cont.*
    field visual merchandisers' performance
        224–25, *226*
    in-store service schedule *219*
    in-store survey 219–20, *221*, 233
    major milestones 211
    merchandising service reports 218–23
    quarterly reviews 223
    real-world situation 226–29
    report distribution 223
    resource needs assessment 212–14
    status/progress reports 215–16
    tricks of the trade 230–34
    weekly store visit summary 220, *222*
    see also strategic plan
MJH & Associates 2
    *Partners for Growth: The new role of
        merchandising service organizations*
        2–3
MockShop software 36, *37*, *38*, 83
    benefits of 39
    look book and *41*

National Association for Retail Marketing
        Services (NARMS) 2
Nielson, Karla 61
Nike 13

outsourcing xvi, 2–3, 88

patterns 63–68, 158
    mixing 67, 68, 72
    types *65*
Pegler, Martin M 10
plan *see* strategic plan
planograms 11, 34–36, 50, 129
    compliance 225
    components 141–42
    example *35, 36, 83*
    fixture layout *22, 257*
    product placement *23*
    T-shirts *227*
    training 133, 140–44
problem-solving 42–46, 50
product features 135–36, 244
Product Features and Benefits Manual
        (catalogues) 172
product knowledge seminars 244–45, 251
product listing *144*
project management 29–32, 50, 169
    example *30*
    phases 169
    plan 29–30
    schedules 30
    software 30, 173
    timeline *31, 78, 79*, 169

Project Management Institute (PMI) 32
proposal *see* strategy proposal
request for proposal (RFP) 119–22
    content 119–20
    evaluating proposals 120
    scorecard 120, *121*
    statement of work (SOW) 119
    see also merchandising services
        organizations (MSOs)
resource needs assessment 212–14
retail battlefield, the 1–2
Retail Merchandising and Marketing
        Conference 10–11
retailers 3, 162–68
    corporate contacts 163–64
    documents from 173
    feedback from 225
    letter of introduction 164–65, *166*
    management contacts 164
    'sales floor rules' 167

sales analysis per market 225
sizing instructions *25, 98, 197, 201*
special projects 245–50
    checklist 250–51
    'flawless floor set' 251–61
    hit-and-run projects 246–47, 251
    reconnaissance 249
    questions to ask 246
    shop installations 249–50
    SWAT project 247–48, 251
    tricks of the trade 251–61
sponsors 93–95, 107, 163, 223
    communication with 214–16
    examples *94, 95, 95*
    expectations 95–96, 112
stakeholders 114
stockroom captain 252
stockroom team 252
store layout 1
store manager 252
store opener 251–52, 261
store visits 92, 107, 167–68
    alert/red flag issues 220–21
    before and after photos 220, 234
    defining requirements 103–06
    example *81*
    guidelines *21, 79, 139, 181, 194*
    photographs 100
    report checklist *233*
    schedule *219*
    surveys 187–88, 219–20, *221*, 224,
        233
    time estimates/study 99–100, 102
    training 132, 138–40, 181

visual assessment   100–01
weekly summary   220, *222*
strategic plan   169–90, 229
    checklist   194
    communicating   169
    example   *17, 19, 31, 171*
    execution phase   179–81, *182–83*
    goals   170
    initiation phase   170–73, *174*
    kick-off meeting agenda/topics
        177–79
    launch directives   172–73, 179
    milestones   211, 229
    monitoring phase   184–90
    phase progression   169–70
    planning phase   175, *176*, 179, *180*
    real-world situation   191–93
    tricks of the trade   194–205
strategic thinking   14–24
    co-ordinating the execution   15, 47
    developing road map   15, 18, 47,
        169
    example   15, 16
    field communication   15, 47
    identifying risk   14–15, 22–23, 47
    researching   14, 47
strategy   13–14, 27, 85–111, 162–205
    definition   13
    development process   26, 112–22
    example of plan vs strategy   16–24
    strategy scope statement   163
    tactics and   24–26
    see also field visual merchandising (FVM)
        strategy, strategic plan
strategy proposal   112–22
    checklist   123–24
    content   113–14
    example   115
    key questions   117–18
    outline   114–15
    preliminary timeline   115, *116*
    selection of MSO   118–23
    scenario   124–29
    sign off   119
    tricks of the trade   124–29
SWOT analysis   211, *212*, 229

tactics   24–26, 27, 235–45
    checklist   250–51
    in-store   243–45, 250
    merchandising seminars   245, 251
    product knowledge seminars   244–45,
        251
    programme blitz   239
    shock   242–43, 250

snail tactic   *236–37*, 238, 250
sneak attack   243, 250
swarm   240, 250
wave   242–43, 250
task breakdown evaluation   104
task duration estimates   105, *106*, 112, 113,
    228, 257
    example   *258*
    monitoring   187
    real-world situation   226–29
    training   132, *140*
    'tricks of the trade'   107–11
task list   *101, 102, 103*
Taylor, David   61
Ternus, Kate   10
trade publications   10–11
trade shows   10–11
training   130–61
    administering   152–54
    certification test   136, *138*
    checklist   156–57
    documents   135
    frequently asked questions   147–48
    implementing   145–56
    log   154, *155*
    materials   133–34
    merchandising directives   140–44
    merchandising standards   *137*
    needs assessment   132–33, *134*
    planograms   140–44
    principles of repetition   131
    product features/benefits   135–36
    programmes   11, 27, *153*
    setting expectations   130–31
    skills gaps in the field   154
    store visit guidelines   138, *139*
    task duration estimate   140
    'The game of mix and match'
        159
    tricks of the trade   157–61
    see also evaluation test
truck team   253
'Tuscan Villa' concept   74

vendors   25
    sourcing   12, 27
visual merchandisers
    compared to field visual merchandisers
        7–8
visual merchandising   55–56
    checklist   72–73
    colour   68–70, 159–60
    culture   10, 27
    directive   *80*
    example   *57*

visual merchandising   *cont.*
  skills   57
  team   253
  see also merchandise presentation
visual retailing software   37–39
  see also MockShop

Wal-Mart   3
wall presentation   *62*
  20ft wall   *128*
  options for 4ft wall   *127*
warehouse team   253

window displays   11–12, 27, 70, *161*
  documentation   79
  example   7284
  initial concepts   *52, 53, 54*
  product selection   *80*
  see also design concepts
World Alliance for Retail Excellence and
    Standards   2, 3, 88–89, 107
  Gold Certification   89

zone captains   252, 261
zone field visual merchandiser   252

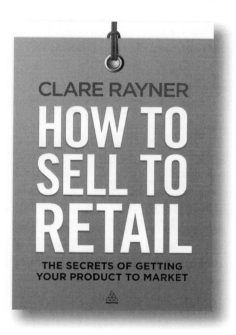